SPARE PARTS

SPARE PARTS

A Marine Reservist's Journey
from Campus to Combat
in 38 Days

BUZZ WILLIAMS

GOTHAM BOOKS

GOTHAM BOOKS
Published by Penguin Group (USA) Inc.
375 Hudson Street, New York, New York 10014, U.S.A.
Penguin Books Ltd, Registered Offices: 80 Strand, London WC2R 0RL, England
Penguin Books Australia Ltd, 250 Camberwell Road, Camberwell, Victoria 3124, Australia
Penguin Books Canada Ltd, 10 Alcorn Avenue, Toronto, Ontario, Canada M4V 3B2
Penguin Books (NZ) Ltd, Cnr Rosedale and Airborne Roads,
Albany, Auckland 1310, New Zealand

Published by Gotham Books, a division of Penguin Group (USA) Inc.

First printing, March 2004
10 9 8 7 6 5 4 3 2 1

Gotham Books and the skyscraper logo are trademarks of
Penguin Group (USA) Inc.

Library of Congress Cataloging-in-Publication Data

Williams, Buzz.
Spare parts : a marine reservist's journey from campus to combat in 38
days / Buzz Williams.
p. cm.
ISBN 1-592-40054-X (hardcover : alk. paper)
1. Persian Gulf War, 1991–Personal narratives, American. 2.
Williams, Buzz. 3. United States–Armed Forces–Biography. I. Title.
DS79.74.W55 2004
956.7044'2'092–dc22   2003025031

Printed in the United States of America
Set in Berthold Baskerville with Copperplate 32bc
Designed by Sabrina Bowers

3/ 19/ 12   26·00

This book is printed on acid-free paper. ♾

FOR GINA MARIE—

For signing every note, card, and letter with the words
SEMPER FI, and more importantly for meaning it.

FOR TYLER AND SOPHIA—

So you may answer knowledgeably,
should the yellow footprints call.

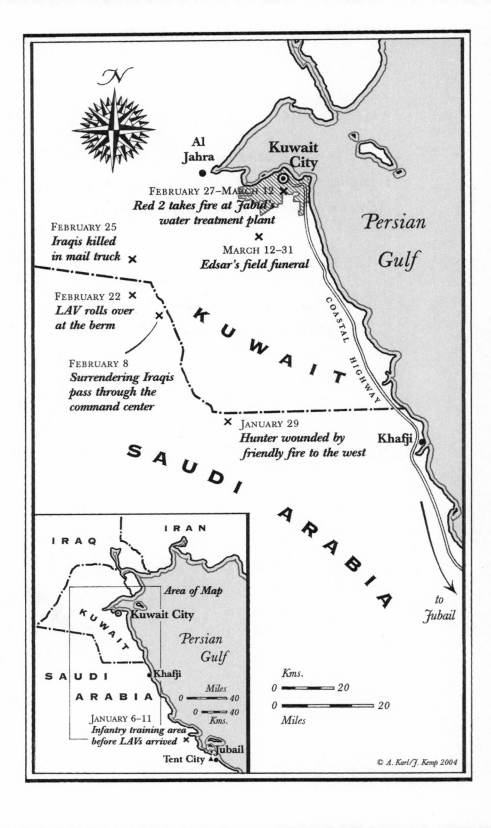

N

Al
Jahra

**Kuwait
City**

FEBRUARY 27–MARCH 12
*Red 2 takes fire at Jabul's
water treatment plant*

FEBRUARY 25
*Iraqis killed
in mail truck* ✕

*Persian

Gulf*

MARCH 12–31
Edsar's field funeral ✕

FEBRUARY 22 ✕
*LAV rolls over
at the berm* ✕

K U W A I T

COASTAL HIGHWAY

FEBRUARY 8
*Surrendering Iraqis
pass through the
command center*

✕ JANUARY 29
*Hunter wounded by
friendly fire to the west*

Khafji ●

S A U D I

A R A B I A

*to
Jubail*

IRAQ   I R A N

Area of Map

K
U
W
A
I
T

◎ Kuwait City

*Persian
Gulf*

S A U D I
● Khafji

A R A B I A   *Miles*
0 ━━━━━ 40
0 ━━━━━ 40
Kms.

JANUARY 6–11
*Infantry training area
before LAVs arrived* ✕

Tent City ▲● Jubail

Kms.
0 ━━━━━ 20

0 ━━━━━ 20
Miles

© *A. Karl/J. Kemp 2004*

GLOSSARY OF MARINE TERMS

AP Rounds . . . . Armor Piercing Rounds

ATD . . . . Annual Training Duty (two-week reserve duty in the summer)

Butts . . . . The belowground target area of the rifle range

CO . . . . Commanding Officer

Cover . . . . Marine Corps hat or cap.

Dog Target . . . . A target shaped like a person's head and shoulders from front

FO . . . . Forward Observer

Guidon . . . . The pole that bears a unit flag

Head . . . . Outhouse or bathroom

HE Rounds . . . . High Explosive Rounds

H-harness . . . . Suspenders that hold combat gear

I & I . . . . Inspector and Instructor (active-duty Marines of a reserve unit)

Ilum Rounds . . . . Illumination rounds

LAI Bn . . . . Light Armored Infantry Battalion

LAV . . . . Light Armored Vehicle

LZ . . . . Landing Zone

MCI . . . . Marine Corps Institute (Marine self-study training)

MOPP . . . . Mission Oriented Protective Posture (NBC suit)

MOS. . . . . Military Occupational Specialty

MPs . . . . Military Police

MRE. . . . . Meal, Ready-to-Eat

NAP Pill . . . . Nerve Agent Protection Pill

NBC. . . . . Nuclear, Biological, Chemical

NCO . . . . Noncommissioned Officer—corporal and sergeant

PMIs. . . . . Primary Marksmanship Instructors

Rack. . . . . Military bunk bed

Skivvies. . . . . Underwear

Snapping in . . . . Aiming rifles for practice

SOI. . . . . School of Infantry

Staff NCO . . . . Staff Noncommissioned Officer—staff sergeant—sergeant major

TA. . . . . Training Area

TOW . . . . Tube-launched Optically-sighted Wire-guided (missile)

UA . . . . Unauthorized Absence

VC . . . . Vehicle Commander

Vision Blocks . . . . Windows in the LAV

PROLOGUE

The yellow footprints called.

They first called as I read that initial letter from my older brother, Lenny, back in June of 1975. I was eight years old, and had lost my only brother, ten years my senior, to something he called "the Corps." It was devastating, but the letters helped, and they came weekly. Each one was a transcript of boot camp life that carved itself deeply into the tablet of my young mind. The first letter described how scared he was, standing on the yellow footprints. I couldn't believe that my invincible big brother Lenny could be scared of anything.

Much of what my brother wrote I didn't understand, but that didn't stop me from emulating it as best I could. I marched everywhere, because Lenny wrote that marching was the only way recruits were allowed to walk. Any adult who talked with me was bombarded with sirs or ma'ams, as one of the letters described how my brother had been poked with a rifle butt for forgetting to say "sir." After I read the letters describing Lenny's rifle training, my mother never saw her broomstick again. I imagined shooting across the creek with it so I, too, could qualify "expert" as Lenny had.

After thirteen weeks and a dozen letters, I would finally be able to see Lenny on the parade deck for his boot camp graduation. Or so I had expected. But that day at Parris Island I saw someone new, someone capable of pushing his new wife away, robotically reciting a rehearsed phrase about not showing public affection. Everything was different—the way he walked, the way he talked, and especially the look in his eyes.

In the decade that followed, Lenny occasionally visited, but he would never be the same. He was now a stranger with a rank instead of a name. His visits were never more than a few days, and my curiosity about the man he had become remained with me long after he left.

Missing my big brother became a familiar feeling for me, and nostalgic recollections a favorite pastime. I missed him at dinner when I couldn't reach the potatoes, and at night when the dark scared me to sleep. But I missed him most of all on the streets of West Inverness, the working-class suburb in Baltimore County, Maryland, where my family lived. Our neighborhood was a place where a chubby kid like me, without a protective older brother, was easy prey for bullies.

As I read and reread the letters he had written from boot camp, I tried to imagine transforming myself as he had.

In 1980 we moved to Harewood Park in rural Chase, Maryland. At the same time, Lenny transferred from his active-duty station at Cherry Point, North Carolina, to a new civilian position as an ordnance specialist at Patuxent River Naval Air Station in Maryland. This meant he could return home on weekends, and it felt as if I had my big brother back at last. During our time together Lenny taught me the Marine way to do just about everything. I ran with him while he sang cadence, made my bed like a rack in a squad bay, and even cut my hair in Marine buzz-cut fashion. More than anything else, though, was the confidence I gained by learning how to fight. He bought me boxing gloves for my twelfth birthday, and spent countless hours sparring with me.

I got the chance to test my new skills that winter when Butch, an eighth grade bully, threatened to kick my ass after school. During our bus ride home, I exited at his stop instead of mine, after which the entire bus emptied. Remembering what Lenny had taught me about the element of surprise, I drove my fist into Butch's nose as he stepped off the bus, sending him under the back wheels, bloody and crying. That fight helped me to make a name for myself in the new neighborhood—literally. Walking away from the bus stop, I over-heard one of the kids say, "That kid with the buzz-cut can fight!"

I've been known as Buzz, or Buzz-Cut to a select few, ever since.

In 1982 Lenny divorced his wife, and soon relocated to an airbase outside Visalia, California. The next year he remarried. I wouldn't see him again until the summer of 1984—I was a sophomore in high school. At sixteen my life centered around my new driver's license and the motorcycle that gave me my independence. But normally it was parked by sunset, as my father considered night driving too dangerous. So when he allowed me to go out cruising on my motor-cycle with Lenny at ten o'clock one humid Saturday night, when my brother was visiting us, it was a big deal.

We toured our old neighborhood, and the greater Dundalk area surrounding it, Lenny in front and me clutching on to him. As we rode, he yelled over the hum of the engine as he pointed out land-marks.

Our old house . . . the apartments where his first wife had lived . . . the woods he used to hide in when he hooked school . . .

We rolled to a stop at a red light in front of the North Point Busi-ness Park. Lenny pointed left to a lighted sign that read ARMED FORCES RECRUITING.

"Is that where you joined the Marines?" I asked.

His helmet nodded in front of me. I was filled with questions about the recruiter and the Marines. That night I expected to be able to talk with Lenny, man-to-man for the first time, and have the chance to see the world through his eyes. But I wasn't prepared for half of what I saw when we stopped at the Circle Bar-B-Q.

The Circle was a favorite weekend hangout, and the parking lot was packed. Lenny reunited with some of his old hippy buddies there, and showed me how his crowd partied. That night Lenny gave me my first beer, introduced me to Led Zeppelin, and if I had not chickened out, he would have gotten me stoned and laid.

When I woke Sunday morning I knew that was the good-bye day—the day my brother drove off to wherever his other home was. After the night at the Circle, I felt as if I had just been introduced to my brother for the first time, and now he was already leaving. I cried as Lenny waved his last wave. It had always been that way on the good-bye day.

On Easter morning 1985 the phone rang and Dad answered, expecting Lenny's voice; he always called during breakfast on holidays. But instead of Lenny, it was his new wife. She told my father that Lenny had fallen asleep at the wheel after a night of partying. He was in shock trauma in critical condition and it didn't look like he would make it.

When the second call came an hour later, I was in my room reading the letters Lenny had written to me from boot camp. For ten years they had been on the ledge of my headboard, ready to be read whenever I missed him.

My father came into my room to tell me the news I had been dreading.

My brother was dead.

As I sat beside the casket at the funeral, I searched for some way to connect with the memory of my brother. As the trumpet played "Taps," the Marines in the funeral detail began moving in unison with the precision of robots. As the solemn notes pierced the brisk morning air, echoing from the grassy hill in the distance, the flag was folded into a perfect triangle. It was amid the finality of the trumpet, and the folding of the flag, that I found my connection. That day I silently promised Lenny that "Taps" would be something

just between us. I vowed that I would never listen to it again as it
played in honor of anyone else.

As our family made our final pass, my father, who had until then
kept his cancer diagnosis from me, touched the coffin and whispered, "You won't be lonely, son—I'll be with you soon."

Throughout the following summer I never admitted to myself that my
father was speaking the truth when he had whispered to the coffin.
Even as he lay bedridden, with a gaping cancerous hole in his side, I
convinced myself he was just in one of his surgery cycles, and that he'd
be well again soon. During my senior year of high school, though, it
became tougher to hide the truth from myself. Dad was losing touch
with reality, and his memory was fading. I still hadn't accepted the loss
of my brother. Losing Dad was just too much. Vulnerable, and in the
throes of depression, I found comfort within a new group of friends
who taught me a new way to cope—with alcohol. The numbness of being drunk was welcome relief from the pain of reality, and the camaraderie among my beer buddies fed my hunger to belong.

During my senior year they had become my surrogate brothers,
and we partied nonstop. My drinking intensified throughout the summer and into the fall, when I entered my freshman year at the University of Maryland. Being away from home and leaving my mother
with the responsibilities of running the house and nursing my father
seemed wrong. But going to college had always been expected of me,
and during my father's last days of cogent thought he made two final
requests of me: Take care of Mom, and graduate from college.

Being *at* college and being *in* college were two different things.
While I resided on campus and was enrolled for twelve credits, I
was hardly a student. On the rare day when I attended class, and
even rarer occasion when I remained awake during class, my mind
was elsewhere. By October my father had been moved to a hospice
suite, where he lay helpless and emaciated.

Back at the dorm there was a red phone on the wall just outside my room. Every time that phone rang I feared that it was the call. There were many false alarms that month: a panicked call from Mom—a ninety-minute drive to the hospital—then waiting, and waiting—and the long drive back to campus to carry on with the college-student charade. My beer buddies never let me down during those dark days. It only took one phone call to rally them, and before long I would once again be comfortably numb.

Dad passed away on November 1, 1987. Although I completed that fall semester successfully, I began to believe that fulfilling his wish for me to graduate from college was out of reach. The only thing I lacked more than motivation was money. My father had never been healthy enough to secure any significant life insurance, and my mother's pay didn't cover the monthly expenses we had. Our modest savings couldn't sustain us through the next year. College would need to wait.

Mom and I grieved differently. She turned toward God. I turned away. That summer I moved to Ocean City, Maryland, with my beer buddies. While I had convinced my mom that it was healthy for me to get away, there was nothing therapeutic about drunken teenagers sharing a beach house for the summer. Most of that summer remains blurry for me, the memories locked away in an unreachable corner of my mind.

When summer ended, my return home shocked me back into reality. Nearly a year had passed since my father had died, and I had honored neither of his wishes: I was neither in college nor taking care of my mother.

As September approached, I managed to pull myself together and enroll at Essex Community College as a physical education major. Being a gym teacher and coach had always appealed to me. While in high school I had looked up to my own gym teachers and coaches as mentors, and I liked the idea of being considered a role model for students.

To complement my studies I worked as a health club trainer,

which also paid my tuition. Although I still drank heavily on the weekends, partying didn't fit the weekday schedule. I attended classes all day and worked in the health club until ten o'clock at night, Monday through Friday. During the week, studying replaced drinking as my escape from reality. Being lost in the books kept my mind too busy to allow my thoughts to drift back to Lenny or Dad, and it had the secondary effect of producing A grades.

Big Ray was a legend at the health club where I worked. He was a hulk of a man whose shaved head made him resemble Mr. Clean. He seldom spoke, but when he did speak he usually had something important to say, and people listened. Occasionally the room would fill with his voice, as he offered some political commentary or philosophical position on the discussion of the day.

Big Ray was interesting to me; he had been a Marine. Although I made it my business to talk with all the former Marines in the gym, telegraphing my obsession with the Corps, I had never talked with Big Ray. It was generally understood that Big Ray was to be left alone. The reason I knew he was a Marine was the faded eagle-globe-anchor tattoo on his right shoulder. I watched him from afar sometimes as he meditated between sets, always appearing to be in deep thought. While others looked at their reflections in the mirrors, Big Ray seemed to look through them, as if there was something on the other side of the glass.

After working at the health club for a year I had never talked with him, and probably never would have if it weren't for my compulsion to keep the dumbbells on the rack in numerical order. One day I had reached down to replace a one-hundred-pound dumbbell, but hadn't noticed that it was one of a set that Big Ray was using. Pushing my hand from the dumbbell, he wrapped his thick fingers around my wrist and jerked me into his face.

"Do you have a death wish, son?" he yelled.

The room fell silent. Petrified, all I could manage to do was shake my head.

"You'd better have a good excuse for fucking up my routine!"

"I'm sorry, sir. I got carried away with straightening up and didn't realize . . ."

Big Ray started laughing.

He looked up at the other lifters still staring, "Oh, c'mon, people. I'm jerking his chain!"

Relieved, everyone joined Big Ray in a laugh at my expense. Helping me to save face, Big Ray called to me.

"Hey, Buzz."

I was shocked that he knew my name.

"I could use a spot here."

Big Ray had always worked out alone. Bracing for another joke, I stepped up cautiously.

After his set he dropped the dumbbells to the floor and spun around to face me.

"I'm sorry about your brother and dad."

Caught off guard, I fumbled for a response. "How'd you know about them?"

"For Christ's sake! I've been listening to your soap opera for a year now. I think I know more about you than even you do."

He was right. I saw some of the men in the weight room every night, and they had become like family to me.

Big Ray finished his last set, dropping the dumbbells to the floor with a crash. "I know that life dealt you some fucked up cards. . . ."

Then he pulled something from his gym bag, and pressed it into my palm with both his hands.

Squeezing my hand closed within his grip, he leaned down, his face softening with a smile. "See my friend if you want to learn how to play your hand."

He disappeared into the locker room.

Looking down, I saw a business card with red and gold embossed letters that read:

UNITED STATES MARINE CORPS RECRUITING

NORTH POINT BUSINESS PARK

STAFF SGT. W.D. STONE

The encounter with Big Ray kept me awake late into the night as I lay in bed thinking about the motorcycle ride with Lenny when we had passed that same recruiting station, and just how far I had drifted away from my childhood dream of becoming a Marine.

Just standing in the doorway of the recruiting office gave me chills. At the center of the room was a large oak desk, polished to high gloss, cleared except for a desk pad, mini–flag stand, and nameplate that read, STAFF SGT. W.D. STONE, USMC.

The far wall was covered with photos of Marines under the sign PARRIS ISLAND GRADUATES. The wall on the right was covered with an assortment of posters:

THE MARINE CORPS BUILDS MEN.

THE FEW. THE PROUD. THE MARINES.

ONCE A MARINE ALWAYS A MARINE.

MAYBE YOU CAN BE ONE OF US.

The left wall was lined with bookshelves stocked with videos and binders with military acronyms stenciled onto their spines. Next to them was a gray metal wall locker with Marine uniforms organized meticulously enough to be on display at a museum. Atop the wall locker rested a white cap (I didn't know that Marines called it a "cover" at this point) with a gold eagle-globe-anchor emblem, and a shiny black bill—the same cap the Marines wore in the photos on the graduation board. As I was imagining how I'd look wearing it, a hand squeezed my shoulder from behind and a powerful voice redirected my attention.

"Good afternoon hard-charger," he said. "I'm Staff Sgt. Stone."

He towered over me, bending over to look me in the eye with a handshake and a Hollywood smile from ear to ear. Although skinnier than the Marines in the posters, everything else was as expected— the square jaw, flattop haircut, perfect uniform, and radio-announcer voice.

"What can I do for you today?" he asked.

"Good afternoon, Staff Sergeant." I said. "I'm ready to enlist."

Staff Sgt. Stone looked at me curiously. "I don't usually hear that kind of commitment from the get-go. What's your story?"

"I didn't want you to think I was undecided about joining," I explained. "My brother was a Marine—aircraft ordnance at Cherry Point."

Then came the rapid-fire recruiting questions.

Enlisted or officer?

What jobs interest you?

Have you taken the ASVAB (Armed Services Vocational Aptitude Battery)?

Any ROTC or college?

Married?

Dependants?

When are you available to ship out?

Who knew there was so much to it? I just wanted to be a Marine, and hadn't thought the rest through. Staff Sgt. Stone spent the afternoon counseling me about my options. After learning that I was only one year from completing my associates degree, he tried to sell me the idea of going to Officer Candidates School. But as soon as I learned that officers didn't go to Parris Island, I dismissed that option. For me, Parris Island was the only passage into the Marines.

Changing his sales pitch to make active-duty enlistment attractive, he started talking about the aircraft ordnance MOS. My interest fizzled when I heard the minimum enlistment obligation was four years. Four years was a long time to be away, and after my tour I'd still have two years of college left to earn my teacher certification. I didn't want to wait six years to begin teaching.

Feeling suddenly overwhelmed, I stood up to leave. "Well, you've given me a lot to think about—"

Reeling me back he said, "Whoa. Don't leave yet. I haven't even told you about the reserve option."

Although skeptical, I returned to his desk and listened.

The staff sergeant explained how being in the reserves was like having a part-time job that would pay me a salary plus provide tuition money through the GI Bill. All I had to do to become a Marine was go to boot camp the summer between the spring and fall semesters. Then I would serve one weekend per month until the following summer, when I would attend my MOS school. After that my obligation would become one weekend per month and two weeks in the summer. Altogether it would be a six-year obligation. It sounded like the perfect option, allowing me to stay in college, experience boot camp at Parris Island, and even get tuition money.

"As a reservist . . . I would still be considered a real Marine, right?" I asked.

The staff sergeant hesitated. "If you graduate from Parris Island, then you're a Marine."

"Is there a special boot camp for reservists?"

I wanted the same experience that Lenny had. I needed to stand on those yellow footprints.

"All recruits are mixed together," he said. "You'll all be treated the same."

"Can I go to boot camp this summer?" I asked.

"Nope; you missed the window for reservists this summer," he answered. "But if you sign up in the delayed entry program today, I can guarantee you a boot camp slot next summer—June of '89."

Satisfied with his answers, I asked what MOSs were available. He flipped through some papers on his clipboard, stared at a chart on the wall, and then back to his clipboard.

"Looks like the only reserve billet available right now is armored infantry—0313, LAV Crewman."

I was disappointed there were no aircraft ordnance positions, but in seconds my hands were filled with stickers, book covers, posters, and videos featuring the LAV. It looked like an amphibious tank with four wheels on each side instead of tracks. The clincher, though, was the latest edition of *Leatherneck* magazine. His pointing to that LAV on the cover sealed the deal.

"Makes my dick hard just looking at it. Can you see yourself firing that bad boy?"

"Yeah—where do I sign?"

★

A few days after enlisting in the Marine Reserves I first saw Gina, a petite Italian girl with silky black hair, tan skin, and an angelic face. She smiled whenever she passed me in the health club where I worked. Not only was she my type, she was the most beautiful girl I had ever seen. Gina was a beauty pageant winner, and way out of my dating league, which is why I never approached her. One evening, however, I took the advice of the health club matchmaker and asked her out. To my surprise she said yes.

Gina embraced the idea of being a Marine's girlfriend. During the six months leading up to boot camp she remained my steady girlfriend. It felt good to have someone who understood me, accepted me, and listened. Moreover, neither she, nor her parents, tolerated drinking. Since I wanted her more than I wanted to get drunk, I distanced myself from my beer buddies and dried out. With Gina's support I was able to face my feelings about my brother's and father's deaths for the first time. She was the only person with whom I had ever shared Lenny's boot camp letters, and she understood their significance.

In the months leading to my departure for Parris Island I read them regularly. They transcended written words and became portals into the past. Their pages fueled my passionate desire to experience that mysterious place where my brother had been transformed, and as June approached, the yellow footprints began to call louder than ever.

SPARE PARTS

PART I

RECRUIT

ONE

THE CONDENSATION FROM INSIDE the bus window made the foreign world outside barely visible. It was fitting that the first time I saw Parris Island it would be cast in a surreal haze. The interior lights came on, blacking out the windows. There was absolute silence. Then reality stepped aboard—a poster-perfect drill instructor.

"Get off my friggin' bus!" he barked.

Suddenly there was mass hysteria and a panicked rush for the exit. I made my way out of the bus, riding a wave of human momentum that crested and crashed down right on top of them—sixty sets of footprints stenciled onto the road with bright yellow paint. To everyone else they were training aids laid out to teach disoriented recruits how to position their feet in the platoon formation. To me they were launch pads into the world I had longed to be a part of for most of my life.

There we stood for the first time on Parris Island, four columns of fifteen bodies, perfectly aligned and covered. While most were shivering from fear and anxiety, I was in ecstasy. I was finally standing tall on the yellow footprints, as my brother had fourteen years before. The emotional rush lifted my spirits and cushioned my ego from the verbal assault being dealt by the receiving drill instructors. The rush was intoxicating. I was no longer just reading about recruit training. I was living it.

The yelling and shouting of the drill instructors became muffled as my thoughts raced forward. We were arranged tallest to shortest, which placed me farther back in formation than Lenny had been. If nothing else, I had to remember to say "sir" to avoid being jabbed with a rifle the way Lenny was. But none of the drill instructors had rifles. That thought reminded me that I hoped to qualify as a rifle expert too—if genetics played a part, I might.

The pain that shook me from my thoughts didn't register until I was facedown on the asphalt. I felt a dull ache at the back of my head from the drill instructor's blow, then strangulation as the back of my collar was yanked upward. My feet never touched the deck on my way up to vertical, and as I hung suspended by my cotton shirt I came face to face with the man who would make me a Marine.

Recruit Bell stood shaking at attention as Drill Instructor Sgt. Talley's boots stopped and left-faced directly to his front. It was the first evening with our forming drill instructors, but each of the sixty rigid bodies of our platoon had already learned the bitter lesson that recruits should only look straight ahead. Bell's skinny frame wobbled from anxiety directly across the squad bay from me, and I struggled to stay focused on the nothingness just beyond his head.

Drill Instructor Sgt. Talley was a thick-framed, muscular Marine, with dark brown skin. Standing over six feet tall, he towered above most of us. His face was rigid, and his eyebrows seemed to be permanently fixed in anger. Although his entire uniform was immaculate, the thing that stood out most to me was the way his sleeves were folded so tightly that the veins bulged in his forearms.

The uneasy silence ended with a room-jarring bellow directly into Bell's face.

"Why did you join my Corps, recruit?"

I glanced for an instant to see his eyes widen, as his mind raced for a response.

"I asked you a friggin' question, boy . . . Now, why did you join my Corps?"

A second hesitation evoked an explosive reaction from the drill instructor, who snatched Bell from his feet, clenching the front of his collar with two fistfuls of material. Bell's boots rose six inches off the floor, swinging violently. My peripheral vision showed a blur of camouflage as Bell was slung around into the side of the top rack. The metallic ring echoed as the right side of his cheekbone caught the steel frame squarely. Bell shriveled to the floor, instinctively regressing into the fetal position. Drill Instructor Sgt. Talley stood above him, hands on his hips, looking around to catch any undisciplined souls giving in to the temptation to glance over at Bell's misfortune.

"Now, listen up, recruits! Bell here is a nonhacker who apparently stumbled into our recruit training center without really knowing why he is here!"

My eyes darted down as Bell wiped the blood dripping from his mouth and nose onto his sleeve. Jesus, I thought. . . . Staff Sgt. Stone had told me we wouldn't be hit, or touched, or called names. This had to be a mistake.

"How about you, Nasty One?" Drill Instructor Sgt. Talley demanded of the next recruit.

Recruit Hart stood scared, eyes wide, as he searched for the words caught somewhere deep in his throat.

Leaning into Hart's face, nose to nose, Drill Instructor Sgt. Talley continued to escalate his volume with a rigor that shook the barracks' window frames.

"Well, any day!" he screamed.

In desperation Hart blurted, "Sir, the recruit joined to be tough, sir!"

Smiling wryly as if he finally had some new material, Drill Instructor Sgt. Talley backed off. He began pacing with his hands behind his back, staring at the floor as his heels struck the deck methodically with a hypnotic thud, thud, thud.

Drill Instructor Sgt. Talley was just warming up. "So you joined to be tough . . ."

He paused to let silence work its evil.

"Well, I wouldn't want to disappoint you there, now, would I?"

More anxious silence.

"Well?" he screamed, waiting impatiently for a reply.

We did not know yet that this was the standard cue prompting us to answer in unison. It was a new skill, and one in that was paramount in the world of recruits.

"Sir, no, sir!" rang out as every recruit gave it his best effort.

Drill Instructor Sgt. Talley refocused on Recruit Hart.

"What's your name, tough guy?"

"Sir, the recruit's name is Hart, sir!"

"Pick up your footlocker and hold it over your head, tough guy!" Drill Instructor Sgt. Talley commanded, smiling. His evil grin widened when he ordered the other fifty-nine of us to raise our footlockers over our heads. "Look at all these tough guys!"

The smile, we learned, was a deception. It always preceded a hellish series of games. The games were rote tasks, repetitive acts, and physical punishments designed to illicit frustration and rage within recruits. School was in session. Today's lesson was "Why join the Marine Corps?"

Sixty recruits wobbled under the stress of their twenty-pound wooden footlockers. The sweat cascading down my forehead and through my eyes made the footlockers look blurry green.

"Deck!" he ordered, and sixty footlockers slammed to the mirrorlike reflection of the squad bay floor. "Nope, too slow. Get 'em back up, tough guys."

The looks of fatigue from the first few repetitions were soon replaced with frustrated faces. Sensing our insubordinate thoughts, Drill Instructor Sgt. Talley prepared to take us to the next level of game play. We stood frozen from anticipation in our places on-line. "On-line" is the default position for all recruits in the barracks—the position of attention with your boot heels touching the straight yellow line in front of the racks. The squad bay was a long rectangular room with thirty racks on each side, called starboard and port. That was where we stood, empathizing with Atlas under the increasing weight of our footlockers. Finally Drill Instructor Sgt. Talley gave us our next command.

"Pass!"

Each of us handed our footlocker on to the next recruit to our right. The last recruit on the right passed his to the recruit opposite him to keep the suffering cyclical and continuous. The first few passes were rhythmic and orderly, resembling a human chain organized to move things efficiently. Only, there was no efficiency. There was, however, the futile passage of rough wooden footlockers that scratched and splintered against our forearms, exposed by rolled camouflage sleeves. I naively believed we would stop after about a minute. We were pitiful.

I would learn that pity was a foreign emotion to drill instructors. Drill Instructor Sgt. Talley growled, "Feeling tough yet, girls?"

A mixture of sir-yes-sirs and sir-no-sirs communicated our mounting confusion and signaled a breakdown in unity. Like trained dogs we would perform on command.

"Move!" snapped Drill Instructor Sgt. Talley.

Sixty salivating dogs barked, "Faster, sir!" reinforced by an accelerated series of commands.

The directions came faster. "Move!"

Our response kept pace. "Faster, Sir!"

"Move!"

"Faster, Sir!"

Meanwhile the rhythm and order were giving way to the lactic acid building in our muscles and the desperation building in our minds. I was tossing each footlocker to my right and looking left without knowing, or caring, if Watkins managed to receive it. Wilson to my left was rushing, too, and I wanted to be ready.

Drill Instructor Sgt. Talley's threats were painful to hear. "Go ahead . . . drop one of my footlockers . . . and I guarantee there will be hell to pay!"

Those were the last words before the inevitable happened. In hindsight it's clear that the goal of this was never success. Our drill instructors would push us to the physical, mental, and emotional breaking point many times at Parris Island over the coming weeks—in this case that point was a dropped footlocker. Failure fragments personal security. Consistent failure replaces self-confidence. Absolute failure erases identity.

But the mind of a recruit tells him that he should have been able to meet the drill instructor's expectations. We had believed success was possible, and we had failed, yet again. Thus the punishment that followed was just and deserved. Lesson one. We were inadequate. We were worthless. We were the myriad of condescending insults that Drill Instructor Sgt. Talley sent washing over us like floodwaters that drowned our very being.

"Fine. We just want to piss off the senior drill instructor by abusing his gear. Oh, we are gonna play, girls. The games have just begun."

I felt tears begin to well up. My muscles ached and my head was spinning. I knew that some of the smaller recruits were ready to pass out from heat exhaustion. The temperature on Parris Island in June was routinely in the high nineties, and the unbearable humidity left us sweat soaked from morning until night.

Drill Instructor Sgt. Talley pressed on. "Get 'em up. Now!"

Mustering enough momentum from the help of a lifted knee, my footlocker loomed overhead once again.

He sounded the next order. "Quarterdeck!"

Confused recruits stood, gasping for air, hoping someone knew what to do. It was the first time we had heard that command.

"Goddammit!" yelled Drill Instructor Sgt. Talley. "Run to the quarterdeck!"

He pushed recruit Lambert into recruit Lyons, and like dominos sixty recruits learned that falling and crawling toward an objective was preferred over standing and wondering. A chain reaction of scurrying bodies headed for the front end of the squad bay just outside the drill instructors' office—the quarterdeck. I was close to it and among the first recruits to enter the lobbylike area. Relief at such a short move was soon replaced with the realization that sixty recruits and their wall lockers could not fit into the space. Nonetheless, the last recruits to charge were not going to be caught disobeying an order, so they rammed full force into the herd of camouflage. Wooden boxes crunched against flesh and bones, manufacturing bruises by the gross. I was smashed against the far wall and squeezed until I lost my breath. Over the sounds of agony and pain we heard the next command:

"Rear hatch!" called Drill Instructor Sgt. Talley.

The pressure released as the accordion effect reversed itself and the outer recruits headed for an equally small area on the opposite end of the squad bay. Before the last of us were able to avenge ourselves with our own violent assault on the group, he called out, "Quarterdeck!"

Back and forth we ran, then hobbled, and ultimately limped. We had been reduced to a human slinky spring with which Drill Instructor Sgt. Talley could amuse himself.

Finally back on-line we were given a reprieve while the inquisition continued.

"Do we feel tough?"

"Sir, yes, sir!" gasped sixty winded recruits.

Drill Instructor Sgt. Talley stopped at the middle of the platoon and left-faced smartly. "What's your name, tough guy?" he asked.

"Sir, the recruit's name is Simons, sir!"

"What question am I going to ask you, boy?"

"Sir, the drill instructor is going to ask why this recruit joined his Corps, sir!" Simons answered.

"So you've been thinking of an answer, right?"

"Sir, yes, sir!"

I was praying he would give the right answer, if there was such a thing as a right answer. I know each of the others was saying that silent prayer, too, in the uneasy silence that follows such questions.

"Well! Don't keep it to yourself, there, Simons. Let us all in on the secret."

Not so sure about himself anymore, he hesitated before answering. "Sir, the recruit joined for discipline, sir."

I looked across at Bell's face, flushed with emotion, one side still swelling from the earlier collision with the rack. His lip was the size of a golf ball, and his eye was already purple. Bell, like most of us, was fighting back tears. It was the kind of rolling emotion that starts in the pit of your stomach and crawls its way upward into your throat. Each time it creeps up you swallow hard to suppress it for a few moments, only to have it come back again even harder, forming a lump in the back of your throat.

Drill Instructor Sgt. Talley turned to look at his partner, Drill

Instructor Sgt. Wagner, just entering from one of the hallways emptying into the quarterdeck.

Drill Instructor Sgt. Wagner was as tall as Drill Instructor Sgt. Talley, but much skinnier, and looked less threatening. His blond hair was long enough to part on the side, and his glasses made him look more like an accountant than a drill instructor.

"It seems as if Simons joined for discipline, Drill Instructor," sneered Drill Instructor Sgt. Talley.

Simons, realizing that his response was about to result in more punishment for the platoon attempted to recant. "Sir . . . Recruit Simons—"

But he was immediately stifled by the charge of Drill Instructor Sgt. Talley.

"Shut your suck-hole, you nasty thing. Did I tell you to run your suck?"

Again, Simons attempted repairs, but the damage had been done, and his attempts only worsened the storm headed our way. "Sir, the recruit thought—"

This time his words were cut short by the thick fingers of Drill Instructor Sgt. Talley's right hand as he snatched Simons from the safety of his place on-line. He was gasping for air as the material of his collar closed in tightly around his throat. His feet were kicking and thrashing. The sheer strength of Drill Instructor Sgt. Talley left us in awe. He was able to handle a 150-pound man like a rag doll. Moreover, he carried out his barbaric acts without remorse or sorrow, or any of the traits we attribute to humans.

"He's right about one thing, Drill Instructor Sgt. Wagner . . . he is an undisciplined fuck!"

We were left standing at the position of attention, straining to hear Simons's fate as he was pushed out of the rear hatch. The metal stairs rang loudly as Simons's body was dragged unwillingly down three flights to some unknown fate. As we listened in horror, Drill Instructor Sgt. Wagner noticed a recruit swaying from the dizziness that came from locking one's knees for long periods of time. Knowing it wouldn't be long before we had a body fall out unconscious, he ordered us into the head to fill our canteens.

On his command, "Ready . . . face!" fifty-nine bodies pivoted toward the head while sounding off the ditty, "Cock and drive!" These ditties were the verbal cues that helped new recruits move in unison while facing and marching. The next command followed—"Ready . . . move!"—and the recruits on the right side of the squad bay stepped off quickly to file in front of the sinks. We waited at attention with our canteens clenched in our left hands, braced against our forearms, bent at the elbow ninety degrees, and held parallel to the deck. We moved like robots.

On the command "Ready . . . fill 'em," we hurried to turn on the faucet and jam our canteens in to get them filled. God help the poor son of a bitch who failed to get his canteen filled. Filling canteens and drinking lukewarm water were high-priority rituals for recruits at Parris Island. It was considered a sin to get sick from dehydration. We learned that heat casualties, as they were called, were the lowest form of scum on the island. They embarrassed the platoon with public failure. Worse yet, the senior drill instructor, or "senior," as he was more commonly called, would catch hell from the company commander, and probably be investigated for negligence. Not a day went by that Drill Instructor Sgt. Wagner didn't threaten us for even thinking about embarrassing the senior by falling out with heat stroke.

So we filled our canteens and waited to hear "You're done!" After capping our canteens we faced and moved back on-line, but, as expected, not quickly enough for Drill Instructor Sgt. Wagner.

"So we want to take our sweet-ass time getting on-line . . . fine. We can play." He opened the rear hatch and called out, "Got room for fifty-nine more bodies? We've got ourselves some lollygagging slackers!"

"Send 'em!" invited Drill Instructor Sgt. Talley.

Once we were told to get out, we charged the rear hatch. Fifty-nine racing frantic lunatics clawed and scratched to get through a thirty-six-inch hatch, afraid to be accused of not putting forth a maximum effort.

While sprinting for the hatch, and observing the futility of such an exercise, I flashed back to my first days of school. I thought of how my kindergarten teacher had worked all year to teach us to exit and enter doorways in an organized, safe, and linear fashion. In a single afternoon one Marine drill instructor had managed to undo twelve years of learning, and unleash the beast within all of us. Darwin would have been delighted to witness the fittest survive, and the weakest suffer, in the doorways of our squad bay that day. I was elated to fight my way out of last place, and stepped onto the bodies of those who fell before me.

Once bottom-side, we staged our canteens on the deck and fell out into the pit, a twelve-foot-by-twenty-four-foot rectangular sand-pit bordered with railroad ties. We joined Recruit Simons and fell into formation. The next ten minutes would be the most painful and miserable of my life to that point. Every time Drill Instructor Sgt. Talley called out a new exercise, we performed it. Not just performed it, but executed it with a life-and-death passion.

The drill instructors called this type of forced calisthenics "digging." Although our introduction to digging took place in the sand pit, we soon discovered that recruits could be dug anywhere—the most common site being on the quarterdeck of the squad bay. Digging was a brief and embarrassing ordeal at best, but a long and excruciatingly painful one at worst. Our first time being dug in the pit happened to fall in the latter.

Drill Instructor Sgt. Talley's voice faded in and out of my consciousness.

"Go ahead and slow down, you lazy maggots! The slower you go, the longer you'll stay! We quit when I get tired, and you're not making me tired, ladies!"

When he grew bored with the insults, he switched exercises.

"Mountain climbers!"

As we threw ourselves facedown, the heel of a boot caught me in the nose. I screamed out in pain, only to have my mouth filled with spraying sand. I could feel the warm blood mixing with the abrasive crystals covering my lips and chin. It didn't matter.

What mattered was getting the job done and meeting the drill instructor's expectations of performance. Faster. Harder. Higher. More. Sand had entered every orifice of my body. I felt it scratch under the

lids of my eyes, cake inside my ear canals, and clog my nose, rob-
bing me of the air I needed to continue. Scoops of it entered my
trousers from behind, each time we transitioned from our backs to
our bellies or our backs to our feet. It was grinding away under my
arms and at the tender flesh between my legs. It was like being in a
carwash where sand was being blasted into my body instead of water. Side-straddle hops, push-ups, sit-ups, bends-and-thrusts, mountain climbers, knee bends, and leg raises.

The transitions continued.

"On your belly!"

"On your back!"

Belly . . . back . . . belly . . . back.

After calling out a series of seat and feet commands, Drill Instructor Sgt. Talley gave up using words and just moved his index
finger up . . . then down. It amazed me that that one man could hold
such amazing power. Simply flexing one joint of his finger resulted
in sixty grown men flopping, flipping, sweating, and bleeding, all
with the common goal of making the torture end.

As an education major I had studied instructional methods, but
nothing I had been taught resembled the methods of Marine drill instructors. In this school, teachers didn't muddle through lessons
with "disruptive behaviors" and "noncompliant attitudes." There
was no "developmental appropriateness" to lesson planning and no
endless search for "motivational activities and strategies." Drill instructors relied exclusively on traditional direct instruction. They focused on one objective at a time, gave instructions, and provided
practice until everyone demonstrated mastery. The reward for
learning was an absence of punishment. The consequence for failure was pain and suffering.

As I continued whaling away in the sandpit, I tried desperately to
figure out a good answer in case I was asked why I had joined. A
plethora of inane reasons flashed through my mind like a slide show
in slow motion. I remembered specific posters and pamphlets, ad-
vertisements on the television and radio, and the recruiter who had
visited my high school. I didn't have a good answer. My thoughts
began to take a cynical turn.

It wouldn't be long before we would trade the numbness of the culture shock of joining the Marines for rage and resentment. We had been fooled by the military marketing masterminds. Honor. Courage. Commitment. The uniform. These clichés have stood the test of time and have led even the brightest of scholars to stand on the yellow footprints. I had already learned that the truth of Parris Island was not as glamorous as my fast-talking recruiter had portrayed. Nor was it the adventure that the posters claimed. If the truth were printed, and naive young men were not blinded by promised pageantry, I thought few would volunteer. The truth hurt.

The next command, "Leg raises!" offered a glimmer of hope. "Keep those legs off the deck for one minute and we go home—but if one of you nasties drops his boots, the clock restarts."

At that moment home seemed a million miles away. By the end of this day it would be a challenge to remember it at all. Then Drill Instructor Sgt. Wagner started humming the tune of the Olympic games. I think this was supposed to piss us off, but it actually took my mind off of life in the pit. I was only beginning to learn how to use my mind to get through the misery and pain. It would become a necessary skill for survival in the days, weeks, and months to come.

"On your feet!" directed Drill Instructor Sgt. Talley.

He walked around the platoon to assess the damage, silhouetted against the orange glow of the setting sun. We were weary and emotionally spent. Most of us were in pain, and all were now saturated with the legendary Parris Island sand. We crudely turned and walked out of the pit, characteristic of raw recruits who have not yet mastered the precision of marching drill movements. The privilege of drilling was reserved for recruits farther along in their training, and even then they marched only when the drill instructor was pleased with their performance. Since neither case applied with us, we moved out with the finesse of a herd of cattle. We stopped when each recruit stood over his respective canteen. It seemed like such a long time since we had put them down.

"Prepare to drink!" was the next order.

Our bodies tingled as synapses fired in our brains, alerting even the most dense recruit to anticipate the coming command.

"Redaaayyyy, drink!"

Sixty recruits simultaneously bent over, unscrewed their canteen caps, and began to guzzle. We remembered the punishment of a past lesson. No one removed the canteen from his lips until the next command was given, even if the canteen was empty.

"Redaaayyy, two!"

Sixty hands dropped as we screwed the caps on and returned the canteens to their resting positions atop our left forearms.

"Get upstairs!"

This time the fight to reach the top was complicated by the fatigue from our battle with the pit. Endurance was the criterion for success and a totally different group of recruits lay bewildered at the foot of the stairs, brandishing tattoolike bruises from the soles of their comrades' boots.

The safety of being back on-line was reassuring, because it signaled a transition of some sort. Hopefully the games would cease, and we would discover the answer the drill instructors harbored. Even though the drill instructors arrived thirty seconds behind the last recruit, we didn't dare speak to each other. Noise discipline was a must for recruits, and only the bravest, or most stupid, ever dared to squeeze in a spoken word without permission. Instead we used gestures to communicate, but even those were limited to the recruit directly across the squad bay. Recruit Bell made eye contact with me and nodded his head toward the rear hatch to signal the entrance of the drill instructors. Our eyes snapped to the front. Drill Instructor Sgt. Wagner repeated the sequence of commands that led us into the head to fill our canteens. Once back on-line we received our next lesson in gamesmanship.

The silence ended far too soon.

"You've got one minute to sound off the correct reason for enlisting in my beloved Corps, recruits!"

Drill Instructor Sgt. Talley stalked us with his hands on his hips, his elbows antagonistically brushing the chests of the recruits as he moved, and heels deliberately driving into the tile floor. It was like a violent game of roulette and none of us knew who would be the next recipient of the tyrant's wrath.

"Ten . . . nine . . . seven . . . three . . . one," he counted. This was the typical counting sequence of an impatient drill instructor, over-anxious to move on to the consequence for failing the clock.

Then Drill Instructor Sgt. Wagner joined in the fun and games. He often took a more sarcastic approach than did Drill Instructor Sgt. Talley.

"Oh, I'm sorry, ladies, but it appears our time is up," he said. Using his most exaggerated television-game-show-announcer voice, he followed with "Drill Instructor, tell them what they've won!"

Drill Instructor Sgt. Talley interrupted the satire.

"Prepare to drink. . . . Drink!"

Up went the elbows and down went the water. Throats contorted and abdomens bloated as unnatural volumes of water were forced down against gravity's best wishes. We had consumed two quarts of water in less than five minutes, and the smaller recruits were struggling to keep it down. We were now ordered to file into the head a third time to fill our canteens with the bitter lukewarm water.

Once back on-line he continued with his rhetorical questioning. "Were you all on drugs? Is anyone's brain working here? I can't believe it! Not one of you numbskulls can tell me the reason . . . the purpose . . . the function . . . of Marine Basic Training!"

Our minds scanned. We weighed the pros and cons of answering. Would it be an act of courage, or stupidity? Should we risk it?

My knees weakened. I felt a shiver in my spine that sent a wave of muscle spasms through my limbs. It is the kind of sensation that occurs when the inevitable is about to happen and nothing you can do will stop it. I closed my eyes when his voice boomed again.

"Prepare to drink. . . . Drink!"

Reluctant arms twisted caps and elevated canteens. The first to go was Carr, a short and skinny recruit, who was no more than 120 pounds. I risked looking to the side to see his diaphragm heaving. His lips could not contain the bile that was pumping from his guts.

The dam burst with a pressure that sent vomit spewing across the squad bay onto the recruits on the starboard side. No one laughed. It was pitiful. Worse yet, it was contagious. The stench began to waft and permeate the air surrounding the rest of us.

A second recruit let loose, and the remnants of dinner made their way across the once shiny floor. The odor, combined with the grotesque kaleidoscope of regurgitated food chunks, acted as the catalyst for a massive chain reaction of projectile vomiting. Somehow I managed to keep my water down, although most around me did not.

Where were the drill instructors during all of this sickness? I imagined them high-fiving each other on the quarterdeck, laughing and trying to keep their perfect uniforms from getting splashed. After about two minutes of vomiting the recruits returned to their vertical positions on-line. Surprisingly, the drill instructors walked right down the center of the floor, their boots sloshing through the mess as they would through puddles on a rainy day. It was a rainy day for us. Certainly it was the most difficult day of my life up to then. And it was about to get worse before it got better. We filed into the head to fill our canteens for a fourth time.

Drill Instructor Sgt. Talley lowered his voice. "Now, recruits, the senior is coming in to tuck you babies in tonight, and the squad bay will be spotless."

I could barely stand still and avoid throwing up. There was no way I could clean this floor, I thought. I rationalized I would not be involved, since the mess wasn't mine. That was the faulty thinking of an egocentric civilian.

Drill Instructor Sgt. Talley faced Recruit Carr and challenged, "Well, what are you going to do about this friggin' mess you made, boy?"

Recruit Carr stood stiff and scared. "Sir, clean it up, sir?"

"Are you asking me or telling me?"

"Sir, the recruit will clean up his mess, sir!"

"Oh, you bet your sweet ass you're gonna clean. But it's not *your* mess. It's *our* mess."

Drill Instructor Sgt. Talley had introduced another tenet of recruit training: There are no individuals in the Marine Corps, only the platoon as a whole—the team.

Drill Instructor Sgt. Wagner approached Recruit Carr and leaned into his face, apparently disgusted with the situation. "Well, any friggin' day!"

Dazed, Carr blurted, "Sir, the recruit needs a mop, sir."

Drill Instructor Sgt. Talley guided Carr by his shoulders to the center of the squad bay. "Recruit Carr has disrespected our house. He has embarrassed himself, and the platoon."

Carr's eyes closed slowly, as he steeled himself for whatever was coming. Our training's unpredictability was devastating for me, and I assumed it was the same for my fellow recruits. We functioned more like animals than people, reacting without logic or rationale. The higher levels of thinking and feeling had already atrophied, leaving only our brain stems to govern primal instincts and survival reflexes.

Surely the drill instructors couldn't have expected such a small recruit to absorb that much water. Were they crazy? It seemed like abuse! My curiosity turned to anger, and adrenaline fueled the rage developing within us all.

But now there was only silence.

Drill Instructor Sgt. Talley walked to the quarterdeck and executed an about-face maneuver. "You don't rate a mop," he commanded. "Use your blouse!"

Carr slowly started unbuttoning his camouflage jacket, only to be jolted from his stupor.

"Goddammit! Did I say take your blouse off? Now, drop and start pushing!"

Carr must have turned something off inside. He flopped from his belly to his back in the pungent puddles. Although it was still wet and sandy from the pit, the material in his cammies still managed to absorb most of the moisture on the deck. Pleased with his creative solution to cleaning the deck, Drill Instructor Sgt. Talley ordered the remaining fifty-nine of us to join Carr in the housekeeping efforts.

Within seconds the floor was covered with camouflage-covered bodies writhing on the floor.

We then were ordered to do calisthenics for a few minutes, and
then low-crawl under the eighteen-inch space between the racks and
the floor. It wasn't so easy for me to turn the switch that Carr had
found. I gagged repeatedly, and struggled to choke back vomit.
Worse, I could no longer hold back the water in my bladder. I
briefly considered requesting a head call, but quickly dismissed the
thought. After surveying the mayhem I chose the less confronta-
tional alternative. As my bladder drained, a warm sensation spread
down my legs, further saturating my trousers and socks. I wasn't as
embarrassed as you might expect. The standards of conduct were
different on the Island. It didn't seem wrong to me, and not a single
recruit in the platoon would have acted differently.

"Get on-line!"

Once we were on our feet I glanced briefly to see the faces of
those across the squad bay. Bell, with his swollen lip, was angrier
than ever. To his left Brady was grinding his teeth and flexing his
jaw muscles to ebb his frustration. On the other side of Bell, Ander-
son stared with an absence of emotion, restraining his anger with
clenched fists hidden tightly by his side.

My observations were cut short by Drill Instructor Sgt. Wagner's
voice.

"Readyyy, face!"

We collectively pivoted toward the quarterdeck and filed off into
the showers, wearing our uniforms. I shared the shower stream with
two other recruits I didn't know. We didn't make eye contact to
avoid the perception that we were talking. The water was liberating
and refreshing as it washed away the slime and sand.

Drill Instructor Sgt. Wagner's voice sounded sharply over the
hiss of falling water. "Strip your filthy little uniforms off and start
scrubbing your bodies. You've got five minutes."

We worked feverishly and silently. Not stripping would have assured that I made it back on-line in time, but the others were risking
it, and the thought of keeping that putrid sand-encrusted uniform

on made me gag again. With my uniform in hand I rinsed my body for thirty seconds and then sprinted to the clean cammies in my footlocker.

We could hear the threatening countdown from the quarterdeck as Drill Instructor Sgt. Wagner called out. "Four minutes left!"

The nearest recruits to him then called out the same, "Four minutes!" Then every recruit repeated the call, "Four minutes!" until we were certain that the drill instructors had heard our affirmation. When the one-minute warning sounded I was nearly dressed, determined not to be late. Being dressed on time would keep the drill instructors and Recruit Morrison, my squad leader, off my ass.

As squad leader, Morrison was responsible for the performance of fourteen of us in first squad. Whenever any of us was dug, in groups or as individuals, the drill instructor would dig him too. That was how the drill instructors motivated the squad leaders to keep the recruits under their charge "squared away." Morrison hated to be dug. But instead of teaching us, or leading us, he preferred to threaten us.

Acting more like a junior drill instructor than a recruit, he screamed his mantra, "I better not have to pay for you, First Squad! If I pay, you'll pay!"

Morrison wasn't half the leader that Guide Carey was.

As guide, the drill-instructor-appointed recruit platoon leader, Carey was responsible for all sixty of us. Because he was usually punished whenever any recruit in the platoon was punished, he endured more digging than any of us. Yet, he never seemed to take it personally. Even with only half of the recruits dressed, and punishment looming, he calmly walked from one end of the squad bay to the other, showing the faster recruits how to help the slower ones get dressed.

It was an amazing sight, really. Following Carey's directions Recruit Myers was fastening Brock's belt, while two other recruits were tying his boots, and a fourth was buttoning his blouse. It was a lesson in sacrifice and teamwork, with the ultimate goal of accomplishing the mission together and avoiding punishment.

By the time the countdown from ten seconds had commenced, all sixty recruits were standing tall on-line in clean cammies.

"Outstanding!" beamed Drill Instructor Sgt. Talley. "There may be hope after all here, recruits."

He continued to pace while the stagnant odor of lingering vomit filled the air. I hoped he would be bored with the questioning, and allow us to clean up the barracks and hit the rack. But he seemed more deliberate than ever.

"Recruits, think long and hard before you answer. Get it right, and we'll clean the barracks and hit the rack. Get it wrong, and we'll play."

In the movie *Full Metal Jacket* Recruit Joker impresses the drill instructor with his psychological insight when answering a similar question. The answer he gave was a possible answer, but wasn't worth the punishment if I was wrong. While I debated, the boots stopped and left-faced in front of me. My heart sank and suddenly I knew the fear that Bell, Hart, Simons, and Carr must have felt.

All that existed was the drill instructor and me.

"Why did you join my Corps, recruit?"

This was it. The fate of the platoon rested in my hands. My answer would either bring relief or misery, and there was no turning back. Silence would bring punishment. I had to say something, so I thought hard and fast. I could sense his impatience as I searched for my response. It was about to be too late. Then a burst of awareness passed through my mind and my voice started without getting permission from my brain.

"Sir, the recruit believes that any answer he gives will be wrong, sir!"

I was sorry immediately after I said it. Drill Instructor Sgt. Talley sighed a deep breath and rubbed his chin.

"You think this is some kind of mind game, recruit?"

I was sure he saw me swallow hard before attempting a reply.

"You a college boy, recruit?" he asked with contempt in his voice.

Knowing it was not the favored answer, I struggled just to tell the truth. "Sir, yes, sir."

His words now came faster and louder. "No shit. So this is a goddamned psychological experiment, huh?" Silence. "So the United States Government is paying thousands of dollars per recruit to allow drill instructors to shrink their heads?"

I didn't know what to say. I stood there lifeless, blankly staring at the drill instructor's chevrons. The least any recruit could do in this situation was keep his military bearing. It was all I had and I clung to it.

"Ever take a psychology class, college boy?" he snorted.

"Sir, yes, sir."

He was reeling me in. Only, I couldn't stop it and had no idea where he was going with his line of questioning. I felt like a witness on the stand being badgered by an expert prosecutor. Ignorance was my crime.

"Well, here's a little brain teaser for you."

He paused a moment to let reality set in. Nothing good could come of being singled out and addressed by the drill instructor.

Drill Instructor Sgt. Talley reached out with his fist and gently tapped me in the chest. Then he whispered in my ear, "Hit me back, or the platoon will pay."

While I was thinking, he called out the command, "Eyes!"

All of the recruits replied, "Snap, sir!" while turning their heads and eyes toward us.

This command usually preceded a period of instruction that required recruits' eyes and full attention. It was the only time a recruit was permitted to look at a drill instructor directly. Now I was the object of the platoon's attention and the next period of instruction.

I could either punch the drill instructor or let the platoon down. The former was risky, with fifty-nine recruits and a fellow drill instructor witnessing my assault. It was brilliantly applied psychology, forcing me into a no-win situation. Feeling like it would be better to save the platoon some grief, I took the high road. With all eyes upon me, I extended my fist and tapped his chest.

He turned to the platoon with animated disbelief. "I think I was just hit by a belligerent recruit."

"Eyes front!" returned the recruits' eyes to their front and away from me.

"Now, we can't tolerate insubordination. It would lead to a breakdown in order and discipline in the platoooooon!" With the last word he reared back and thumped my chest with his fist, making me take a step back to regain my balance. It was a hard punch, but nothing that I hadn't endured in the back alleys of West Inverness.

The second whisper came, "Hit me again."

"Eyes!"

I mustered up enough courage to punch him again, this time more assertively.

"Eyes front!"

All of the recruits snapped their heads and eyes forward, so they couldn't bear witness to what was about to happen. Drill Instructor Sgt. Talley approached me like a shot-putter shuffling forward to generate power from his legs. After rearing back with his right arm he launched his open palm into my sternum, driving me up off of my feet and in between the racks. I crashed down on my coccyx bone and arched my back to keep from splatting on the deck. My momentum carried me over into a back roll and into the base of my wall locker, which came crashing down on top of me. Gasping for the air that had been sucked from my chest, I lay still and silent, angry enough to kill him.

The next sound was the platoon forwarding a call, "Attention on deck!" as Senior Drill Instructor Staff Sgt. Parsons entered the squad bay. Several recruits righted my wall locker and helped me to my feet.

The senior was a short, stocky Marine with a round face. His hair was beginning to turn gray above his ears, which contrasted with his black skin, making him look old and wise.

Once back on-line I could see that our senior was pacing and observing. How would he react to the acidic stench in the air, the disarray of gear, and the hardened looks on our faces? By the look on his face he was pleased: Blood. Sweat. Tears. Urine. Bile. Adrenaline. Testosterone. These were the ingredients he had requested of Drill Instructor Sgt. Talley—the master warlock simmering the cauldron of hatred.

Bell, Hart, Simons, Carr, and I had experienced the first of many hard lessons. We were the examples—the demonstrators for the lab. It was basic psychology. In one afternoon Parris Island had eradicated the civility, socialization, and self-respect of sixty grown men.

It is a phenomenon commonly referred to in psychology as "stripping." The rules of life changed in one day. We were forced to forget all we had learned about personal conduct, social interaction, limits of morality, and logical consequences. We were no longer *thinking* individuals. We were *reacting* animals. We stood on-line, silently staring and getting in touch with the primary emotions that drove us—anger, frustration, and hatred.

After walking around the barracks several times, the senior addressed us.

"Apparently you have been training very hard with my drill instructors. They tell me there is some confusion about why you enlisted in the Marine Corps."

I tried to think of what would happen next. Drill Instructor Sgt. Talley had told us the senior would be ashamed to find out his recruits were so misguided. I imagined the worst of course. This was only our first official training day and it had been pure hell. The senior, however, had a different role than the other drill instructors. He was tough, but he seldom punished us, leaving that task to his drill instructors. He demanded as much or more than the others, but his relationship was that of strict father to his sons. His tactics were more clever than bullying, and his influence more powerful.

"So we are all wondering why men join the Corps?"

Sixty voices boomed, "Sir, yes, sir!"

"Well, this will be the fifth platoon that I trained, and none has ever figured it out on their own."

The senior always put things in perspective. Though the universality of our ignorance was a relief, I was anxious for this sixteen-hour lesson to end. The senior explained the importance of training with a purpose, and validated our quest for the answer.

"If you pass your inspection I will teach the class my way. But if you fail the inspection, Drill Instructor Sgt. Talley will continue teaching you his way." As he pivoted and turned away he bellowed, "Is that understood?"

Our "Sir, yes, sir" reply reverberated in the barracks as the senior disappeared through the quarterdeck hatch.

We spent the next ninety minutes scrubbing the floor, the head,

our uniforms, and our bodies. Every recruit had a job, and every recruit worked with life-and-death urgency.

First squad worked especially hard under Morrison's badgering:

"That's not how to make a rack, stupid—"

"Are you blind? That mirror's still smudged—"

"We'll be up all night if that's the best you can do—"

Drill Instructor Sgt. Talley got off on Morrison's antagonism and
enjoyed fueling his fire. "If we don't pass the senior's inspection,
Morrison, it'll be your squad's fault!"

It is this passion that visitors to Parris Island observe in awe.
They see recruits busting their asses because of supposed pride and
commitment, but few know the real reasons for our motivation—survival. Our drill instructors watched as we worked like dogs to make
our deadline. By 2000 hours the squad bay smelled as sterile as a
hospital. We were proud to earn the privilege of sleep. We remained
still, lying in our racks at the position of attention, waiting for the senior to pass judgment.

The lights clicked off, leaving the barracks dark, with only a
glimmer of light from the head reflecting on the polished tile floor.
The concentrated smell of Aqua Velva saturated the air, as it was
both every recruit's mandatory splash-on, as well as the secret in-
gredient to the mop water. A hard summer rain pounded the cinder-
block walls, the asphalt streets, and the metal awning covering the
stairwell just outside the rear hatch. Around the squad bay's perimeter the sound of boot heels striking the deck continued in a monotonous hypnotic way for several minutes before we heard his voice.
Recognizably the senior, but mysteriously sinister.

*"Tonight's the night . . . dark and rainy . . . the perfect night for
killing. They won't expect us tonight. They'll just hear the rain. But we
are ready. Swift. Silent. Deadly. Your rifle is loaded and locked. Your
bayonet is fixed. Your eyes study the shadows. Tread lightly. Watch the
Marine in front. Repeat the signal. We will make the first move. It's a
rush just before it happens. Muzzle flashes and the crack, crack,
crack, of rounds. It's a beautiful thing—a fire-team rush. Face-to-face
with the enemy. Get up close if you can. Thrust the bayonet in. Don't*

forget to twist on the way out. Once you grate ribs you'll know he'll drop. The rainwater mixes with the blood. Dark red at first . . . then diluted to runny lines of cloudy pink. The smell of wet gunpowder . . . Ahhh, you gotta love that. Savor it. You've done your job. It was him or you. That is what we do. Listen to the rain. Stare into the night. Move on. There are others waiting to die tonight."

He spoke with calm conviction. Our fatigue made his message seem cultlike.

As the senior walked to the quarterdeck and clicked on the squad-bay lights, we snapped out of the trance.

"Some of you may have heard that the Marine Corps builds men," he began. *"That's a line of bull that some recruiter made up to tell your mommies and sweethearts. The reality is that we build warriors. Make no mistake here, recruits. You are here to learn to kill. Embrace the way you feel right now. Savor the taste of hatred you have for Drill Instructor Sgt. Talley. Remember it. Anger and hatred are necessary tools of the trade. And our trade is killing.*

"So from now on when anyone asks you why you joined the Corps, you sound off loud and proud, 'Sir, to kill, sir!' And when anyone asks, 'What makes the grass grow?' you sound off, 'Blood! Blood! Blood!' "

Then he ordered us out of our racks to the position of attention. He told us he was proud of our effort. As a reward he taught us a good-night ditty he had made up just for us. Each recruit waited for the command.

"Readyyyyy, face!"

Sixty bodies robotically pivoted and stepped adjacent to each rack. Each pair of recruits faced off with arms outstretched and palms down on the taut green blankets. It was as if we were learning a new religion, with a new god, and new prayers.

On the senior's cue—"Who are we?"—we began the ritual.

We slammed our arms down on the rack three times—*boom, boom, boom*, echoed throughout the empty corridor and down the stairwells. Then we professed our faith:

Marine Corps!
We romp and stomp, bringing death and destruction!
We're ass-kickin', Woman-lickin', tough as nails and hard as steel!
And the best senior drill instructor on the Island is—our senior drill
instructor, Staff Sgt. Parsons.

Following our chant the senior called, "Prepare to mount. . . . Mount!" We clambered to our backs into the position of attention. Under the cover of darkness we lay still and licked our emotional wounds.

As the sound of the senior's boots disappeared into the distance, I could hear the muffled sounds of young men attempting to silence their tears as they, too, cried themselves to sleep.

TWO

THE FIRST ROUND FROM my rifle traveled straight through the heart—a confirmed kill. Round two drilled the forehead—another kill. Rounds three through six all in the chest—all kills. Round seven pierced the neck. Eight and nine were abdomen kills. The last round I fired found its mark in the heart.

Ten shots.

Ten kills.

I was proud to be a killer. I was different.

All was quiet until the safety officer's voice echoed through the rifle range loudspeaker, "Cease fire! Cease fire! All clear on the firing line. Shooters keep your muzzles pointed downrange and clear your weapons. Instructors, check 'em!"

As I moved from my belly to my knees, marksmanship instructors surrounded me. I stood at the position of attention with my eyes down-range.

The primary marksmanship instructors wore campaign covers like drill instructors, but their relationship with us was educational; we were students and they were our teachers. In fact, drill instructors were not permitted on the range while recruits possessed loaded rifles. The rationale was that recruits with loaded M16s, filled with first-phase hatred, might shoot their drill instructors. Unexpended rounds were accounted for individually to ensure that none found its way back to the barracks and into a rifle chamber. Every recruit was searched individually by a handheld metal detector before leaving the range. The Marine Corps understood that our hearts and minds were hardened, and it was possible that a recruit with a bullet might very well kill a drill instructor if given the chance.

First I felt a pat on the back. Then I received a handshake from my marksmanship instructor. Then smiling, happy faces approached from all sides. Then a captain extended his hand to me. Recruits do not speak with captains. Officers were off limits to recruits. He was smiling too. He grabbed my hand and squeezed it tightly, nearly shaking my shoulder out of its socket.

"Congratulations, Recruit Williams. You are the high shooter for your platoon!"

"Thank you, sir!" was my simple response. The significance of my accomplishment was sinking in gradually.

I had successfully mastered the paramount task of Marine basic training—to train riflemen who specialize in the "one-shot, one-kill" doctrine. Marine rifle training is unmatched worldwide. Prior to Parris Island I had never touched a firearm. After only fourteen days on the rifle range I was able to put ten rounds in a man's trunk and head from a distance of five football fields.

I was singled out from the platoon and paraded around the rifle range with the other high shooters. We were treated like royalty that afternoon. In retrospect we were actually only treated like human beings, but in comparison to the standard treatment on Parris Island it felt like royalty.

Once we returned to our platoons, we fell into formation and marched off from the safety of the rifle range and back into the hands of our drill instructors for the evening. Drill Instructor Sgt. Talley met us, clipboard in hand, studying what I assumed were our rifle qualification scores.

"Get up here, Guide!" snapped Drill Instructor Sgt. Talley.

"Guide Carey reporting as ordered, sir!"

"You're fired. Fall in at the end of formation," Drill Instructor Sgt. Talley commanded, surprising everyone in the platoon.

I wondered if he'd failed rifle qualification. It had to be something extreme for him to lose the guide position this late in training. He was a model recruit.

Recruit Carey, confused, sounded off hesitantly, "Aye, sir," and turned in his guidon.

Carey's demotion was as sudden and unexpected as what happened next.

"Morrison! Take the guidon and assume the guide position," ordered Drill Instructor Sgt. Talley.

What had Morrison done to take the guide position from Carey? He must have scored high on the range, I thought. But then again, if rifle scores were used to determine billets, then I would have been promoted to squad leader. After facing right and marching off to the barracks I guessed I was wrong about being promoted. There must have been some other reason for the leadership change. But what?

Back at the barracks Morrison was reveling in his new role as guide, delegating work and barking orders. While the other recruits were scrubbing rifles, I was scrubbing toilets. That wasn't surprising to me. Morrison and I had become rivals, so I knew he wouldn't let my accomplishment as high shooter go unpunished.

Morrison had assigned me to permanent head-scrubbing duty early in first-phase training, when he was my squad leader. It was payback for my telling him that scrubbing toilets sucked, and that he should rotate us through different jobs. That was the beginning of our mutual dislike—and with help from our drill instructors and a few twists of fate it would grow into hatred.

During our first-phase physical fitness test Morrison padded his sit-up score to make it appear as if he earned the maximum eighty repetitions. When the drill instructor called for Morrison's score, I reported it, which was my role as his test partner. But while I was calling out, "Seventy," Morrison was calling out, "Eighty." Drill Instructor Sgt. Wagner berated us with an integrity lecture and then counted as Morrison repeated the sit-up part of the test. Because he performed fewer than eighty sit-ups during his second trial, Drill Instructor Sgt. Wagner made Morrison dig in the pit while screaming repeatedly, "I am a cheater! I am a cheater!"

As squad leader Morrison had been able to use his authority to get even with me, which he did every time I bested him. My punishment for having embarrassed him during the fitness test was being sentenced as permanent "late-chow recruit." As late-chow recruit I was required to stand guard in the squad bay until the designated early-chow recruit returned to relieve me from guard duty. Because I was required to fall into formation whenever our drill instructor dismissed the platoon from the chow hall, I seldom had time to finish my meals, and occasionally I'd be called to formation before making it through the food line.

Morrison and I would continue to clash throughout the eight weeks of first-phase training. While the majority of this phase was spent mastering close order drill, the monotony of marching was interrupted every few days for specialized physical training. This was the training that most people associate with Marine boot camp—obstacle courses, confidence courses, assault courses, and hand-to-hand fighting.

This training required us to compete against each other in groups or as individuals. Drill Instructor Sgt. Talley humored himself by pitting recruits against their rivals, so Morrison and I battled frequently. Fortunately for me I usually faired better than Morrison.

The first time I went head-to-head with Morrison was pugil stick fighting. I knocked Morrison onto his back and drove the padded end of the pole into his chest, ending the fight with a simulated kill.

"You call yourself a squad leader, Morrison?" Drill Instructor Sgt. Talley said. "I ought to fire your lame ass!"

Following that win Morrison assigned me to fire-watch duty for three consecutive nights. Although missing an hour of sleep to walk guard was not difficult, doing it repeatedly had a cumulative fatigue effect. As squad leader Morrison had the power to make my life miserable. He was the reason I was constantly hungry, and now sleepy. But beating him was always worth the punishment that would follow. No victory over Morrison was sweeter than the one during our day on the confidence course.

It was a special day because it marked the end of first-phase, and was one of the few times when the entire company—all 240 recruits—

had come together to train. Morrison figured a public victory would be just the thing to avenge his honor, and challenged me to race him on the centerpiece of the confidence course—the slide-for-life obstacle.

The slide-for-life is a high-wire obstacle on the confidence course that features a single steel cable stretched from a platform several stories high, over a body of water. Recruits are required to slide along the top of the cable, headfirst and belly down, until they reach land (finishing dry) or fall into the water (finishing wet). Those who finish wet are nabbed by the drill instructors and harassed as prisoners of war.

Morrison and I lay on parallel cables, before hundreds of recruits and dozens of drill instructors. When we reached the midway point, though, drill instructors began shaking the cables to make us lose our balance. We both slid off the top, left hanging under the cable by our hands. I managed to swing my legs up and hook them over the cable. Morrison wore himself out trying to do the same, and eventually dropped. I pulled myself along the cable like an inchworm, until I made it to land. I knew that any retaliation I would later face from Morrison would have been worth the sight of him, humiliated, hands over his head in surrender, being led away to dig in the muddy pit with the other prisoners.

After I finished scrubbing toilets I sat on my footlocker and started writing a letter home about my good fortune on the rifle range.

No sooner had I started writing it Guide Morrison's voice interrupted. "Williams! Report to Drill Instructor Sgt. Talley's office!"

I knew the good times on the range that afternoon would have to end sometime, and it looked like that time was now. I loathed knocking on his hatch.

Pounding the wall outside his door with my open palm, I screamed, "Sir, Recruit Williams reporting as ordered, sir!"

And I waited. Nothing good ever came of being sent to see Drill Instructor Sgt. Talley. Punishment . . . games . . . sarcasm . . . looks of disgust . . .

"Get in here, Williams."

"Aye, sir!"

I executed three pivots upon entering and stood tall before his large oak desk, staring through the sergeant chevrons on his collar. I was unflappable.

"Sit down, Recruit Williams."

I hesitated. Recruits did not sit down in the drill instructor's office. I thought I must have heard the command wrong.

"Sir, the recruit requests to hear the direction again, sir."

He smiled. I didn't know the bastard could smile.

"Williams, just sit down."

Robotically, I eased myself to the edge of the seat. My elbows formed perfect ninety-degree angles as my forearms rested along the top of my thighs. My fingers were together and pointed with palms down just over my knees. I was ready for anything.

Drill Instructor Sgt. Talley pushed a white piece of paper, called a chit, across his desk.

"Congratulations, 'High Shooter.' Read the chit."

It read, *This pass authorizes Recruit Williams to make a phone call home.*

I read it, and read it again.

"Sir, the recruit does not understand, sir."

"A phone call home is a privilege reserved for the high shooter. You'll find the phone booth just outside the rear hatch. Dial zero and ask the operator for help placing a collect call. Understand?"

"Yes, sir. Thank you, sir."

I could tell there was more.

"Williams, you and the other recruits enter third-phase tomorrow."

The two weeks on the rifle range had flown by. I couldn't believe second-phase was over so soon.

"Life on the Island is going to change for you," he said. "Things will be different."

Different? I didn't understand, but I knew better than to ask. That would be conversational, and way out of bounds for recruits.

He continued, "Tomorrow morning you will be part of a detachment for a one-day duty assignment in the base laundry facility. Do you understand?"

I didn't. *Was it a punishment? Was it a privilege?*

"Sir, the recruit will be ready for instructions in the morning, sir."

"Good. Make your phone call and turn to personal time."

"Aye, sir. The recruit requests permission to leave the drill instructor's office."

"Get out!"

I left reassured that our relationship was back to normal because he was screaming again.

I walked out of the rear hatch, clutching my phone chit and dealing with emotions that had been stirred from hibernation. Remembering my family meant dredging up feelings and memories of life before the transformation. The simple act of making a phone call was stifling. My fellow recruits would be jealous that I could make a phone call, but they didn't realize the dilemma.

I stood in the booth, staring blankly at the receiver. I considered just turning around and going back to my safe recruit world. I felt suddenly vulnerable in the booth. I was about to hear a voice that would transport me back home, and I wasn't ready. I had spent ten weeks being distanced from everything I was.

What would I say? I didn't even remember how to speak in the first person. Should I tell how proud I was that I could now kill a man with a bayonet? Should I tell them how the heel of my boot could drive the bones in the enemy's septum through the frontal lobe of his brain, killing him instantly? Should I explain that I had earned this phone call by being the best killer?

"This is the operator. How may I help you?"

It was strange hearing a woman's voice. "Good afternoon, ma'am." Guarded, as I had been for months, I hesitated to speak. Was it a base operator? Civilian? "I request permission to make a collect call to Ms. Mary Jane Williams."

"Your name, sir?"

"Recruit Williams, ma'am—make it, Buzz, ma'am."

"And the number you wish to call, sir?"

The number? I knew my combination lock number, and my social security number, and my rifle serial number, and dozens of other numbers that had been branded into my memory—but I couldn't remember my own phone number.

"I'm sorry, ma'am . . . I just need a minute." Home seemed so far away and so long ago. Once I got the first digits, the remaining four came easily. The phone rang once . . . twice . . . again, and again. My mother wasn't picking up.

Finally the operator interrupted. "There is no answer, sir. Would you like to try another number?"

It was nice being called "sir" for a change. "Yes, ma'am. This number is for Gina."

The thought of speaking with Gina rattled my nerves. Although she had promised to be faithful while I was away, and had written to me daily, I was still insecure. I, too, wrote to her daily, hoping that she would still be interested in me when I returned, whoever "I" might be at that point. Gina answered on the second ring.

"Hello."

It was unreal to hear her voice.

"This is the operator. Will you accept the charges for a collect call for Gina from . . . your name again, sir?"

"Gina Marie, it's Buzz," I announced impatiently.

"Oh, my God! Buzz?"

"Do you accept—"

Gina cut off the operator, "Yes! Yes! I accept!"

"Buzz?"

"I'm here" was all I could say.

"How are you? Where are you? When are you coming home?"

I tried to talk like the person she remembered. "I'm OK. I only get one call, and I tried Mom, but she wasn't home. Would you tell her I tried?"

"You sound funny. Are you sure you're OK?"

Silence. Neither of us knew what to say.

Suddenly I froze at the sight of a strange drill instructor approaching me. I could hear Gina's voice. "Buzz? Are you there?" but I put the phone down as he approached. The drill instructor stood in the threshold of the booth, hands on his hips, eyes burning holes into mine like a magnifying glass focusing the sun's rays. Then he leaned into my face and let loose with a scream that vibrated the glass in the booth.

"Just what in hell do you think you are doing?"

I snapped to the position of attention, stretching the phone cord to its limits. I could still hear Gina's voice in the handset by my thigh, but I did not dare answer her.

"Sir, the recruit has a chit for a phone call, sir."

He snatched the chit from my hand. After he reviewed it he asked, "Did you make a phone call?"

The son of a bitch, I thought. Gritting my teeth I responded, "Sir, yes, sir."

"You're done! Get off."

"Aye, sir!"

Trembling at the hand and voice, I lifted the handset to my ear. There was so much to say, and no time for any of it.

"Gina Marie?"

"Buzz, What is going on? Are you sure—"

Knowing that she didn't understand my predicament made matters worse. Would she think I no longer cared for her? "I can't talk any more. My time's up."

"But we didn't get to talk yet."

The drill instructor was inside the booth now. "You got about a heartbeat to get off the friggin' phone, boy."

"I have to go now. I'll write tonight. Bye."

The last thing I heard her say was "I love you," before the phone was ripped from my ear. Never had I ended a phone call with Gina without telling her I loved her. I regretted not telling her, despite the drill instructor in my face. What could he have done to me that hadn't already been done?

As I attempted to scurry away he held on to my sleeve and spun me around to face him.

"You owe me a thank-you," he said.

I stared back blankly.

"She's fucking your best friend. You just don't know it yet."

Snapping to the position of attention, I pulled my arm down to my side and out of his grasp. I forced the words out, "Sir, thank you, sir," then quickly about-faced and double-timed back to the barracks.

Afterward I thought that a phone call was the worst possible way to reward recruits. It had been an emotional detour that I really didn't need. I couldn't get Gina's voice out of my head. It kept reminding me of the person I had become at Parris Island.

After morning chow the next day, just as Drill Instructor Sgt. Talley had explained, I boarded a five-ton truck at 0700 hours for duty in the base laundry facility. We were told that the truck would transport us back to the barracks at 1900 hours and were instructed to report to the drill instructor's office upon our return.

Upon entering the laundry facility we were greeted by an old man in civilian clothes. He introduced himself as Charlie, and we learned that each day a small group of recruits from a different platoon are tasked with laundering recruit uniforms.

"In the old days," he explained, "recruits would spend hours cleaning their own uniforms—by hand! These days, recruits can spend their time training while only a handful of recruits run the machines. The machines do all the hard work!"

Charlie was amused when I explained how Drill Instructor Sgt. Talley had made a game out of bagging our laundry. Back at the barracks, we were required to count aloud as we stuffed each garment into the giant mesh bags. All the while though, Drill Instructor Sgt. Talley hovered over the bags, leaned into our faces, and screamed out random numbers to confuse us. Then, when our final clothing counts were wrong, he would punish us in the pit for being too stupid to count correctly. Sometimes it took us all afternoon to fill our laundry bags.

Charlie explained the procedures for each of our stations in the assembly-line laundering process. I was positioned at the drying station, where I put giant carts the size of commercial Dumpsters in front of the dryer door. At the end of its cycle the dryer would tilt forward using hydraulics, and eject the bags of dry clothing into the carts. I would then push the cart to the next recruit's station, where he would sort the bags for shipping by platoon. Because of the drying time, my station afforded me the most "idle time" of the bunch, and Charlie spent a good part of the day talking with me. By the end of the day I would think of Charlie as the Laundry Sage.

"So what's your name?" asked Charlie.

"Sir, the recruit's name is—"

"No," Charlie interrupted, "I'm not a drill instructor. Hell, I've been retired for twenty years, young man. Just talk to me like you do back on the block."

There was silence from me.

Charlie laughed. "I know you think I'm fucking with you. I'm for real. There aren't any drill instructors hiding around the corner to punish you for talking to me."

The whole exchange reminded me of the time I found a wild dog running the streets back home. He visited occasionally, waiting under my dad's Chevy pickup truck. Every time I tried to pat his fur he would back away and posture in a defensive crouch. I didn't know how to communicate that I wouldn't hurt him. He just didn't trust people, period. The closest I ever got to him was an arm's length. That was when he was busy eating food that I brought him.

Charlie interrupted my memory, offering me a Baby Ruth candy bar. "I bet it has been a while since you had one, huh?"

"Yes, sir." I took it but held him at an arm's length.

As I chewed, Charlie took advantage of the silence.

"It's amazing to me how you boys all come in here the same way, day after day . . . spouting off to me like I'm gonna send you to the pit if you fuck something up. I get paid to run a laundry shop, not to train recruits. It's a hell of a lot nicer to work here if you just drop the recruit act."

I shot a pissed-off look his way.

He disarmed me with a chuckle. "Well, go ahead and say what's on your mind."

Again, there was silence from me.

"Let me guess. You didn't like that I used the word *act,* right? You might be one of them hardheads that would rather keep his head in the sand about the truth. Life on the Island could be a lot different for you if you understood."

As he walked away he added, "By the way, you're welcome for the candy bar."

I sat and listened to the hypnotic rattle and hum of the dryer and wondered what Charlie meant by "the truth." I thought I understood what was happening on the Island. I had entered into a contract when I hit the yellow footprints. The drill instructors agreed to provide emotional and physical stress. We agreed to take it. The payoff for the drill instructors was the satanic pleasure of making life hellish for recruits. The payoff for recruits was the hatred that fueled a desire to kill that would make a man into a Marine. What more was there to understand? *That old man,* I thought to myself, *has been out of the Corps too long.*

At midmorning Charlie passed by, checking on my progress. As he passed, my guilt from my past absence of manners kicked in.

Just slightly louder than the dryer noise, I called out, "Mr. Charlie."

He stopped and turned around.

"Thanks for the candy bar."

I wanted him to stay, but he simply acknowledged me with a nod and kept on his way. Months had passed since I'd been able to have a normal conversation with anyone on the Island, and I really did want to hear what he had to say.

At 1200 hours Charlie brought me my brown-bag lunch. He had a lunch, too, and he sat down on an empty crate beside me. I prepared myself for more awkward tension. As I opened my bag he began to tell me a story. Years later, in college, I would learn that Charlie's story was a version of Plato's Allegory of the Cave. This is how I remember him telling it:

> *"There were four people, imprisoned since childhood, who lived in a cave below the ground. Their bodies were chained so that they could only look at a blank wall straight in front. There was a fire at a dis-*

tance behind them, and a low parapet between the fire and the prisoners backs. Behind the parapet were puppeteers who moved statue figures along its top and spoke in echoed voices. Reality for the prisoners was limited to the shadows of the puppets on the wall before them and the echoes that they heard from a distance. One day the prisoners were re-leased and left free to explore the world of the cave. One was prompted by an instructor to examine the fire. Along the way he observed the parapet and was asked to identify the statues that he had known for-merly only as shadows. And the instructor then dragged the reluctant caveman up a steep ascent to the mouth of the cave and forced him to look at the brightness of the sun. The caveman's eyes were irritated and he was confused. Just as his eyes grew accustomed to the brightness, his mind grew accustomed to the realities that existed beyond the shadow world—and he was enlightened. He was different."

I thought I understood the message of the story.

"I'm wondering what you meant earlier when you said I need to understand the Island," I said.

"Son, I have spent my entire adult life in the Marine Corps. I served in Korea and Vietnam. I understand what happens when boys go to war. And I understand how to prepare boys to go to war. I was a drill instructor in 1975 just after my tour in Vietnam."

Jesus, I thought. *He was a drill instructor when Lenny was in boot camp here.* He had my full attention now.

"What is the worst thing the drill instructors have done to you?" he asked.

I immediately flashed back to our forming night. There was so much to choose from.

"We were forced to drink water until we puked, and then we ex-ercised in it."

"And why was that so bad?" he asked.

"It seems like abuse, not training. Our drill instructor knew that we could not hold three canteens of water. And then to make us ex-ercise in it . . ."

"You're still wearing your chains, I see," he responded, taking an-other bite of his sandwich.

After he finished chewing he added, "Everything your drill instructors do for you and to you has a purpose. More than that, every minute of the day is calculated and planned on a training schedule. Drill instructors follow very specific objectives, and are held accountable by the series commander for everything they do—everything."

"So you are telling me that drinking until we puked was on the training schedule."

"Every drill instructor on the Island understands the physiology of dehydration, and they are trained on techniques for increasing your body's ability to use water."

I gave a blank stare.

"By the time you leave this Island, your body will be accustomed to consuming three gallons of water per day. Most of the military hot spots in the world are in jungle or desert climates. If you dehydrate, you can't fight. And isn't that why you are training?"

It was taking me a while to process the logic. "OK. What about the vomit?"

"Know what happens when you get seasick?"

"I get nausea, but I don't get seasick."

"Then you've never been on a troop carrier making a beach landing. Inside, a squad of Marines sits shoulder to shoulder—all squeezed together in a floating metal box. When that thing hits the waves, Marines will start to puke their guts up. If the waves don't get to you, the vomit in your lap will. Dealing with stench is just the beginning of being ready for combat. Your drill instructors are giving you the tools you will need to survive. It would help you to graduate if you started thinking of the drill instructors as doing things for you instead of to you."

This was not the kind of information that I could digest and accept without a great deal of reflection. I just sat and thought about our training schedule, the endless games, the rote drills, and the mindless repetition. Were there reasons for it all? Did the tasks lead us to accomplish objectives?

"What about sitting on the deck for hours of classes instead of using chairs?" I asked.

"Did you sit in a chair on the rifle range?"

"No."

"The cross-legged position used for classes helps to prepare your legs and trunk for the muscle tone and control necessary to make a steady firing platform for your rifle."

"They tell us we need our sleep, and then wake us up to play games in the middle of the night."

"Do you think the enemy sleeps when you sleep? Nobody gets regular sleep in combat."

"What about digging us in the pit for punishment?"

"You say punishment, we say conditioning. There are no showers in the field. You get filthy, and you live with it. Physical comfort is a commodity that you need to learn to live without."

Our dialogue continued throughout the afternoon. It was fascinating to hear the rationale that placed my experiences on the continuum between torture and training. In only one afternoon of dialogue I had developed a new appreciation for the work of our drill instructors.

When the workday ended, Charlie pushed a button on the wall, which started the whine of an electric motor. As the overhead door of the loading dock shook, a stream of daylight flashed across the floor. As the door rose, the darkness in which we had worked all day gave way to the blinding light of the setting sun.

As Charlie shook my hand he looked me in the eye. "Consider yourself unshackled." And he sent me off into the uncomfortable sunlight. Like the caveman in the story I, too, was excited about the realities that existed beyond my recruit world. I was becoming enlightened.

The twenty-minute ride home in the bed of the five-ton truck was liberating for me. I listened to the woes of the recruits as they lamented the return to hell. I, however, was anxious to get back to the platoon and enjoy my new status as high shooter. The paradigm shift that I was experiencing gave me confidence and optimism that set me apart from the others. While the others were complaining of the inevitable three-mile run in the morning, I was thinking of how I couldn't run a mile before boot camp, and now I was looking forward to proving I could do it faster than ever. They bitched about being sent to the pit for calisthenics, while I saw definition developing in my biceps and abdomen for the first time in my life. Most of all they traded horror stories of the cruelty of their respective "heavy" drill instructors.

Before my time with the laundry sage I would have joined right in. Instead I was feeling the pride of emotional hardening to the point where I did not think that Drill Instructor Sgt. Talley could bother me anymore. I understood, with amazing clarity, that the heavy drill instructor, more than any other factor on the Island, was what gave newly graduated Marines their steely look.

The squeal of the air brakes interrupted my thoughts. I was the first to jump from the bed of the truck and sprint to the rear hatch of our squad bay. Just before entering I collected myself mentally and squared away my uniform. I was prepared to report to the drill instructors' office and show them the new Recruit Williams . . . the unchained Williams.

After my time with Charlie, life on the Island never seemed better. The first-phase games had ended, rifle qualification was behind us, and we were all ready for the perks of third-phase training: a short patch of hair atop our heads, fewer trips to the pit, combat training in the field, and then graduation. The best part, though, was the camaraderie we shared. Helping each other to survive ten weeks of hell on Parris Island had formed the strongest of bonds between us. We were brothers.

Nothing, I thought, could change that.

As I crossed the threshold of the hatch I wondered if I was in the wrong squad bay. Things didn't seem quite right. The lights were off, except the light emanating from the drill instructors' office side window. As the hatch slammed behind me, I saw the blinds of the drill instructors' office separate and then snap back into place. I surveyed the surroundings carefully. Some recruit spaces were vacant, their wall lockers and footlockers open and empty. There were two fully packed seabags in front of Guide Morrison's rack.

The drill instructors' office door crashed open and Drill Instructor Sgt. Talley barked at the guide, "Report!"

Morrison belted out his the response. "Sir, the count on deck is fifty-two recruits, sir!"

Fifty-two? I thought. *This morning there were sixty . . .*

"Stand by there, Morrison. There's soon to be only fifty-one recruits on deck."

"Aye, sir!" Replied Guide Morrison.

"Front and center, Williams." Drill Instructor Sgt. Talley spoke with calm conviction. I heard his command, but was still mired in the mathematics of his last statement . . . *soon to be fifty-one . . .* someone was getting dropped. I remembered the seabags in front of Guide Morrison's rack. Could it be that Morrison was getting dropped back in training to another platoon? I knew I had beaten his score on the rifle range, but I didn't think he went unqualified.

A scream interrupted my thought. "Any friggin' day there, Williams!"

I ran to within the specified arm's length from his front and reported at the position of attention. "Sir, Recruit Williams reporting as ordered, sir!"

"You know how Morrison earned the guide position, Williams?"

Still confused, but lucid enough to reply as trained, I sounded off, "Sir, Recruit Morrison earned the position of guide because he is the most squared-away recruit in the platoon, sir."

I spewed the rhetoric to him, even though I did not believe it.

Guide Morrison stood at parade rest at his guard post within earshot of the quarterdeck.

"Guide, are you the most squared-away recruit in this platoon?"

Guide Morrison yelled confidently, "Sir, yes, sir!"

"Really," he asked sarcastically. "Guide, did you negotiate the slide-for-life obstacle dry or wet?"

"Sir, wet, sir," snorted Morrison.

"You, Williams?" asked Drill Instructor Sgt. Talley.

"Sir, dry, sir!" I replied proudly.

Drill Instructor Sgt. Talley upped the ante with the next question.

"Refresh my memory. Who beat whose ass with the pugil sticks?"

After an uncomfortable silence and mounting tension I boasted, "Sir, Recruit Williams beat Guide Morrison's ass with the pugil sticks, sir."

The redemption felt liberating. I reflected on all of the shitty duties that the guide assigned to me out of jealousy. It was coming clearer to me now. I was going to become the guide tonight.

"You beat his ass in the boxing ring, too, didn't you, Williams?" asked Drill Instructor Sgt. Talley, rubbing salt into Morrison's wounded ego.

"Sir, yes, sir!" I replied.

Drill Instructor Sgt. Talley added the final insult. "And—correct me if I am wrong, Guide Morrison—but didn't Williams outshoot you on the rifle range too?"

"Recruit Williams scored two points higher than Recruit Morrison on the range, sir!" Guide Morrison shouted defensively.

He followed up in a condescending tone, "So I asked you again, Guide Morrison. Are you the most squared-away recruit in this platoon?"

Silence.

"Well, it is not a trick question there, Nasty! Answer me!"

I was reveling in the thought of assuming the position of guide and beginning to think that Charlie was right. Drill Instructor Sgt. Talley wasn't so bad after all.

Recruit Morrison was choking back his anger. "Recruit Morrison believes that Drill Instructor Sgt. Talley knows what makes a good Marine and trusts the drill instructor's decision to make this recruit the guide, sir!"

I thought that was a pretty good answer.

"You are right, Morrison. I do know what makes a good Marine, and Williams has it all. Well, almost all. You see . . . Williams didn't want to be a Marine all of the time, so he joined part-time. A reservist . . . a friggin' reservist."

I was frozen. His words stung my ears.

Drill Instructor Sgt. Talley commanded, "Get Williams's seabags to the quarterdeck, Guide."

Oh, shit, I thought. *Those are my bags, not Morrison's.* I didn't understand what was happening. I knew I was on my way out, but had no idea why I was leaving or where I was headed.

Drill Instructor Sgt. Talley continued to speak to Morrison as if I were invisible. Apparently I no longer rated the privilege of being seen.

"It is a shame too. I knew in first phase he had what it took to be a squad leader—maybe even the guide. But reservists ain't like us full-timers, Morrison. Well, with all of the studying, keg parties, and sorority girls, it's sometimes hard to fit in being a Marine."

I summoned the courage to ask, "Sir, Recruit Williams requests permission to know what is happening, sir."

Drill Instructor Sgt. Talley turned toward me with contempt in his voice and disgust on his face.

"What is happening, Recruit Williams, is that you, and eight others like you, are being fast-forwarded to another platoon so you can graduate a week earlier and start college on time."

Eight others? While I wondered who else would be joining me, Morrison dropped my seabags at my feet. His eye contact lasted longer than it should have, and he remained in my face, toe-to-toe, and chest-to-chest.

Drill Instructor Sgt. Talley pulled me away by the material in my collar and continued. "What is happening, Recruit Williams, is you are about to get your nasty ass off my quarterdeck and out of my face! Pick up your trash and move!"

To my surprise Recruit Carey was positioned directly across from me, as we stood on-line for the first time with our new platoon. Until then I hadn't known he was a reservist. Then I realized the reason he had been fired from the guide position had had nothing to do with his shooting score. It was because he, like I, was leaving the platoon.

Assimilation into the culture of the new platoon never fully occurred. It was reminiscent of first-phase training all over again. The
drill instructors, as well as other recruits, treated us like black sheep
throughout third-phase training. Worse yet, I mourned the loss of
my identity and my recruit buddies in my former platoon. I was so
distraught that I spoke with my new senior drill instructor and requested permission to return to my former platoon and delay my
entrance to college. I was informed it was not an option. It was the
first time, but not the last, that I questioned my decision to join the
Marines as a reservist.

Graduation day was bittersweet for me, as I suspect it was for the
other black sheep who were fast-forwarded. Although I was glad I
had survived Parris Island, my graduation was anticlimactic.

As we stood ready in our dress uniforms, the senior drill instructor talked of how proud he was of us, which meant little to me. He
wasn't my senior. It wasn't my platoon. Looking on, I saw the
crowd in the bleachers, relieved that Gina and Mom were there. But
as we started marching toward the parade deck, the sky suddenly
turned dark and the clouds opened. The rain was so torrential that
the base commander called off the ceremony, sending families to
take cover, dismissing us hurriedly with the wave of his hand. It was
no real loss. It didn't feel like graduation to me anyway.

After fifteen minutes of wandering amid the chaos of disoriented
graduates and rain-soaked relatives, I finally found Gina and Mom.
It was now I who stood rigid and robotic, uncomfortably accepting
the hugs that I thought might get me sent to the pit.

My mother's boyfriend—who I did not get along with—congratulated me with a handshake. Mom was laughing and crying at the
same time. She was happy for me, but I knew a part of her was reliving Lenny's graduation, as was a part of me. Gina stood close,
held on to my arm, and waited for me to start talking. But talking
would have to wait.

What I remember most vividly about our rainy reunion was the
insecurity I felt without the drill instructors' supervision. We had
been micromanaged twenty-four hours per day, seven days per
week, for three months. Now we were on our own. There were so

many ways to screw up. I began to wonder if my uniform was still squared away—whether the officers nearby were close enough to salute—and how I would speak to my drill instructors if they approached. Paranoid of being dug in front of my family, I excused myself and headed back to the barracks to collect my bags.

As I walked away from the parade deck I heard the familiar voice of Drill Instructor Sgt. Talley calling, "Hey, Marine!"

I stopped and looked around. Directly to my front were the recruits of my original platoon, halted and positioned at parade rest—apparently for my benefit. I assumed they were returning from the tailor, as all were smartly dressed in their dress green alpha uniforms. They looked at me enviously, knowing that I had just graduated.

Drill Instructor Sgt. Talley motioned for me to come over to the platoon as he stood impatiently with his hands on his hips.

"Get over here, Marine," commanded Drill Instructor Sgt. Talley.

I second-guessed my ears. Had he just called me, Marine?

It sounded too good to be true, and it was.

I responded with the reflex, "Sir, Recruit Williams reporting as—"

"At ease, Williams," he interrupted. "You did graduate today, didn't you?"

I remained at the position of attention and took a risk. "Yes . . . Sgt. Talley!"

"Well, then, you're a Marine, not a recruit," he sneered back. "Act like one!"

I did not respond, for fear of saying the wrong thing.

Recognizing my anxiety, Drill Instructor Sgt. Talley directed me to stand in front of the platoon, "Form them up, Marine."

I looked at him for a clue, and he motioned with his hands for me to address the platoon. Only drill instructors addressed platoons from the front, and I had no idea of how to proceed. I walked cautiously around to the front and stared at the recruits whom I had missed since we parted.

Just as the nostalgia started to set in, Drill Instructor Sgt. Talley tore into the platoon.

"Do we not see a Marine in front of you? So we just want to be disrespectful to a United States Marine? How about snapping to attention! How about offering a proper military greeting? How about locking your bodies and showing some respect!"

I instinctively snapped to attention and braced for the storm. Only, the storm wasn't directed at me—it was aimed at them. Did he really expect them to treat me as they would a Marine? Drill Instructor Sgt. Talley, clever as always, had one last game to play. He apologized to me for the disrespect of the recruits, as they stood at full attention in the blazing midafternoon sun, sweat starting to show on their dress uniforms.

"This mob needs a little discipline. I think you should dig them."

I couldn't believe my ears. He was asking me to punish my brothers with calisthenics, in the street, in their dress uniforms.

I responded unassertively, "Uh . . . no thank you, sir."

"Oh! You thought it was a choice?" Drill Instructor Sgt. Talley yelled. "Let me be clearer . . . I am giving you a direct order to dig this platoon. Now!"

I locked eyes with Guide Morrison, standing in his dress blues, positioned before a standing puddle of water left over from the rain. His eyes dared me.

"Get on your faces!" I screamed, in my best drill-instructor voice.

Every recruit dropped to the street in the push-up position. Guide Morrison's uniform soaked up the muddy water like a sponge. After a minute of the familiar grind I ordered the platoon back to the position of attention.

Then Drill Instructor Sgt. Talley ordered Guide Morrison in front of the platoon with me.

"I want you two to shake hands," he said, physically positioning our hands together in a handshake fashion.

"You two never know when you might see each other again. Someday, Morrison, if we are fortunate enough to have another war, the Marine machine might break down and Uncle Sam will have to send out for spare parts! Oh, I am sorry Williams. . . . I meant call up the reserves."

I never heard from Drill Instructor Sgt. Talley again.

I wish that I could say the same for Morrison.

PART II

RESERVIST

THREE

WHEN THE LIGHTS CLICKED ON, waking me from my sleep, I exploded from my bed with life-and-death urgency as I had during each of my mornings on Parris Island, which nearly gave my unsuspecting mother a heart attack. When I landed on my feet I saw her frozen, eyes wide and startled, with her hand still plastered on the light switch to my bedroom.

"Jesus Christ, Mom!" I yelled.

These were words she never heard from my mouth, rendered in a tone and volume I had never before used in her presence. She looked at me in a state of horror, as if I were the son of Satan and not her own. My waking reflex was so out of context, it was shocking. One night home was not enough to clear Parris Island from my subconscious.

I understand it better now in hindsight. Newly graduated Marines do not get embarrassed. Emotions like embarrassment, grief, sadness, and vulnerability are all converted into anger—the omniemotion that helps recruits survive.

It was the same maternal gesture, an innocent flick of the light switch that had awakened me for most of the days of my life, which sent me into a fit of rage. Her dumbstruck stare was making me angrier by the second. After a very uneasy silence, she cautiously backed out of the doorway to leave me alone. And there I stood, alone in my room, looking for myself in the mirror.

This was my first of many recurring experiences with a process I call reintegration—the mental, physical, and emotional transition from being in combat-ready Marine mode to society-ready civilian mode. It is unspeakably difficult when one's boot-camp world collides with one's civilian world. The culture shock of home life is initially just as debilitating to you as recruit life is for those landing on the yellow footprints for the first time. In civil society there are no outlets to exercise the warrior mentality and personality born at Parris Island, and the constant stress this creates results in an antisocial personality. Some return to their friends and family as quiet dissidents; some return as arrogant egomaniacs; but all return dramatically different from the person who had left just three months before.

Active-duty Marines experience reintegration briefly, if at all, as they pass through their hometowns during their ten-day period of leave, before reporting to their new MOS schools. There is little time, and even less necessity, for them to return to civilian ways of thinking, feeling, and acting.

Reservists, however, are unleashed into their communities indefinitely, left alone to cope with their personal reintegration experiences. Our drill instructors had not prepared us for the process of reintegration, as best I can understand, because it is a phenomenon that is unique to reservists. I later wondered whether it was because the drill instructors did not know, or did not care, what reservists did after boot camp. I suspected the latter.

This Friday morning, however, my struggle with reintegration would need to wait. My mind was preoccupied with the remnants of boot camp dreams. My anxiety about the unknown would soon be realized, and my questions would be answered. It was time to shift gears again.

It was time to report for my first drill weekend.

The rumble of my truck tires crossing the old wooden bridge signaled the moment of truth. After parking in the dirt lot of Camp

Upshur I sat in my pickup truck, sweat soaked from anxiety, and watched the dust settle. I had no idea what to expect for the next forty-eight hours.

I walked up to the chest-high counter of the administrative area and reported as the drill instructors taught us in boot camp.

"Pfc. Williams reporting for duty as ordered, sir!" I presented my check-in papers with an outstretched arm while my body was locked rigidly at the position of attention.

A female voice responded as the Marine behind the counter turned to greet me. "I know it has been a long time, Pfc., but you didn't forget the difference between men and women, did you?"

Staff Sgt. Church smiled and introduced herself as the company admin chief. She was a tall, attractive Latina, more feminine than the female Marines I had seen at Parris Island, but a staff sergeant nonetheless.

I stood silently, locked at the position of attention, not knowing how to respond.

Then a corporal leaned over the counter, exaggerating his visual inspection of me standing at attention. "You've got to be kidding me, Dog!"

Dog is the abbreviated form of "Devil Dog," a term of endearment among Marines.

Then came the sarcasm. "Hey, Staff Sgt. Church! I think Chesty Puller's grandson is checking into our unit."

Chesty Puller was arguably the most famous Marine in history, reverently remembered for his bravery in combat in five wars during the first half of the twentieth century.

The office area boomed with laughter as the Marines gathered around the counter to watch me, the new-join, check in. *New-join* was the default label designated for all Marines new to the unit whose names were not yet known.

"At ease, Marines!" commanded Staff Sgt. Church.

The Marines returned to their desk areas under muffled sounds of laughter.

"Come around to my desk, Pfc., I'll get you processed and on your way. You're the only Marine checking in this drill."

I surmised that it was acceptable to refer to the collective drill weekend simply as drill.

She went on to add, "Most new-joins are reporting in October. Were you fast-forwarded?"

"Yes," I answered resentfully, "to make my college start-date."

The staff sergeant smiled. "Well, I guess you'll just have a head start on all the other new-joins next month, now, won't you?"

There was something maternal about Staff Sgt. Church that made me comfortable. In addition to processing paperwork she answered all of the questions I had about the forthcoming drill. I learned that the unit's CO, Capt. Cruz, had a reputation for realistic combat training. The staff sergeant explained that most of the drill weekends for our unit were spent in the field, and that I would need to visit supply to get my initial issue of field gear.

She added that I should not expect to get liberty during my drill weekends. *Liberty* was the Marine word for off-duty, but it didn't mean much to me at the time.

The staff sergeant expected more of a response from me.

"You do understand that this is an infantry unit, right?"

"Yes," I replied. "I'm a light armored vehicle crewman."

"No," she said. "You're a 0311 grunt until you graduate from LAV crewman school next summer."

It didn't matter to me. *Infantry was infantry.* I believed the marketing behind the recruiting poster that read, GO INFANTRY. EVERYTHING ELSE IS JUST SUPPORT. I wanted to sneak through the woods with camouflage paint on my face, paddle stealthily along a river in an inflatable recon boat, and rappel down cliffs with an M16 rifle on my back. I didn't enlist to repair engines, drive bulldozers, or file papers. I wanted to be a fighter, and that meant infantry.

Staff Sgt. Church told me I was assigned to Weapons Platoon under Cpl. Ramsey, the acting platoon sergeant. She explained that I would not be assigned a position with a LAV crew until enough Marines joined to form a second LAV platoon.

I left the admin office with a basic understanding of what the drill weekend would be like, and headed for supply. The supply building was located on the large asphalt parking area called the Ramp. The Ramp was roughly the size of a football field, and contained three rows of perfectly aligned armored vehicles, each covered with a thick green military tarp.

Walking amid the LAVs gave me chills. I had been anticipating this moment for more than a year. I had wanted to be a LAV crewman so much that I had been willing to drive three hours to get to the base for each training weekend. It was the closest infantry unit to my home in Baltimore. Or so the recruiter had said. A year later, halfway around the world in Saudi Arabia, I would meet Marines from a LAV unit in Frederick, Maryland—only one hour's drive from my home.

When I entered supply I met Staff Sgt. Bader, who gave me what I would learn was his standard greeting: "What the fuck do you want?"

After hearing that I needed my initial issue he rolled his eyes and mumbled something about "fucking new-joins." Thirty minutes later he slid a signature card and a pencil across the counter that separated the requisitioners from the requisitionees. On the wall was a crudely drawn picture of a skull with crossbones and the caption WITHOUT SUPPLY YOU WILL DIE. I recall thinking that it seemed out of place for a reserve unit. The base was filled with cryptic messages and symbolism like the supply sign. I knew that in time I would figure it all out, one way or another.

"You going to the field tonight?" grumbled Staff Sgt. Bader.

I gave the automatic reply, "Yes, sir."

Staff Sgt. Bader lunged toward me, grabbed my uniform at the collar, and pulled me up and onto the counter so I was face-to-face with him.

"See these chevrons?"

"Yes"—I hesitated—"yes, Staff Sergeant!"

"I work for a living, Pfc. Don't insult me by addressing me like a goddamned officer! . . . Understand me?"

I managed to squeak out, "Yes, Staff Sergeant!" as he eased me back to my feet on the far side of the counter.

This guy thinks he's a drill instructor, I thought to myself.

I made it through the rest of the gear-issue process without another incident. I left supply with a seabag full of gear, and a heightened awareness that I needed to keep my recruitlike behaviors in check.

As I walked the two hundred meters from the ramp to the barracks area, I observed that our company only occupied four of the dozens of Quonset huts of Camp Upshur. Staff Sgt. Church had explained that Camp Upshur had been an officer training facility during the Vietnam War. As I pulled open the dilapidated door to building 2015, the designated building for Weapons Platoon, it nearly fell from its hinges. To say that the Quonset huts were poorly maintained was an understatement.

Once inside I smelled a strong musty odor. There were twenty sets of steel racks lining each side of the Quonset hut, each with a thick spring-laden mattress. There were no pillows and no linen. Tall green metal wall lockers separated the racks. At the foot of each rack was a green wooden footlocker like the ones in boot camp. The layout of the barracks was hauntingly similar to the ones on Parris Island. Sunlight streamed in through cracks in the boarded windows, spotlighting heavy dust particles that floated through the air. I flicked a circuit breaker on the far end of the wall and the ceiling lit up with the humming glow of long cylindrical fluorescent bulbs.

The wall lockers each had strips of masking tape with last names and first initials labeled on them with a black marker. I stopped at the first unoccupied wall locker and emptied my seabags. I had arrived more than three hours before the 2000 hours formation just to be safe. I had learned all about the significance of formations in boot camp. They were organized meetings in which all Marines were accounted for, and important information was passed along to the troops. I knew it was important to be on time to the first formation, even before Staff Sgt. Church warned me not to be late.

The pressure of being ready and on time made me focus, just like I did in boot camp. It is an intense sort of focus—the kind that filters out everything except for the thing I'm concentrating on. In the squad bay at Parris Island I would spend Sunday afternoon organizing my footlocker, only to empty it and start over again for no reason. Recruit Wilson, my bunkmate in boot camp, said it was like I was in a zone, and it became a running joke between us.

But even after returning home from boot camp I still found myself slipping into that zone. During my first night home I had stayed up late arranging my dresser like my footlocker, and my closet like my wall locker. I couldn't sleep until I had counted everything in my drawers and my closet, and laid out my clothes for the next day. Even after a week home I found it difficult to sleep without this nightly routine.

In the squad bay at Camp Upshur I found it easy to blow three hours, lost in my zone. I inventoried and organized my footlocker, just as it was in boot camp, complete with every item ranging from my *Guidebook for Marines* to my shaving kit. I also arranged my wall locker with all of my issued uniforms and made it ready for inspection. Most of my time, though, was spent labeling, adjusting, and fitting all of the newly issued field gear that we called 782 gear.

Staff Sgt. Bader had told me the numbers 782 were the numbers identifying Form 782, which is the form Marines sign, accepting responsibility for the field gear that they are issued. I didn't know whether he was bullshitting me or not, but it made sense to me at the time. At that point in my development as a Marine, I believed just about everything that higher-ranking Marines told me.

By the time I heard the second set of car tires thumping across the wooden bridge, I was fully dressed in combat gear, including my flak jacket, gas mask, and helmet. Over my flak jacket I fastened my H-harness and war belt complete with filled canteens, ammunition pouches, and a first aid kit. I didn't know what Cpl. Ramsey would expect of me, so I relied on the only experience that I had—all of which was from boot camp.

Shortly after the second car arrived came a second, third, and fourth. I had hoped that at least one of the Marines would be assigned to Weapons Platoon, like me, so he could tell me what to expect. That wasn't the case. Before our barracks door opened the bridge was humming with a steady stream of vehicles, and the dirt parking area outside the barracks filled with the growing roar of

voices, laughter, and cursing. I kept myself busy, ritualistically organizing, counting, and reorganizing the gear in my footlocker and
wall locker. At approximately 1930 one voice boomed over the others, "Thirty minutes to fall in!" Other Marines echoed the order as
it was relayed across the parking lot in a matter of seconds.

First I heard the crash, and then I saw the splintered wood fragments as the fragile door was ripped from its hinges. "Fucking piece-
of-shit door!" exclaimed the first Marine as he threw it outside the
barracks in the grass. I stood rigidly at my footlocker as the rush of
civilian-clad Marines flooded the barracks. Boom-box style radios
filled the room with all kinds of music. Most of them entered with
convenience-store bags filled with snacks, candy, and sodas. The
mood was one of feverish urgency as Marines changed into their
uniforms. I noticed their wall lockers and footlockers were empty
except for the gear they brought with them to drill.

Finally I got the nerve to interrupt the Marine next to me. "Hey,
Pfc.! Could you show me who Cpl. Ramsey is?"

He yelled over the music, "Yeah, his rack is at the end of the
squad bay—the light-green Marine with the glasses."

Light green was the Marine way of saying "white." This was the
Marine Corps's way of promoting racial acceptance. According to
the theory all Marines were considered equal, and thus all Marines
were green, albeit different shades of green. White Marines were
"light green" and black Marines were "dark green." The theory
sounded better than it worked.

As I walked through the center of the squad bay to find Cpl.
Ramsey, I observed that the platoon was made of mostly privates
first class (Pfcs.) and lance corporals, about half dark green and half
light green. Small cliques of Marines formed around certain racks to
celebrate their monthly reunion. There was a sense of brotherhood
among the Marines of Weapons Platoon. It was a sense of belonging
that I hoped to be a part of one day.

Cpl. Hoffman looked way too young to be in charge of a platoon of Marines—he was no more than twenty years old. He stood
about five feet nine inches tall, and his uniform hung loosely on
his skinny frame. He, like the others, was in the frantic throes of

changing into his uniform to be on time for formation. One thing that was crystal clear to me was that being on time to the formation was of paramount importance to the Marines of Weapons Platoon. I thought that there would be no better time to introduce myself to the platoon sergeant, so I stepped into his space and interrupted his routine.

I considered snapping to the position of attention, but remembered Staff Sgt. Bader's reaction and simply extended my arm for a handshake. "I am Pfc. Williams. . . . I've been assigned to your platoon."

Cpl. Hoffman squinted his eyes and looked in my direction. He fumbled blindly through the tangle of clothing and snack wrappers on his rack to find his glasses, which he pushed onto his nose with one finger in a scholarly manner.

As I came into focus he shook my hand. "Welcome aboard, Pfc. Got a sponsor yet?"

"No, I'm not sure what that is."

"You know, a buddy," he explained, "—to show you around and answer your questions. Lance Cpl. Baker's fire team is short one man, so you can fill in. Baker will be your sponsor."

Cpl. Hoffman was still preoccupied with dressing, but I had a few questions.

"I need to know what to do to get ready for the formation," I stated matter-of-factly.

One of the lance corporals next to Cpl. Hoffman laughed sarcastically, and called down the corridor of dressing Marines to Lance Cpl. Baker. "Hey, Baker! The new-join wants to know if he is ready for formation?"

Baker was a short, dark-green Marine whose muscular upper body, thick from weight lifting, looked mismatched when compared to his scrawny legs.

"Ready for formation? That mu-fucka ready for combat, yo!" laughed Baker.

I realized that I did look out of place among them wearing every piece of gear issued to me. A cascade of laughter rolled through the barracks. Cpl. Hoffman laughed too.

Just as the embarrassment was setting in, a hulking dark-green Marine bolted through the doorway. "Three fucking minutes till formation, ladies!"

There was immediate silence in the squad bay.

Cpl. Hoffman broke the silence saying to me, "That's our acting platoon commander, Sgt. Pitts. He does not play. . . . Don't fuck with him."

I watched as Sgt. Pitts walked along the center of the squad bay, hands on hips, surveying the progress of his troops.

"I don't have one stinking body ready to fall out? First Platoon and Headquarters Platoon are ready and waiting."

"We got one hard-charger ready, Sgt. Pitts," Lance Cpl. Baker called out. "The new-join is ready to storm the mu-fuckin' beach."

Muffled laughter rumbled again. It was obvious that Sgt. Pitts did not like the challenge to his authority. "Baker, you can drag your sorry ass to the end of the formation. The new-join can take your place as first squad leader."

He stared Lance Cpl. Baker into the position of attention. "Aye, Sergeant!"

Sgt. Pitts drove the point home. "Any other comedians want to try out their material?"

The Marines of Weapons Platoon joined together in boot-camp-like manner, "No, Sergeant!"

As he exited through the hatch he ordered, "Cpl. Hoffman, form them up!"

Sgt. Pitts's visit changed the Marines of Weapons Platoon. It was as if a switch had been thrown, shifting the undisciplined civilians into Marine mode. It was instantaneous and lasted for the duration of the drill weekend. Even Lance Cpl. Baker, the joker, grew serious.

Cpl. Hoffman threw the remainder of his trash and gear into his wall locker and led me outside to show me my responsibilities.

"Was he serious about me being squad leader?" I asked naively.

"Did he look like he was kidding?" answered Cpl. Hoffman. "He likes to make examples out of shit birds. But don't worry, Baker's only a shit bird in the rear. . . . He's good-to-go in the field."

I was way out of my comfort zone assuming the responsibility of squad leader, and Cpl. Hoffman knew it.

He patted me on the shoulder. "Just do your best, Pfc."

That was all the training he had time to provide. I was on my own, at the front of the formation. I knew I would be asked for a headcount, so I walked to the end of the row and asked Lance Cpl. Baker how many Marines were on the roster for first squad. He reported ten total, including me. I counted only nine.

Lance Cpl. Baker told me, "Just report, 'All present!' Nobody checks the numbers."

I knew better. Marines hold true to the principle of troop accountability and the doctrine "Leave no Marine behind."

The formation was all business and ceremonial in nature. When it was my turn to give my report I drew a deep breath and summoned the loudest bass my voice could offer. "Nine present. One UA!"

During the formation Capt. Cruz briefed us on the training schedule for the drill. Nearly one hundred Marines stood silently and attentively as the CO laid out the blueprint for our next forty-eight hours of training. The briefing was not that of a practice or simulation. It was a realistic brief of a combat mission that we were expected to carry out, and all eyes and ears were focused. I sensed another shift among the Marines as the mission was explained. Whereas Sgt. Pitts provided the incentive to find our military bearing, Capt. Cruz provided the common purpose that motivated the Marines to perform. In a little less than an hour the weekend warriors of Weapons Company were restored to combat readiness, undoing a month's work of civilian reintegration.

Following the formation Lance Cpl. Baker approached. I braced for the retribution of being responsible for his loss of the squad leader position. Instead I received a handshake.

"That was what we call an integrity check."

I had no idea what he was talking about.

"You know, the report you gave," Lance Cpl. Baker explained. "Instead of bullshitting Cpl. Hoffman with a phony headcount, you gave it to him straight up. You allright, Will."

Lance Cpl. Baker was an influential favorite among his peers. He was that special type of Marine who could dance between being an undisciplined joker in garrison, but highly skilled in the field. Even as a new-join I understood that performance in the field made up for incompetence in the rear.

Capt. Cruz ended the formation by calling out, "Platoon sergeants! Take charge of your Marines and carry out the plan of the day!"

All of our attention was focused on Cpl. Hoffman for direction. He informed us that we had until 2300, approximately two and one-half hours, to get all four vehicles prepped and on the road ready to roll. Once we arrived on the Ramp, every Marine pursued his task with an inspiring sense of urgency. Marines swarmed over the four vehicles assigned to our platoon. I shadowed my sponsor, Lance Cpl. Baker, to learn the way business was conducted on the Ramp.

Within the first thirty minutes the tarps were stripped from the hulls of the vehicles, hatches were opened, gear was laid out and inventoried, and the weapons systems were inspected. I recognized that one of the vehicles had a TOW-firing system—a tank killer. It looked like the LAV on the cover of *Leatherneck* that Staff Sgt. Stone had shown me in the recruiting office. I was awestruck standing next to the real thing.

Lance Cpl. Baker called out, "Fire in the hole!" and the diesel engine on our LAV erupted.

Thick black smoke flowed from the exhaust pipe on the side of the hull and shrouded the vehicle in a dark billowing cloud. It was my first inhalation of LAV diesel exhaust, and it was intoxicating. Our vehicle was one of two that included the mortar weapons system. It had a 60mm firing platform built into the center deck of the LAV, as well as a removable ground-mounted 80mm mortar gun.

I was disappointed that I was not assigned to the TOW vehicle, because it had been the object of my combat fantasies for more than a year. Until then I hadn't known that there were different variants of light armored vehicles. Ironically, during my six years of service in the Marines I would never operate the TOW variant that had been responsible for my original fascination with the LAV.

At approximately 2130 the crewmen turned their attention to

reassembling and strategically placing the gear, weapons, and supplies back on the vehicle. There were Marines hovering over every inch of the LAV. I was overwhelmed by the technicality of it all. They worked feverishly to perform the required radio checks, engine services, hull maintenance, weapons inspections, ammunition placement, map reconnaissance, and personal gear storage. It was dizzying.

At 2230 Cpl. Hoffman ordered all hands to mount up and prepare for movement. I followed him into the darkness that was the belly of the LAV hull. It was pitch black and crowded with gear and troops. I sat sightless and waited. And waited. It was the familiar hurry-up-and-wait phenomenon that I remembered from boot camp.

The glow from my wristwatch showed the time was 2345 when I heard Cpl. Hoffman's voice competing with the hum of the engine.

"Those fucking slowpokes in Headquarters held us up . . . but we are Oscar Mike!"

Oscar Mike represented the phonetic names for the letters *O* and *M,* which together stand for "On the Move." Being on the move felt great, even though I had no idea where we were headed. I recalled from the CO's briefing that tonight's mission was to set up a base camp at a mortar firing range.

I hoped it was close. I was growing tired in the vibrating darkness of the hull.

The faint squeal of the air brakes and the deceleration of the diesel engine continued until we halted forward movement. After a few clanking sounds of metal on metal the two overhead hatches swung outboard, exposing the entire hull to the glow of the moonlight and the dampness of the midnight air. Instinctively, the Marines exploded from the vehicle into a flurry of activity. Gear and people poured from the top and backside of the LAV. I had no idea what to do in the midst of it all. I found Cpl. Hoffman just outside the vehicle, using his hands to ground-guide a five-ton truck into our perimeter. When the truck stopped, he handed me an M16 rifle and told me to stand guard. I pulled on his sleeve to stop him from leaving.

"Cpl. Hoffman, what am I guarding?"

He walked me around to the tailgate and showed me the stack of wooden crates that filled the bed of the truck.

"That's our ammo for the drill—five hundred mortar rounds. Don't let anybody fuck with it until I get back."

I looked down at the M16 and realized it had a full magazine clip in it. It was the first time I had held a loaded M16 outside the safety constraints of the firing range, and it was unsettling. There were no Marines checking to see where the muzzle was pointed, no one to ensure that my rifle's safety mechanism was engaged, and nobody to watch my finger on the trigger. Cpl. Hoffman trusted that I knew what to do. I didn't. I started to panic.

I thought about the sentry classes that Drill Instructor Sgt. Wagner had taught. I couldn't believe I was wishing Drill Instructor Sgt. Wagner were with me. For a moment I thought even Drill Instructor Sgt. Talley would have been a welcomed sight. Then I silently recited the words from the Marine "general orders." They were no longer just words, the way they had been to this point.

1. *To take charge of this post and all government property in view.*
2. *To walk my post in a military manner, keeping always on the alert and observing everything that takes place within sight or hearing.*
3. *To report all violations of orders I am instructed to enforce.*
4. *To repeat all calls from posts more distant from the guardhouse than my own.*
5. *To quit my post only when properly relieved.*
6. *To receive, obey, and pass on to the sentry who relieves me, all orders from the commanding officer, officer of the day, and officers and noncommissioned officers of the guard only.*
7. *To talk to no one except in the line of duty.*
8. *To give the alarm in case of fire or disorder.*
9. *To call the corporal of the guard in any case not covered by instructions.*
10. *To salute all officers and all colors and standards not cased.*
11. *To be especially watchful at night, and during the time for challenging, to challenge all persons on or near my post and to allow no one to pass without proper authority.*

These general orders are tattooed into every Marine's brain. But reciting the words and assimilating their meaning are two very different processes. I rationalized that all Marines must feel anxious the first time they hold a loaded weapon on guard unsupervised.

I recited the general orders in my head over and over. Then it dawned on me. *The "corporal of the guard" provides all orders and instructions to sentries. I need to find the corporal of the guard.*

I stopped the first Marine that passed.

"I need the corporal of the guard."

"You mean Cpl. Hoffman?" he asked.

"I mean the Marine in charge of this guard post."

I was sweating profusely and my hands were wet against the rifle.

The Marine in the shadows seemed annoyed. "You got rounds in that rifle?"

"Yes," I said.

"Then you are the Marine in charge of this guard post," he replied, and walked away.

He was right. I was the Marine in charge of this post. I walked around the truck so that I could keep all of it in view. I walked my post in a military manner as I had been taught in the squad bays of Parris Island. It was actually more marching than walking, around a square perimeter, pivoting at each corner, with the rifle on my right shoulder. The rifle fit differently into my shoulder with the magazine in place.

At approximately 0130 the monotony of guard duty ended. I heard footsteps and voices from a distance. I could make out two silhouettes approaching on foot. I questioned what I was about to do, but did it anyway. Once I started, it was automatic and instinctive.

I called out into the darkness, "Halt! Who goes there?"

The voices stopped and the footsteps slowed, but did not stop.

A second time I commanded, "Halt! Identify yourself!"

The footsteps stopped. I moved the rifle from my shoulder to the port-arms position in front of my chest, loudly slapping the hand guards for the warning effect.

The body on my left started moving toward me. "You got to be fucking kidding me?"

I gave a third and final warning, by the book. "Halt, or I'll shoot!"

I heard one more footstep. They heard the bolt slam home, driving a 5.56 round into the chamber of my M16. I clicked the safety switch to the fire position, and sighted the muzzle at the earth in front of their feet.

A third body approached from behind the silhouettes. "Just what is the holdup here?"

"Sir, the Marine on guard just locked and loaded on us!"

Silence.

"Marine, this is Capt. Cruz . . . your commanding officer. I have placed my ID card on the deck for you to inspect." He then backed away with the others.

I was shaking when I picked up the ID. Sure enough, it was he.

After I clicked the rifle's safety switch back into place, I called out, "Aye, sir. All clear!"

Capt. Cruz walked right up to me and asked for my rifle. I gave it up cautiously. He emptied the chamber and performed a procedure called inspection arms to ensure there were no rounds left in the chamber.

He returned my rifle and asked, "What are your instructions for guarding this post, Marine?"

"Sir, Cpl. Hoffman's instructions were to not let anyone fuck with this ammo until he returned."

One of the Marines snapped, "So you're going to shoot us over some ammo?"

"I was following orders!" I defended.

"At ease!" Capt. Cruz interrupted, extending his palm for emphasis.

Cpl. Hoffman returned just in time to hear the commotion.

Capt. Cruz turned toward him. "Cpl. Hoffman, the guard you assigned did an outstanding job protecting the mortars, but the Marines in my work party almost got their asses shot off."

Capt. Cruz quizzed me again. "Do you know why I authorized rounds for your rifle?"

I didn't.

Cpl. Hoffman helped me out with his explanation. "Sir, this is an open base. You always tell us any yahoo with a pickup truck could make off with a shit load of ammo if the supply point was left unsecured . . . and that would mean a court-martial for me and you."

Nodding his agreement, Capt. Cruz gave Cpl. Hoffman more instructions. "These Marines are going to unload mortar crates for the remainder of the morning. Post guards as needed to secure them."

He leaned into the two lance corporals. "And the next time an armed guard tells you to halt and identify yourself, fucking halt and identify yourself!"

It was a relief to know that I had passed yet another test.

After assigning a new guard to the ammo, Cpl. Hoffman walked me back to the mortar gun position he and his crew were busy setting up. He gathered the other two Marines in the pit, a waist-deep hole surrounded by sandbags, and told them the story of how I almost shot two Marines and the CO. By daybreak the story would make its way all across the range.

It was nearly 0230 by the time Cpl. Hoffman told me to hit the rack. I had too much adrenaline in my system to sleep, so I fashioned a sandbag chair and thought about how much had happened since I left home just a few hours before. I recognized that there was still a lot of boot camp left in me, and it was confusing to figure out which parts of recruit training were assets and which were liabilities. I would need to be more consciously selective in the future. I had already figured out that drill often required difficult choices to be made—sometimes life-and-death choices.

After the adrenaline rush subsided, I lay back into my sandbag chair and covered myself with my poncho to keep warm and dry. My slumber ended at 0445. Capt. Cruz's briefing explained that predawn is the best time to launch an attack on the enemy. The logic was that morning light would arrive before the enemy could regroup for a counterattack. Thus, they would lose the advantage afforded by the cover of darkness. Our predawn mission was to fire mortars to support an ambush being conducted by the scouts of

First Platoon. Although I knew the enemy was fictitious, nothing that I observed would make the exercise seem like a simulation.

I hated training at night. Trading the warmth of a sleeping bag for the freezing night air was miserable. Waking up after only two hours of sleep was unnatural, and fumbling around in the dark with loaded weapons was insane. We were tired, cold, wet, and blind. There were no flashlights to assist us, and no fires to keep us warm. Those amenities were for camping, not combat. Light of any sort would compromise our position and make us an easy target for the enemy. We relied on our sense of touch, and familiarity with the terrain, our gear, and our weapons systems.

We all hated training at night, but to Capt. Cruz it was the most important thing we did. Looking back, I realize that his emphasis on night training saved a lot of lives in the war to come. Infantrymen are told the harder they train in peacetime the less they will bleed in war—but knowing that doesn't make it suck any less.

A crackled message on the radio in the mortar pit started the action. As the stand-to order was passed from position to position, bodies quickly sprang from their dew-laden sleeping bags. The stand-to order was the infantry's version of full alert. It required that all Marines stand ready to fire their weapons in preparation for an imminent attack. Cpl. Hoffman leapt into the mortar pit where Baker and I huddled. He was breathing heavily from making his rounds to ready the Marines and their 80mm mortar tubes. Prior to this I had never even seen a mortar round before. With only a five-minute crash course in the dark, I was opening crates, positioning charges, and stacking HE mortar rounds for my first live-fire mission.

As I worked I listened to all of the radio chatter, which sounded garbled and unintelligible to me. Lance Cpl. Baker was hovering over the mortar tube, cranking and winding its parts. Cpl. Hoffman was hustling between the two mortar pits, and communicating with the radio on his back. Without warning a deafening thump vibrated my innards as the first tube fired its round, leaving my ears ringing painfully. I covered my ears and hunched over. Another thumping blast came, and another. Then the second gun exploded to life. My hands offered little protection against the thunder that surrounded. Finally, after what seemed an eternity, the mortar tubes fell silent. Before the smoke had cleared Cpl. Hoffman jumped into our pit to check us.

"I feel like my ears are bleeding!" I screamed.

He put his finger to his mouth as if to say, *Be quiet!* Though I could see his lips moving, I couldn't hear his words. He reached into his pocket and pulled out two bright yellow foam earplugs. He rolled them between his fingers to make them long and thin, then placed one into each of my ears. As the foam expanded, it filled the cavities in my inner ear. The ringing was louder than ever.

The next series of rounds that left our pit still vibrated my guts, but didn't faze my ears. I took the initiative to hand the prepped rounds to Lance Cpl. Baker, who worked tirelessly to drop them into the mortar tube. The shelling continued, with brief periods of silence and adjustment, until the sun showed on the horizon. As daylight illuminated the landscape, I could match the visual explosions of earth with the distant rumbling of the mortar-shell impacts. It was hard to believe that two mortar tubes could inflict such devastation.

When the tubes stopped firing, I removed the earplugs and was relieved to be able to hear radio transmissions. The mortarmen were silently huddled around their radios, straining to hear the FO. The FO was the Marine forward observer on the ground positioned close enough to the target to observe the impacts of the rounds and call in adjustments as needed to destroy it. He was also the Marine who described the outcome of the fire mission, which was called the battle damage assessment report. It was morbidly gratifying to receive the news.

"All enemy bunkers collapsed, break. . . . Vehicles immobilized, break. . . . Enemy headquarters destroyed and in flames, break. . . . Burning bodies everywhere, over."

The graphic details from the FO motivated us for our next fire mission. The gorier the details, the more psyched we became. I was a killer again.

The swell of pride and accomplishment washed over the Marines of Weapons Platoon. Smiles and congratulations were shared along the gun lines, and officers visited to thank the troops for a job well done.

More missions came throughout the day, each with a delay so we could clean the mortar tube and restock ammunition. There was no scheduled personal time. We had to hope the pace of the missions provided enough time to drink a canteen of water, swallow a few chunks of dehydrated MRE, or make a quick head-call to relieve our bladder or bowels. Cpl. Hoffman visited occasionally to keep us motivated and communicate the progress of First Platoon. He never let us forget that there were Marine scouts on the ground in the valley who needed our support. He impressed upon us that we did not get to decide when our mortar tubes went hot. We understood that a fire mission could come through the radio at any time, and we had to be ready.

By 1300 that Saturday, Lance Cpl. Baker was growing tired, and for me the novelty of watching the mortars fire was giving way to boredom. When the next fire mission alert woke us from our doldrums, we assumed our positions with much less enthusiasm than we had in the early morning. So when Lance Cpl. Baker asked me if I wanted to drop the mortars for the mission, I welcomed the challenge. It didn't look difficult. I had watched Lance Cpl. Baker drop over a hundred rounds already. That simplicity changed when the next call-for-fire mission came across the radio.

Lance Cpl. Baker called out, "Hang an HE round, Will."

I looked at the splintered mountain of wooden crates and the Styrofoam trash that had accumulated at the base of the ammunition point. Finding the HE rounds wasn't so easy with the pressure to perform and the litter that buried the ammunition crates. The first rounds I touched were white phosphorous. The second were illumination rounds. Finally I found them. The HE round was designed to explode into thousands of steel fragments upon impact, theoretically killing every person within a forty-meter diameter. I had seen the impacts of the HE rounds turn rubber tractor-trailer tires into confetti all day, and now I was holding one in my hands. This thought process lasted only a second, because Lance Cpl. Baker was screaming for me to hang the round. I straddled the base of the mortar tube and squatted so my outstretched arms held the steel fins of the round at approximately eye level.

Lance Cpl. Baker corrected me by placing his hands over mine and repositioning the round. "Fins in the tube, not over the tube!"

Now the mortar round was half inserted, suspended by my hands, which cupped the mouth of the tube.

I called out, "Hanging!" as loud as I could over the sounds of the second gun, which had already fired its first round. Lance Cpl. Baker didn't like being second, and he made up for lost time by forgoing the safety instructions on dropping procedures.

I heard the command, "Fire!" and I immediately dropped the mortar round into the tube. I watched Lance Cpl. Baker instinctively bend at his waist toward his left foot while covering his ears. I had watched him repeat this procedure dozens of times. The obvious fact that I should have done the same didn't register. My hands still hung at the mouth of the tube, and my torso remained upright . . . until the blast came.

I remember the flash of white light and the heat on my face as the mortar exploded upward. The force of the blast blew me backward into the cushion of sandbags.

I recall Lance Cpl. Baker clenching my flak jacket and yelling into my face, "You hurt, Will?"

I didn't think so. I wiggled my fingers and felt my face.

I looked up at him and yelled back, "That was close!"

After he realized I was uninjured, his panicked expression changed to anger.

"Close? You could've blown your hands off, you stupid fuck!"

Exasperated, he pushed me backward into the sandbags and stormed back into his firing position. Lance Cpl. Baker continued to fire, and completed the mission. I was left to think about my mistake and nurse my injured pride.

I learned a few valuable lessons that day in the mortar pit. I learned that realistic combat training sometimes required us to perform with little, inadequate, or no instruction or experience. I would later learn the same is true for combat itself.

I also learned that some Marines' egos affect their judgment, especially under fire. I came to realize that Lance Cpl. Baker had sacrificed my safety so that he could fire the first round of the mission.

From that moment on I challenged the practice of blindly following orders from senior Marines. For me to follow an order without hesitation, the Marine issuing it would first have to earn my trust. My struggle with trusting leaders would become a recurring theme throughout my Marine Corps experience—in training and in combat. Without this judgment filter I would not be here to tell this story.

I also learned that combat training does not afford you the opportunity to develop aversions to traumatic events. Immediately following the fire mission Lance Cpl. Baker had me back in the pit practicing the proper body movements for dropping mortars. I repeated the drill hundreds of times, until the next fire mission. There was no time to think about my anxiety once the commands started coming. Before I knew it, I had successfully dropped my first barrage of mortars. The simulated killing continued for hours.

At 1500 hours the daytime firing ceased and the mortarmen turned their attention to gun maintenance. The next time Cpl. Hoffman made his supervisory rounds, he instructed me to attend something called a hip-pocket class. They were called hip-pocket classes because the NCOs and officers were responsible for carrying various instructional materials in their pockets, so that classes could be held anytime or anyplace. Oftentimes these classes were held during downtime, between missions.

My first hip-pocket class was a call-for-fire class taught by Sgt. Pitts. During the class we practiced the verbal radio procedures to request a mortar attack on the enemy. While some of the Marines were content to simply learn the commands, I was focused on mastery, so that I could teach others how to call for fire in the future.

After an hour of practice and feedback from Sgt. Pitts, I started helping other Marines to understand the steps. My instincts as a teacher took over, and I developed a training model of the firing range in the dirt using rocks and sticks. Before long I had turned the hip-pocket class into a game that allowed Marines to see the effectiveness of their fire requests. A small group of Marines gathered to watch as I lobbed rocks toward simulated targets as each student practiced his commands. Sgt. Pitts even called Capt. Cruz over to see the model.

It felt great to be a contributing member of the company, and I enjoyed the adulation of being considered "the instructor." As reservists we all brought unique talents and expertise from our civilian lives to drill. At the time I was in my junior year as a physical education major at Towson State University, only one year away from my student-teaching internship. It didn't take long for the others to recognize my passion for teaching. By nightfall I had worked with most of the Marines in the company as they rotated through the class. I had found my niche.

After my short-lived notoriety I found myself back in the mortar pit as the crews prepared for our next predawn attack. Lance Cpl. Baker assigned me to stand the first fire-watch duty from 2100 to 2300 hours. Marines on fire watch were required to remain awake so they could sound the alarm if they observed enemy activity. He gave me instructions to open a dozen mortar crates and prep the rounds for firing. Then he instructed me to wake Pfc. Adams for fire watch from 2300 to 0100, and himself from 0100 to 0300. He told me we would all need to be awake for the stand-to order at 0300.

When I started opening the crates, I had the intention of stopping after prepping twelve mortar rounds. After I finished, however, I started analyzing the way we processed the rounds when the fire missions came over the radio. I flashed back to the mess of ammunition I faced when I had to pull rounds under pressure. It was clear to me that we needed an organized system of readiness for the ammunition. So I created one. I became so involved in grouping, opening, and prepping the rounds that I forgot to wake Pfc. Adams at 2300 hours. I told myself that I would just finish half of the hundred remaining rounds, and then wake him for duty. But after I finished half, I felt compelled to finish the rest. I was in my zone again.

I knew it was in my best interest to wake the next Marine for duty and get some sleep, but I felt that it was necessary to finish every last round before I could stop. I rationalized that I would finish and still have time to sleep. But I never slept that night.

At 0300 hours I woke Lance Cpl. Baker and Pfc. Adams. They expected to be awakened for fire-watch duty, and they looked confused when I told them we were at full alert.

Staring at the newly designed ammunition area, Lance Cpl. Baker asked, "What happened to all the ammo?"

"I . . . uh . . . organized it last night on watch."

He surveyed my work. At the nearside of the pit there were sixty prepped HE rounds, stacked and ready to be hung. Next to them were forty illumination rounds—also prepped and ready.

Lance Cpl. Baker looked surprised. "Where is all the trash?"

"I repacked it in the crates and stacked them near the five-ton truck." I replied.

He sat down on his pack and sighed. "A-fucking-mazing!" a favorite exclamation of Marines.

I vaguely remember hearing him ask, "Why?" I was too tired to respond.

There wasn't a lot of time to dwell on it. I recognized the calls-for-fire on the radio, and before I could think twice, we were sending illumination rounds into the sky to support First Platoon's second predawn ambush of the weekend. My system worked well, and Capt. Cruz and Cpl. Hoffman recognized the efficiency of our crew. Lance Cpl. Baker shared the praise with us, and explained how I had stayed up all night to prep rounds.

I really didn't expect kudos. After all, I had no idea why I had been driven to work through three fire-watch duties. I was more embarrassed than proud, and beginning to think that being in my zone was nothing to laugh at.

The sweat-salted Marines and muddy LAVs of Weapons Platoon returned to the Ramp at Camp Upshur in an anticlimactic fashion, at approximately 0900 Sunday. The ride home afforded me two hours of uninterrupted sleep in the hull of the LAV. I felt fortunate to get any rest at all, even though I had to sleep while sitting upright.

Sundays were all about the business of washing vehicles, cleaning and organizing gear, and final formation. Being dismissed from final formation is the goal of every reservist on Sunday afternoon. For us to earn it every LAV and its contents had to pass a cleanliness and maintenance inspection. Each of us worked tirelessly. After eleven hours of hosing, wiping, disassembling, counting, and reassembling every part of the LAV and its weapons system, Sgt. Pitts informed us that we could muster for the final formation. I felt that 2000 hours was late for a final formation, but I was told to be grateful. Some of the more experienced Marines told us of drill weekends in which crews failed their inspections, and everyone was required to stay until they passed. Rumor had it that the latest final formation was held 2300 Sunday. As it was, I wouldn't arrive home until after midnight, and my college classes started at 0900 on Monday.

The final formation lasted approximately thirty minutes. Capt. Cruz addressed the company with accolades for a safe and successful operation. He offered details about the performance of the scout squads of First Platoon, and the mortar crews of Weapons Platoon. After his comments he turned the formation over to First Sgt. Little. The first sergeant announced that he had selected the month's Outstanding Marine of the Drill—a monthly morale incentive. He spoke of the Marine's initiative and judgment, his technical proficiency, and his unselfish devotion to duty. He went on about the Marine being an example for others to follow and on . . . and on.

I tuned out and was on the verge of falling asleep standing when he called me to come to the front of the formation.

I earned the award? I thought. I wished I had paid attention to what I did to earn it.

As I accepted the plaque and T-shirt, the first sergeant shouted, "Ooh rah!" The entire company echoed his cheer, and the ground shook from the vibration.

Receiving the award on my first drill was a defining moment for me as a Marine. From that moment on, for better or worse, everyone in the company knew my name. The bar of expectations was set high, and I was determined not to disappoint. I left the formation thinking that my brother would be proud.

As I hopped into the front seat of my truck for the drive home, I was ecstatic. I had not only completed my first drill, I had done it with style! I couldn't wait to get home to tell my stories, but I questioned whether anyone would believe half of them. I could barely believe them myself!

The three-hour drive back to Baltimore provided plenty of time to wind down and drain the adrenaline from my body. As the glow from the entrance to the Fort McHenry Tunnel grew on the horizon, I let out a sigh of relief. It was after midnight and I was anxious to get home to bed. I had always considered the McHenry Tunnel to be a portal that benchmarked my official arrival home. I remember focusing on the glow of the lights—how it morphed and swirled as my eyes trained on them.

My eyes opened wide and strained as the traffic cones separating the tunnel entrance lanes began bouncing from the front bumper of my pickup truck. I spent critical seconds struggling to refocus from the fog clouding my thoughts and senses. I could see the entrance to one tunnel peripherally on my right, and the other to the left. My momentary doze put me on a collision course with the concrete dividing wall that separates the tunnels. The lights of the tunnel entrance were blinding, and the wall was approaching quickly. I closed my eyes tightly, pulled the steering wheel hard to the left, and jammed my foot as hard as possible onto the break pedal.

Officer Brooks looked up from his notes. "And then what happened?"

I thought for a moment. "The last thing I remember is the truck spinning out of control."

Officer Brooks shook his head in amazement. "You're a lucky man, Mr. Williams." He removed his glasses and pointed through the rain-streaked window of his car. "That's where your truck ended up. . . ."

It was facing oncoming traffic, about fifty meters from the concrete divider.

I shivered when he stated the obvious. "Another couple of seconds asleep and we'd be peeling you off that wall."

Officer Brooks left me alone in the car to join another trooper who had arrived on the scene. They were close enough that I could hear bits and pieces of their conversation.

"No drugs or alcohol. . . ."

"Coming back from Virginia. . . ."

"Fell asleep at the wheel. . . ."

"Yeah . . . Weekend Warrior. . . ."

FOUR

MY FIRST DRILL WEEKEND had shown me that the Marine reservists with whom I trained were true warriors, and that Weapons Company was a warrior culture. And as with any warrior culture, leaders emerged, lines of loyalty around those leaders were drawn, separations developed among the followers . . . and tribes were born.

The tribes within our company evolved through predictable life cycles. Their longevity was a function of the loyalty toward their respective leaders. These leaders included the platoon sergeants, squad leaders, and vehicle commanders. It was not so much the position of the Marine that mattered, as it was the loyalty of his following. This loyalty was the air that breathed life into the lungs of the tribes.

Some tribes had survived since the unit began in 1988, some were in their infancy, and some were on their deathbed when I arrived. But none would survive the upheaval that loomed on the horizon. During the winter of 1989 a sudden influx of Marines would more than triple Weapons Company's numbers, which sent shock waves through the ranks, and wiped out its tribes like the plague.

The company's renaissance afforded me the chance to experience two newly formed tribes led by very different leaders. It took me months to determine where my loyalties lay. In the process I struggled to discover the Marine I wanted to be, the tribe to which I belonged, and ultimately whether I wanted to be a Marine at all.

★

The greatest tribal tensions within our company existed between first-year Marines (privates and Pfc.'s) and second-year Marines (lance corporals). "Private" and "private first class" are the first two positions in the enlisted rank structure. The privates in our company were just out of boot camp, and not viewed very differently from the Pfc.'s. Some Pfc.'s earned their rank by meritorious promotion in boot camp (I graduated as a Pfc. because of college credit), and some by default with about six months of service. The distinction between Pfc.'s and lance corporals, however, was much more significant.

The lance corporals had graduated from their MOS schools and were two years removed from boot camp. They were the original Marines who had started the unit—the members of the first tribe. They were condescending, arrogant, and tightly united. I understood, after experiencing only three drills, how that could happen. They had been through a lot together.

The reorganization of the December drill disbanded them. Moreover, the influx of NCOs and officers stripped the lance corporals of the temporary positions of power they had acquired in the former vacuum of qualified leaders. This was a source of dissension among the ranks of the lance corporals. Their separation from each other, combined with their loss of power within the company, put chips on their shoulders.

No shoulders held bigger chips than those of Lance Cpl. Nagel and Lance Cpl. Draper.

They believed they were the top dogs of the company, and they were not afraid to let everyone else know it. Lance Cpl. Nagel reminded me of Morrison from boot camp. Like Morrison, Nagel was a redneck punk, with a foul mouth and a sarcastic tongue. Draper was Nagel's patronizing sidekick. He was a pompous snob with an attitude. Early on I had no doubt that I would grow to dislike them both.

We started the December drill gathered in the newly renovated big classroom to learn about our company's reorganization. The big classroom was actually nothing more than a rectangular steel warehouse left over from the Vietnam era, but it had lights and propane heat (unlike some of the smaller classrooms that we used). For infantrymen it was like a conference room in a four-star hotel. It even had metal folding chairs and tables—pure luxury.

Capt. Cruz didn't believe in micromanaging his Marines, so he provided only the necessary information to get our training started. He explained that the reorganization of the company included the development of two LAV-25 line platoons, known as First and Second Platoons, respectively. Each of the four LAV-25s that formed a line platoon had a 25mm main gun supported by a four- to six-man infantry scout team that rode in the troop compartment.

The line platoons also included new platoon commanders, platoon sergeants, and a mixture of first-year Pfc.'s and second-year lance corporals. I was assigned to First Platoon, located in barracks number 2016, under the new platoon commander, Second Lt. Street, and Platoon Sgt. Krause. It wasn't as simple for the lance corporals. Nagel and Draper bitched, complained, and bitched some more. I was glad to see the end of their reign as the self-proclaimed honchos of the company.

I said good-bye to Cpl. Hoffman with a handshake, and thanked Lance Cpl. Baker for helping me through my first drills as a newjoin. I left the comfort of the big classroom and headed into the bitter December air to meet the Marines of First Platoon.

As I approached building 2016, I noticed a Marine painting the door to our barracks. There were new hinges and a knob installed on the door, which seemed very out of character for the dilapidated barracks of Camp Upshur. Over the door hung a plywood sign with stenciled gold letters on a red background that read FIRST PLATOON—FIRST TO FIGHT. Next to the entrance was a red platoon guidon leaning outward on its pole, resting in a steel sleeve that had been driven into the earth. The guidon, too, read, FIRST PLATOON.

I entered slowly, not sure what to expect when I crossed the threshold of the hatch. Inside, Marines were gathered in a semicircle formation around a makeshift podium of stacked footlockers at the foyer entrance in the middle of our squad bay. The space was set up like a classroom, complete with seats, a chalkboard, and bookcases. Training aids and posters lined the walls. It looked very different from Weapons Platoon's squad bay, which was barely habitable.

The back right corner of the classroom had a uniform and appearance station. The gear locker was filled with ammo cans labeled, CLIPPERS, HYGIENE, IRONS, BOOTS/BRASS, AND UNIFORMS. On the wall to the right of the locker were laminated photocopies of selected pages from the Marine guidebook illustrating the Marine Corps's standards and regulations for haircuts, hygiene, and uniforms. On the left was a wall-mounted full-length mirror, over which hung a stenciled sign, CHECK YOUR APPEARANCE.

Throughout the squad bay wall lockers were pushed together into various configurations to create partitions, which subdivided the squad bay into three spaces. The third of the barracks to the left of the classroom was designated as the NCO area. The wall locker barricade was clearly intended to segregate the troops from the leaders. The sign next to the opening read, NCO'S ONLY.

To the right of the classroom was the openly accessible nonrate area. This third of the squad bay included the more familiar boot-camp-style setup of aligned racks, wall lockers, and footlockers. The nonrate area was also segregated. The starboard side was designated the scout side, while the port side included only crewmen. There were computer-printed labels with our names on the wall lockers. Mine read, PFC. WILLIAMS.

There was a lot of nervous energy as Marines waited for the arrival of Sgt. Krause. The word among the troops was that he was a shit-hot infantryman, direct from active duty in the Fleet Marine Forces. The teacher in me was impressed by the layout of the squad bay—I liked the structure and organization of the place.

As I returned to the group, the separation of ranks was more apparent to me. The lance corporals were talking and laughing. The Pfc.'s were standing around, feeling out of place, like awkward boys at a middle-school dance.

Nagel's eyes met mine as I approached. He hushed the Marines and held his arms out like a Roman soldier saluting an emperor, "All hail! Super-Marine is on deck!"

I got mixed reactions from the group. Only some understood the allusion to my award from the September drill. I knew Nagel's type, and feeding his ego with attention was the last thing I wanted to do. I decided to avoid the confrontation and made my way to check out my personal space while I waited for Sgt. Krause to arrive. As the rusted lock gave way to my tug, the flimsy metal wall locker door swung open and crashed into the adjacent metal rack. When I looked up I saw that I had disturbed a Marine, lying on the top rack, reading a book.

Lowering the book below his eyes he nodded and offered a simple "Welcome aboard."

I extended my hand in friendship and introduced myself. "I'm Pfc. Williams. Sorry to interrupt your reading."

"Pfc. Dougherty" was his response, as he maneuvered to dangle his legs down over the edge of the mattress.

"Why aren't you with the group?" I asked.

Dougherty smiled. "Same reason you're not."

Apparently he had heard Lance Cpl. Nagel's jab at me. Dougherty and I connected instantly, and we would become inseparable over the next two years.

Our conversation was cut short as the door to the squad bay opened.

"At ease, Marines!" the strange voice commanded.

The Marines gathered anxiously in the classroom area to meet our new leader. As he removed his cover, I noticed it remained perfectly formed and flat on top. I had always wondered how to make my cover look like that, instead of the wrinkled mess that it was.

Sgt. Krause stood behind the footlocker podium and checked his notes. He had a commanding presence. Standing well over six feet tall, he embodied the lean and mean standard of the infantry. His high and tight haircut looked like he had just walked out of the barbershop. His camouflage uniform was heavily starched and sported razor-sharp creases. His duty belt was connected with a spotless brass buckle, featuring the eagle-globe-anchor emblem. Even from the back of the room you could see the mirrorlike reflection of his spit-shined boots. There wasn't any noticeable difference between

Sgt. Krause and any drill instructor I had ever seen. There was no doubt in any of our minds about his prior service in the fleet. He was the real deal. He clearly understood the power of the first impression, and had capitalized on his.

"I am Sgt. Krause, your platoon sergeant." He paused to scan the group. His eyes burned holes into a few Marines along the way.

"This is my first time serving with reservists, and what I see so far is not impressive. Nasty uniforms . . . long hair . . . laziness . . . and bad attitudes."

Nagel was leaning back against the wall, bouncing his leg nervously, and spitting tobacco into an empty Coke can. As far as I could tell, he was all of the above.

"As of right now each and every one of you is a representative of First Platoon," he continued. "I expect you to look better, train harder, and think smarter than any other Marines in this company. I have posted the training schedule on the board, and have briefed squad leaders Nagel and Lyle on what needs to happen before lights-out. If there are any questions, see your squad leaders."

And he was gone. I surmised that he depended on the chain of command for delegating responsibility. That was not a problem for me as long as there were good leaders in charge. I was grateful to be assigned to Second Squad with the scouts under Lance Cpl. Lyle, a thick-framed Marine with a quiet, confident manner. He had completed 0311 infantry school during the past summer, which explained why he was in charge of the scouts.

As I understood it, the vehicle commander of the LAVs could use the weapons system to engage targets, as well as deploy the scouts to engage targets on foot. Some of the scouts, like Dougherty and me, were assigned to Second Squad temporarily, because we had not yet completed LAV school. In essence, the scouts were first-year Pfc.'s, while the crewmen were second-year lance corporals. The disparity in rank, experience, and perceived importance created a class system that separated our squads in spirit. It seemed like a poor way to organize a platoon, but I figured that Sgt. Krause knew what he was doing.

Our next mission included a junk-on-the-bunk inspection of our gear, so I returned to my former squad bay to get all of my gear. It was the new home of Second Platoon, but just as run down as I remembered. I laughed to myself as I stepped on the door, which still lay in the grass outside the entrance to building 2015. In its place hung a poncho, taped to the top of the door frame, which did little to keep the cold out. Inside, a group of Marines were standing on a table, fumbling to ignite the overhead gas furnace. The floor was cluttered with gear, strewn about haphazardly. Music from several boom-box radios competed with loud voices and the rise and fall of laughter. As I made my way to my former wall locker I noticed a Marine in my old space.

"How the hell are ya?" he said, smiling, and grabbed my hand to shake it. "Excuse all my shit. I'm Corporal Moss. Well, for a few more hours anyway. . . ." He puffed out his chest and hiked up his trousers, as he boasted, "Yeah . . . I'm finally going to be promoted to sergeant."

He seems too friendly to be a sergeant, I thought.

"I just need to get my gear and I'll get out of your way."

"Take your time," said Cpl. Moss. "Just kick my shit out of your way."

Kick his shit? It looked like a surplus store exploded. He had all of the top-end field gear. It was not the issued kind, but the kind you have to buy from catalogs. He had a waterproof winter jacket, gloves, a ski mask, and boots that looked like those worn by arctic explorers. All of his gear was labeled with brand names—Thinsulate, DryMax, and Gore-tex.

"Where's all of your issued gear?" I asked.

"Issued gear? Have you met that asshole running supply?"

I started to laugh, and he laughed too. I was not used to hearing NCOs talk like that.

Cpl. Moss pulled me aside as if to share some insider information. "You want to survive out here in these woods during winter, you gotta have Gore-Tex."

His seriousness about fabric made me laugh again. In front of any other NCO I would have expected a reprimand, but I felt comfortable around Cpl. Moss.

He punched me jokingly in the shoulder, and for the first time I saw it—his resemblance to my brother, Lenny. It gave me chills.

"OK, laugh now, motherfucker. . . . We'll see who's laughing later!" he warned as he turned toward his wall locker.

We continued to talk as I stuffed my seabag. He was really laissez-faire, different from any NCO I had ever met. As with Dougherty, I knew right away we could be friends.

As I dragged my seabag out of the barracks I said, "Hey, when you get promoted, can I call you Sergeant Gore-Tex?"

He threw a canteen at me and responded, "That's Platoon Sergeant Gore-Tex to you!"

I thought he must have been kidding. *This is the platoon sergeant?*

"If you ever get tired of that tight-ass, Krause, running First Platoon," Cpl. Moss said, "I'll have a place for you in Second."

Walking away, I wondered if I would ever have the opportunity to take him up on his offer.

I returned to the barracks to find Sgt. Krause berating Pvt. Hurst, because his haircut did not meet the skin-close standard of the Corps. It looked to me like he had a few weeks' worth of growth. He was a new-join, and my guess was that his last haircut had been at Parris Island. He looked young and embarrassed.

"What squad are you in, Marine?" asked Sgt. Krause.

Pvt. Hurst replied quietly, "Second."

"Get up here, Lance Cpl. Lyle!" demanded Sgt. Krause. He was Pvt. Hurst's squad leader, and thus responsible for him.

Lance Cpl. Nagel reported that Lyle was exchanging gear at supply.

Sgt. Krause turned the clippers over to Lance Cpl. Nagel, the next in command, and said, "When I return I want to see a regulation haircut on this private, understood?"

Lance Cpl. Nagel acknowledged with exaggerated phony compliance, "Aye-aye, Sergeant!"

I was surprised that Sgt. Krause didn't recognize Nagel's sarcasm that obviously mocked his authority. Nagel and Draper often humored each other with inside jokes and juvenile antics.

Prompted by Lance Cpl. Nagel, First Squad Marines gathered to watch the drama unfold.

Then Lance Cpl. Nagel's eyes locked on me. I could tell he was enjoying himself.

"Know how to fade hair, Williams?" Nagel asked me sarcastically. "You can do it all, can't you?"

Fading hair was the process of cutting the hair so that it became progressively longer from skintight over the ears to a maximum of one inch on top.

"No," I said. "I've never cut hair at all."

"Good. That's what I hoped." Then he shrugged his shoulders at Draper as if to explain, *He doesn't deserve one of my fades. . . . I couldn't fuck it up if I tried.*

I challenged his orders by calling out for a volunteer. "I need a Marine who knows how to fade hair. . . ."

There were no takers.

Nagel didn't even try to hide his laughter. "Looks like it's all you!"

I apologized to Pvt. Hurst in advance for the poor haircut he was about to receive. He seemed disturbingly quiet and passive about the whole ordeal—too passive.

"Why didn't you get your hair cut before drill?" I asked.

"I've been having some problems at home, and didn't get a chance."

The hidden message in his reply didn't register.

After thirty minutes of clipping, Pvt. Hurst asked me to stop trying. He looked in the mirror at the crooked line around his head, separating the baldness from the hair. He tried to make me feel better by telling me it looked good when he wore his cover.

I felt badly for Pvt. Hurst. Marines placed tremendous value on their haircuts, which were synonymous with their self-worth. Pvt. Hurst spent the drill being harassed by senior Marines and chastised by peers. I couldn't imagine a worse experience during a first drill. But then again, drill wasn't over yet.

★

The December drill was my first admin drill, the term we used to describe a drill weekend spent in garrison instead of the field. Sgt. Krause was in his element in garrison. We awakened at 0430 Saturday morning and began our three-mile platoon run at 0500. We woke Cpl. Moss and the Marines of Second Platoon as we ran by their barracks singing cadence.

"Hey, there, Second Platoon, where you at? Come on out and lose some fat!"

Lance Cpl. Nagel started out carrying the guidon, but he had the lungs of a smoker and couldn't keep pace. I was happy to see him fall back to the end of the platoon. I reveled as Sgt. Krause gave the guidon to Lance Cpl. Lyle, and threatened to fire Nagel from his position as squad leader if he didn't keep up. Sgt. Krause seemed to discipline his Marines in a consistent and fair manner, and I respected that about him.

As we ran by headquarters, Capt. Cruz called out, "Ooh rah, First Platoon!" It was nice to be recognized by the CO, and Capt. Cruz wasn't known for doling out compliments. The CO liked the way Sgt. Krause ran his platoon, and I was starting to appreciate it as well. I liked the structure, the organization, and the discipline. By the time the newly awakened Second Platoon Marines were stumbling into the head to shave, we had already completed a three-mile run, dressed, and attended a class on land navigation.

As we marched to morning chow we passed Cpl. Moss. He was rubbing the crust from his eyes as he walked to the head wearing his skivvies and flip-flops.

As Sgt. Krause passed him he offered a sarcastic greeting. "Nice of you to join us, Cpl. Moss."

Cpl. Moss smiled, apparently unaffected by the sarcasm. "Save some chow for Second Platoon!"

The exchange frustrated Sgt. Krause, but I found humor in it. There was something endearing about Cpl. Moss's aloofness. Cpl. Moss and Sgt. Krause were as different as night and day. That difference was never more evident than during Cpl. Moss's promotion to sergeant during the final formation on Sunday evening.

Sgt. Krause had assembled the Marines waiting for promotion at the rear of the formation. The senior Marine in the promotion detail was Cpl. Moss. Sgt. Krause coached the Marines on their roles during the ceremony, the most challenging of which was Cpl. Moss's. As the senior Marine of the promotion detail, he was tasked with verbally calling the close-order-drill commands to march the file of Marines to the front of the formation, and to center them on the commanding officer presiding over the ceremony. It is a fairly simple procedure, and one that should be well within the repertoire of marching skill of an ordinary corporal. But the company was about to discover that Cpl. Moss was no ordinary corporal.

As the formation fell silent, Sgt. Krause signaled Cpl. Moss to begin his commands. Cpl. Moss was oblivious. The detail of Marines stood silently at the position of attention, waiting longer than usual for the command "Forward, march." That command never came from Cpl. Moss. Instead he offered the incomplete command "Forward . . ." which primed the Marines for forward movement. While all were poised and leaning forward, he realized he had forgotten the second part of the command and, to everyone's surprise, added the word "Go!" The confused file of Marines started marching forward as the CO and his officers looked on in disbelief.

The first Marine reached the point at which he should have heard the next command, "Column left, march!" That command never came from Cpl. Moss either. Instead, he offered his own perverted version, "Left face, march!" The first Marine in line helped Cpl. Moss by instinctively executing the "column left" maneuver, and the remaining Marines followed in trace. Again, the first Marine helped Cpl. Moss by automatically pivoting left at the correct point to guide the line of Marines directly in front of Capt. Cruz.

Now, however, there was nothing the first Marine could do to help. The first Marine could not simply stop marching. The file of Marines anxiously waited to hear the command "Detail, halt!" It never came. As amazement turned to entertainment, Marines started laughing in formation. It was an unbelievable spectacle.

The Marines continued marching right past the line of officers waiting to award their promotions. Finally, Cpl. Moss called out, "Ready, Stop!" instead of "Detail Halt!" The file of six Marines stopped, but failed to pivot right to face the officers. The line came to rest about thirty yards past Capt. Cruz. Someone in formation called out, "Well, how about calling 'Right, face,' there, you!" The entire company erupted into laughter, and laughing at the position of attention is a virtual sin in the Marines.

Captain Cruz was determined to salvage the dignity of the ceremony. His voice boomed, "At ease, Marines!" His command was echoed by the platoon sergeants until order was once again restored. The Marines in the detail individually pivoted to the right to face the officers awarding their promotions. Captain Cruz, in a most impressive display of bearing, quietly marched the detail of officers to the file of Marines. When he finally faced Cpl. Moss to pin his sergeant chevrons, every Marine strained to hear the exchange.

"Sgt. Moss, I take it your close-order-drill commands are a bit rusty."

Sgt. Moss cleared his throat loudly. "Hmmm. Hmmm. Yes, sir."

"Moss, if you want to keep your sergeant stripes, I strongly advise that you brush up!" The captain raised his voice for emphasis. "Not just on drill, but on everything that is expected of a sergeant in the United States Marine Corps!"

Then Capt. Cruz ordered the newly promoted lance corporal in front of Sgt. Moss to march the detail to the rear of the formation.

Sgt. Krause congratulated all of the Marines except for Sgt. Moss. Instead he quipped, "If I was the CO, you would be a private right now."

"I thought you were the CO!" Sgt. Moss replied, in classic face-saving fashion.

The Marines of Second Platoon smiled collectively at Sgt. Moss's clever response. They were already loyal to their leader—some despite his unorthodox style . . . some because of it. I didn't know whether to pity him or admire him. I would figure it out in the drills to come.

The January drill marked the beginning of a slow downward spiral in my motivation to be a weekend warrior. It began with a long and miserable Friday formation that left us standing, frozen, in the blowing snow. It was my first cold-weather drill, and we were scheduled to be in the field all weekend. I wasn't sure how I was going to survive outside for two days and nights, because after only thirty minutes in formation it felt like my fingers and toes were frostbitten. I was relieved when Capt. Cruz took his post to address the company, until he delivered the sobering news.

"Marines, I have sad news to report."

The snow was blowing hard, and collecting on the right side of the CO's face and cover.

"Last month we tragically lost a member of our Marine family."

I observed a funeral-guard form in front of the formation. The Marines in dress blue uniforms were unfazed by the brutal weather. They mechanically stacked three rifles, leaning the barrels vertically inboard until they met, forming a tripod.

"We ask that you remain at the position of attention for a moment of silence, as we remember one of our own."

And then it dawned on me. I leaned forward to scan the squad. We were short one—Pvt. Hurst was missing.

During our briefing in the squad bay, Sgt. Krause confirmed what I already knew to be true—Pvt. Hurst was dead. What I didn't know was that he had taken his own life on the Sunday following last drill.

Lance Cpl. Draper, with his usual bad taste and timing, added his own morbid commentary. "Shotgun in the mouth!" Draper looked at Nagel to validate his sick humor as he mimed the grotesque act of holding a shotgun to his open mouth. "Can you imagine?"

My eyes locked with Nagel's and I silently dared him to join in. While neither of us believed Hurst had committed suicide over a bad haircut, we both recognized our roles in making his last days on earth worse. I hated Nagel for that.

We had an hour to prepare for our gear inspection, but I needed some time to collect myself. I walked outside to make a head call and passed Sgt. Moss. He understood the gravity of the situation. Sgt. Moss pulled me inside Second Platoon's barracks to offer his condolences. Unlike Sgt. Krause he expressed sympathy, and I appreciated it.

I tried to hide my emotion by refocusing my attention on something other than Hurst. So I decided to compare platoons. Things were a lot different in Second Platoon than in First. The first thing I recognized was that all of the Marines lived and worked together. There was no separation between NCOs and nonrates, scouts and crewmen, or squad leaders and troops. The most noticeable difference was that three lance corporals, instead of the platoon sergeant, were teaching a class. Sgt. Krause taught all of our classes.

Sgt. Moss explained that three of his scouts were experts in cold-weather training. So he asked them to teach the others how to use their gear to survive. It looked like the kind of class our platoon needed.

As I stepped back into the snow I joked, "You know, if I had all that Gore-Tex, I wouldn't need any survival training."

He laughed. "You bet your ass!"

Back in our squad bay Sgt. Krause was getting ready to teach us classes to prepare us for the night's mission. There were classes on fire-team movements, patrolling with noise discipline, and setting up a defensive perimeter—but no cold-weather survival classes.

Pfc. Dougherty and I stared at each other when it was time to pack for the field. We labored over which gear to take and which to leave. Too much gear could make marching unnecessarily difficult. Dougherty consulted with Lance Cpl. Lyle, but he offered little help. He had gone to infantry school during the summer, the way all reservists did, and this would be his first cold-weather drill too.

Lance Cpl. Lyle decided to get his packing list from Lance Cpl. Nagel. What he failed to realize was that Lance Cpl. Nagel was a crewman. None of us in Second Squad understood that crewmen had a much different field experience from the scouts. Lance Cpl. Nagel knew, but he didn't tell. So we packed exactly what the crewmen packed. I didn't like the idea of trusting Nagel, but unfortunately I didn't have a choice. To make matters worse I learned that I was assigned as a scout on Lance Cpl. Nagel's vehicle. Nagel was the vehicle commander, and Draper was the driver. It was a match made in hell. The only thing that made it bearable was that Pfc. Dougherty and Lance Cpl. Lyle were assigned with me.

Although our company census had increased, there still weren't enough Marines to fill all the vehicle positions. Our vehicle was missing the third crewman to assume the role of gunner, but the truth was that our training seldom involved the role of the gunner. Unless we were scheduled to conduct a live-fire exercise on a range, the function of the crewmen was limited to troop transport. As far as I could tell, for the purposes of our platoon the LAV was a fourteen-ton taxicab.

Initially I felt grateful that I was not a crewman. While operating the LAV, both the VC and driver were exposed to the weather from their waist to their heads. While en route to our drop-off point the heater offered little relief to Nagel or Draper's upper bodies, which were exposed to the bitter air and icy snow. While the crewmen were freezing up above, Lyle, Dougherty, and I slept comfortably in the hull. Once we reached our drop-off point, however, things changed.

The luxury of the vehicle heater afforded crewmen less need to pack for sustained cold-weather training. They only needed to endure the elements while driving, and we were only on the road for thirty minutes. What we did not know was that crewmen remained with the vehicles while in the field. Their missions required an occasional brief drive from one point to another. In between movements, however, they had heat and sleep. The next time we scouts would know either would be Sunday morning, after thirty-six hours of exposure to subfreezing temperatures. As we disembarked and gathered at the rear of the vehicle, I could see Nagel and Draper pulling cans of soda and bags of snacks from their packs.

As he climbed into the back of the vehicle, Lance Cpl. Nagel whined, "Close the fucking hatch. . . . It's cold out there."

Inside, they laughed like schoolgirls.

Lance Cpl. Lyle wasted no time assembling the scouts and briefing us on our mission. We were dropped at the south end of Training Area 14 and assigned to patrol the roads leading two miles north to Landing Zone Foxtrot. Second Platoon's scouts were dropped off at the north end of TA-14 to patrol southward. We were advised that we could encounter enemy armored vehicles, which were actually our company's LAVs, driving along our patrol routes.

If we located moving vehicles we were supposed to call in the location and direction of the vehicle's movement to headquarters. If we located stationary vehicles, we were supposed to call in their locations and "destroy" them. During the briefing Lance Cpl. Lyle explained that the CO would consider any vehicle destroyed if scouts approached close enough to hit it with a canteen. The canteen represented a variety of weapons that scouts carried that were capable of immobilizing armored vehicles—like hand grenades. The key was getting close enough without being detected, because the LAV crewmen had night-vision equipment that could see us long before we could get within throwing distance. Once we rendezvoused at LZ Foxtrot we were supposed to form a defensive perimeter, assign Marines to fire-watch duty, and get some sleep.

I was thrilled to be embarking on a real-life infantry scout mission, just like those portrayed in the posters I had studied before boot camp. The excitement made up for the cold conditions. We remained in our assigned vehicle groups, which were called fire teams once we were on foot. Equipped with a radio, map, compass, and red-lens flashlight, the three of us headed out to LZ Foxtrot. It was an arduous two-mile creep in knee-deep snow. Even though the route paralleled an asphalt road, we walked within the wood line for concealment. We were determined to avoid being detected by the crewmen. None of us wanted to deal with Nagel's inflated ego if he was credited with killing us.

After nearly two miles of trudging through the snow in the woods, we had neither seen nor heard a single vehicle. The novelty of the exercise was gone and I became frustrated. My cynicism grew with each passing minute. I imagined the crewmen nestled next to the heater, sleeping in the back of the LAV. Our bodies were dangerously cold. The stinging had stopped in our fingers and toes, leaving only numbness. I was worried about frostbite. Lance Cpl. Lyle was concerned, too, so he called Sgt. Krause on the radio. Lyle lowered the volume and pressed the handset close to his ear.

Lance Cpl. Lyle grimaced when he heard the bad news. "Roger, out." He unkeyed the mike and slammed it into its cradle.

"Sgt. Krause wants us to remain on patrol until we see action."

Roger, out? I thought. . . . *How about "Fuck you, out!"*

I should have expected it, though. Sgt. Krause's ego was always in control. He wanted all of his fire teams to be credited with at least one vehicle sighting before checking into the LZ.

Lance Cpl. Lyle studied the map by the glow of the red-lens flashlight. After a few minutes he shared his plan. The three of us were going to split up and occupy three different posts on three different roads. The plan made sense, as it would increase our chances of seeing a vehicle, but splitting up made me anxious. We were trained to always have a buddy in the field. I trusted Lance Cpl. Lyle, though. I went along with the plan as he promised to remain stationary, so we could find him in an emergency. His radio was our lifeline to the company.

I reluctantly turned my back on my buddies and headed off to my post. I found my road, just as Lyle had said, about a hundred meters east of our start point. I waited just inside the wood line, and shivered. By 0300 I had been in a stationary position for thirty minutes. There were no vehicles. There was only cold. My hands and feet felt like blocks of ice. I could barely move my fingers, and when I did they moved in slow motion. I tried to recall the warning signs of frostbite, but it was difficult to think clearly. It was another predicament, and another big decision. Option one was to put my personal safety first, abandon my post, and report to Lance Cpl. Lyle. Option two was to put the mission first, remain observant, and hopefully see or hear something to report.

Having to make that decision pissed me off. I could not believe the futility of this mission. I shuffled from one foot to another, trying desperately to regain feeling in my legs.

The first time I heard it I thought I was hallucinating. I was cold enough to be delusional. I strained to hear more . . . twigs cracking . . . branches snapping . . . footsteps landing. People were moving in my direction. I hid behind a tree and waited. When the boots passed my position, I peeked around to see. It was just one body.

My shaky shivering voice cut through the falling snow as I strained to point my rifle. "You're d-dead!" I was grateful this was just a war game. My fingers were so cold, I couldn't have made them pull the trigger if my life depended on it.

The stranger's voice answered, "Wee-ams . . . is that you?"

It was Sgt. Moss. I recognized him by the way he bastardized my last name. I was relieved to see him.

"What are you doing in my area?" he whispered. "First Platoon scouts are supposed to be on the west side."

I was too cold to go into details. "We split up to get a v-vehicle sighting. Sgt. Krause wants every fire team to call in a r-report before going to the LZ."

"You're only five minutes away." Sgt. Moss snickered. "I just came from the LZ to call in my last fire team."

I didn't respond. He knew something was wrong. It took all of my energy just to talk.

"I don't think I can walk to the LZ, Sgt. Moss. My can't feel my f-feet."

He wasted no time examining the uselessness of my pack and then tossing it aside.

"Where's all your gear?" he asked.

Clenching my jaw in anger I snapped, "I packed what I was t-told to pack!"

As he pulled gear from his own pack, he gave me some of the best advice I ever received in the Marines. "You've got to pay more attention to who's doing the telling."

He helped me sit on a log while he removed my boots and socks. I was as helpless as a baby. He helped me pull two pairs of socks over my purple feet, and after my boots were on, the feeling slowly returned. I welcomed the sensation of pins and needles in my toes, which signaled the return of blood flow. He also gave me the cold-weather gear that he had been issued at supply—gloves, thermal underwear, a field-jacket liner, and a wool watch cap. Most of what he wore he owned personally. The night would have turned out very differently if he had not rescued me.

As I limped back to Lance Cpl. Lyle's position, I wondered what drill would be like in Second Platoon. By final formation on Sunday I would begin wondering what life would be like without drill . . . without the Marines, period.

The drudgery of drill weekends continued through February and March. It was normal for my motivation to wane as drill Friday approached, but following the March drill my dedication to the Corps was at an all-time low. There were many more instances of incompetence and poor leadership while I served with First Platoon, like the debacle at LZ Foxtrot.

Sgt. Krause continued his inane quest to demonstrate his superiority over us, the inferior reservists. While in garrison he saturated our training schedule with fruitless classes, and filled our minds with military textbook trivia. In the field he carried on like MacArthur, micromanaging every exercise with manic intensity. My feelings about his leadership ran hot or cold, depending on the circumstances. The most disappointing thing was his indifference toward the activities of Lance Cpl. Nagel, who continued to alienate the scouts with his adolescent antics and, worse yet, endangered us with flagrant incompetence, questionable morality, and thoughtless decision-making.

After only seven months I learned to loathe drill weekends. My friends and family knew only that I was growing tired of the way drill weekends interfered with my social life. It seemed that drill always fell on the least favorable weekend. Without fail, whenever something important was happening I missed it because of drill. But that was not the real problem. The real problem was much deeper. Life was happening, and I felt I was missing it because of drill.

I have since come to understand that for me, and many others like me, the resentment I felt about drill was a psychological defense mechanism. As long as I resisted the drill weekend, I could continue with the reintegration process . . . fading away from Marine mode back into civilian mode. But just when being a civilian started feeling natural and comfortable, the drill weekend reared its ugly head.

The calendar dragged us unwillingly, under the threat of a court-martial, back to a place that was physically, mentally, and emotionally painful.

Drill weekends are born from the individual missions assigned to them, and bred by the philosophies of their leaders. The experiences of reservists vary greatly from unit to unit in the intensity, duration, and nature of training. Reserve units and their drill weekends fall on a continuum of challenge and rigor. The drill weekends of some units facilitate the process of reintegration, as their demands are little more than an extension of the civilian nine-to-five workday.

On the other end of the continuum, however, there is the Marine combat reserve unit. These units, and the nature of their drill weekends, inhibit the process of reintegration, as their demands are the antithesis of civility. Their missions focus on death and destruction. For Marine combat reservists the personal struggle with reintegrating into society is a perpetual cycle of mental and emotional turmoil.

The cycle involves the weakening of the combat-ready mind, body, and spirit during the four weeks of soft civilian life that precede each drill weekend. On that one Friday of the month the combat reservist must shift from civilian gears to military gears. For the reservists whose specialties resemble civilian careers, such as office workers, the switch is a smooth transition that mildly interrupts their civilian lives. For Marine infantry reservists, however, that anxious drill Friday eclipses all that is civilian. There is no clutch to ease the shift. The ride accelerates progressively through a sleepless Friday and Saturday, climaxes in the darkness of Saturday night, and crashes on Sunday afternoon. The reintegration back to the civilian world begins on the postdrill Monday and lasts, more or less, until the next drill Friday. Then the cycle begins again.

As the April drill weekend approached, my struggle with reintegration was at its worst. I decided to take action to break the cycle on the Thursday before drill. I skipped Sgt. Krause in the chain of command and made a phone call directly to our platoon commander, Lieutenant Street. I informed him I had a chronic knee injury that was aggravated by the rigors of training. He was surprisingly sympathetic, and advised me to get a medical examination. Instead of reporting to drill on Friday, I reported to Bethesda Naval Hospital. I entered with the goal of securing a medical discharge.

I was convinced that the orthopedic condition that affected my left knee, called Osgood-Schlatter's syndrome, was going to be my ticket out of the Marine Corps. It's a condition in which the patellar tendon pulls the bone away from the tibia, making a painful bony protrusion just below the knee. I'd had surgery to correct the condition a year before boot camp, and had managed to hide it from the doctors at the military entrance processing station. The truth was it was no longer painful, but the protrusion was still noticeable. I wanted out of the Marines badly enough to go through with the charade.

After examinations by several doctors, and a brief counseling session, I was provided with documentation affording me light-duty training status until a fit-for-duty determination could be made. At worst I figured that meant I would stay back in garrison when the others went to the field. But I was counting on the best-case scenario— a medical discharge. I should have known that neither way out would be as easy as it sounded.

A few days after the April drill I received a letter from the commanding officer of Weapons Company. I eagerly opened it, sure that there was a farewell letter in consideration of my pending medical discharge. There was not. On the contrary it was a letter of disciplinary action charging me with unauthorized absence. I read the letter repeatedly to decipher its meaning. *Unauthorized?* I guessed that Lt. Street forgot to inform the CO of my excused absence. The letter closed with the threat, "Failure to meet with the commanding officer prior to next drill will result in further disciplinary action that may include discharge under other than honorable conditions."

I was in shock after reading the letter, but figured that it would be resolved with a phone call to the CO. My fingers trembled as I pressed the digits. Having a confrontation was bad enough. Having it with the base commander was overwhelming. Staff Sgt. Church answered the phone, but didn't entertain my plea for forgiveness. Instead she transferred me directly to Capt. Cruz.

He was all business on the phone. "Williams, did I authorize your absence from drill?"

My reply didn't answer his question. "I called Lt. Street before drill and he told me I could report to Bethesda for a medical exam, sir."

Capt. Cruz didn't pull punches. "Williams, there is only one person in this unit to authorize absence, and you're talking with him. So I am going to transfer you back to admin so you can make arrangements to make up the drill you missed. Understood?"

I knew better than to challenge his authority. "Yes, sir."

Before the transfer he added, "And, Williams . . . I hope this is the last I hear about this lame injury. I expected more from you."

The time on hold seemed like an eternity. Capt. Cruz's words had hit home. He knew I was lying, and he'd dropped the ultimate guilt bomb. He had sounded just like my father, who used the same tactic to hold me accountable to the highest standards of behavior, manners, and integrity. One of his reprimands would send me wallowing in a guilt-ridden funk for days. I had lived to make him proud. Deep down I knew he would have expected more of me too.

I reported for duty to make up the missed drill at 0600 the next morning. I could not wait to resolve my quandary. I was virtually stuck, and unable to think clearly about my decision to follow through with the medical discharge. I reached into my pocket to feel for the papers from Bethesda. One granted me light duty status for thirty days. The other was a form to be completed by the CO that would be used to determine whether my medical condition made me unfit for duty. I was still reeling from the guilt trip after my last call to the CO. Facing him was going to be even more difficult. I didn't know if I would have the courage to give him the papers. I wanted out of the Marine Corps, but I wanted an easy out. Somehow I didn't think Capt. Cruz was going to make it easy.

Staff Sgt. Church greeted me at the admin front desk and processed my paperwork for the makeup drill. She informed me that the CO would meet with me at 0800, and asked me to wait for him in the boardroom adjacent to his office. The solitude was not helpful. It amplified the conflicting voices in my head. One told me to throw the papers in the trash and swear my commitment to remain aboard. The other told me I was only one uncomfortable confrontation away from ending the monthly misery.

There were plenty of reasons to want out. I dreaded the three-hour drive, I hated Nagel, and I loathed the misery of the field. And then there was Gina.

I didn't like to admit it, but one of the forces driving my desire for a discharge was my insecurity about my relationship with my girlfriend. I was completely infatuated with her. She was the center of my universe, but I felt the Marine Corps would eventually pull us apart. Gina didn't give me any reason to be insecure. I manufactured my own doubt. She had waited for me through boot camp, but I wasn't sure she could wait through a second summer of separation. I knew she was starting her freshman year of college, and there would be more opportunities than ever for her to meet new guys.

My anxiety was interrupted as another Marine stepped into the doorway to the boardroom. Before I looked up I heard him call out, "Wee-ams!" and I knew it was Sgt. Moss. He explained that he was processing the paperwork for his summer duty assignment. I confessed that I was making up a drill weekend. I found it easy to talk openly with Sgt. Moss.

He laughed when I told him of the trouble I was in. "Hell, you ain't a Marine until you have a page-eleven entry in your record," he said, referring to how disciplinary action was documented on page eleven of our service record books. "Mine carry over onto page twelve!"

Sgt. Moss was able to put things in perspective for me. I had thought of the page-eleven entry as punishment. He thought of it as a benchmark for coming of age as a Marine.

"So where are you going this summer?" I asked.

"To LAV school with you," he said.

"I'm not sure that I am going."

That led us into a lengthy discussion. I purged my conscience, sharing all of the details of my situation. First I explained my thoughts on leaving the Corps. I showed him my papers and expressed my anxiety about confronting the CO. I talked about the dysfunctional leadership of Nagel, the disparity between the scouts and crewmen, the futility of training, and my angst about leaving Gina. He validated my concerns for all of the above, and even added a few complaints of his own.

Then I explained the reasons I wanted to remain aboard. We talked about the phone call with the CO, my guilty feelings, and the integrity instilled in me by my father. Sgt. Moss added his commentary in between my rambling, which gave me a different perspective. He had a way of reminding me of the pride I had once felt being a Marine. And he described LAV school in a different way than I ever imagined it.

I learned that it was located at Camp Pendleton, California. That meant little to me until he explained why Camp Pendleton was considered one of the best duty stations in the Marine Corps. He talked of the sandy beaches of San Diego, the nightlife of Los Angeles, and the forbidden fruits of Tijuana. I had had no idea that there would be time for anything outside of school—I had thought it would be like revisiting boot camp.

Most importantly, he asked me if integrity was as important to Gina as it was to me. I had always assumed she would be happy if I was discharged. But he helped me to see that I wouldn't really be earning a discharge . . . I would be quitting.

His genuine interest and concern was exactly what I needed to help me think through the decision. When Capt. Cruz finally called me into his office, I was more anxious than ever.

Sgt. Moss sent me in with a smile.

"I know you'll do the right thing," he said.

I was in Capt. Cruz's office for only a few minutes. It was just long enough to hear, face to face, the same message I had received from him on the phone. When I closed the door behind me, Sgt. Moss was looking up curiously. I made sure he was looking as I ripped the papers from Bethesda and threw them in the trash. I shook his hand to say thanks and affirmed my decision with a simple comment: "See you in California."

My trip to Bethesda cost me two days of classes at college, a stain on my Marine record, and a dent in my reputation. But during the journey I gained a new self-awareness. I learned that I had an internal compass that pointed me in the direction of morality. I recognized the conflict created when my actions led me in a different direction from the one to which my moral compass pointed. I understood how that conflict eroded my self-respect and sanity. And I realized that I couldn't live happily without either.

In a matter of months I would be in conflict again, and left to rely on my moral compass to lead me. But the next time navigating the crossroads of integrity would be much more confusing, the decision much more daunting, and the destination even more frightening.

FIVE

As I STEPPED ONTO the TWA commercial jet in June of 1990, I nervously clutched my orders, anxious about what lay ahead in California. I knew this was not going to be a vacation. My seabag was a ball and chain that anchored me to the business at hand–LAV school. I don't think Sgt. Moss felt the same way. He was drinking cocktails and partying in the next row over. While I was sweating in my dress green uniform, he sat relaxed and reclined wearing a T-shirt, shorts, and flip-flops. I was dressed for an inspection. He was dressed for the beach.

There were four of us on the plane from Weapons Company– Sgt. Moss, Lance Cpl. Dougherty (who had recently been promoted), Pfc. Poole, and me. Dougherty and Poole, like Sgt. Moss, had had the foresight to dress in comfortable clothes. They joined Sgt. Moss's party and were on their third round of drinks when we landed. Between the plane and the bus Dougherty and Poole managed to dive into a rest room to change into their uniforms. Sgt. Moss told us he would wait until he arrived on base. I couldn't believe how nonchalant he was about checking into school. I had spent two hours at home preparing my uniform and dressing, laboring over every detail. They threw theirs on in fifteen minutes and managed to look just as good. I envied their casual attitude, but kept myself locked inside the safety of my anxiety.

The ride from the airport to the base seemed like an eternity. It reminded me of the bus ride to Parris Island the previous summer.

This time, though, there were no yellow footprints . . . and no drill instructors. I sprang from my seat as the shuttle bus stopped at the headquarters building. The first order of business on my agenda was check-in. I was focused on getting in and out quickly, and raced ahead of the group. That was my first mistake of the summer.

The corporal behind the counter was a small, squirrelly Marine. He started right in when he saw my military ID card. "Pink! You gotta be shittin' me!" He stepped backward and held the card for the other clerk to see.

The Marine next to him announced, "The reservists have landed!"

Marines all around shared a laugh at my expense.

As he examined my card closer his face grew serious. "Why do you have a hole punched in your ID card?"

I responded matter-of-factly, "So I can wear it around my neck . . ." as I fumbled with my collar trying to locate my ID tag chain.

He looked at me curiously. "You're joking, right?"

I remained silent.

He didn't. This time he was louder as he leaned across the counter for dramatic effect, "Right?"

My silence telegraphed my ignorance. I was completely out of my element among the active-duty Marines. I was at his mercy, trapped in his game. For him, it was time to play with the clueless reservist.

He slammed his hand down on the counter. "This card is unserviceable! You can't just punch a hole in your ID card. It's government property, for Christ's sake!"

"I'm not sure what you want me to do," I replied sheepishly.

He walked away in a huff to collude with his buddy, and then returned with a smile on his face. "The good news is we can make you a new one. The bad news is you'll have to earn it."

I looked around for support, but neither Sgt. Moss nor the others were in sight. Left alone, I decided to play along.

"What do you mean . . . earn it?"

The corporal examined a piece of paper as if it were a price list.

"I think a brand-new pink ID card is going to cost you . . . one hundred push-ups."

The Marines behind the counter laughed. The Marines waiting in front of the counter stared. There wasn't much choice, really. I was a Pfc. He was a corporal. I had to follow his orders—that was how the Marine Corps worked. So I stepped out of line and started paying for my new ID card, with sweat and embarrassment.

It wasn't long before a voice sounded above the crowd. "Get on your feet, Wee-ams."

I stood up to see Sgt. Moss standing tall before me, hands on his hips. His uniform was drill-instructor perfect, and his sergeant stripes stood out among the dozens of school-age Marines.

I was as surprised as the rest at his commanding presence.

"What's going on here?"

I explained.

Sgt. Moss responded more assertively than I had never seen before. "You have to forgive the corporal, Williams. I am sure it sucks being stuck behind that counter, like a little bitch, serving all of the real Marines in the infantry."

The crowd raised a collective "Whoa" as the corporal's face turned the color of my ID card.

Sgt. Moss enjoyed the approval of the crowd. He leaned across the counter and jabbed his finger into the corporal's chest. "Make him a new card. Now!"

I had my new ID card in minutes.

As we left, Sgt. Moss warned everyone within earshot, "Don't fuck with my Marines."

It was déjà vu for me, with Sgt. Moss substituting for my brother Lenny. I could almost hear Lenny warning the neighborhood bullies, "Don't fuck with my brother!"

After turning the corner into an empty hallway, we stopped and looked at each other for a reality check. Sgt. Moss had astonished himself as well as me.

"Can you believe I pulled that off?"

I couldn't. He slapped my hand to celebrate the successful bluff.

Watching Sgt. Moss test his new stripes was like watching someone learning to ride a bike. The summer promised to be a wild ride.

Before we arrived at Camp Pendleton, no one had ever explained to us that we had to earn our way into LAV school. We learned that we were not officially enrolled into the next LAV class until we successfully completed the first ten days of infantry training. If we failed to complete this prerequisite, then the Marine Corps made us 0311 riflemen by default. For me that meant I would be sent home to return to Weapons Company to train as a scout. I thought back to the December drill. The prospect of completing my six-year obligation as a scout made me nauseous. I didn't want to ride in the back of the LAV anymore. I wanted to be a driver—or gunner—and one day, maybe even vehicle commander.

During our ten days in the School of Infantry each of us would pray that we might earn a coveted slot in the next LAV crewmen class. The Marine School of Infantry picks up in intensity where boot camp ends. Active-duty Marines were only ten days removed from boot camp, and at a heightened state of readiness. They were easily identifiable, with their shaved heads, lean frames, and steely attitudes. Reservists were nine months removed from boot camp, and most of us were less than ready for the rigorous training for which we were headed. We, too, were easily identifiable in comparison to those Marines straight from Parris Island—soft in mind, body, and spirit.

Nonetheless the rigor of infantry training did not discriminate, nor did the infantry instructors known as troop handlers. The training was grueling. It sucked equally for all of us. Over the course of the summer the "boots" softened and the reservists hardened. Ultimately we would meet somewhere in the middle.

Word spread quickly that there was a sergeant-student aboard, which was highly unusual. Most students in military occupational specialty schools were privates, Pfc's, and lance corporals who were just starting their enlistments. Occasionally a corporal enrolled if he needed to change his MOS, but that was seldom the case for sergeants.

The instructors questioned Sgt. Moss about his enrollment. He stayed their curiosity with a confounding explanation. He told of how he had graduated from the School of Infantry four years prior, but decided to switch MOSs to join a newly forming LAV company. He shared that he only really needed the academic portion of LAV school, but volunteered to help his troops through SOI—to pass on his knowledge, to keep us motivated, and out of trouble while on leave. Practically speaking, he did not need the prerequisite ten days of infantry training, but our company required it. We joked that his orders came from "the department of redundancy department."

I don't know if the instructors believed his whole story, but they acted as if they did. They welcomed Sgt. Moss aboard and granted him the authority of a quasi instructor. His chevrons demonstrated to them that he was worthy of that responsibility. It was generally understood that the Marine Corps did not promote individuals to the rank of sergeant without rigorous screening and careful scrutiny. But there were exceptions.

In garrison Sgt. Moss neither possessed the proficiency nor exhibited the conduct normally required of sergeants. His ineptitude was magnified by the rigid demands of the school environment. In the field, however, he functioned like a Rhodes scholar. No one was more motivated than Sgt. Moss to don his pack and rifle. But, in the rear, no one was more intimidated to lead. He knew the instructors expected more from him than he could deliver. His worst fear was that he would fumble, as he had during his promotion ceremony, and be ostracized by his fellow sergeants. His moment of truth would come sooner rather than later.

The instructors embraced the idea of having a sergeant aboard to whom they could delegate work. Before we even left our first formation, Sgt. Moss was overwhelmed with responsibilities. Among other things he was asked to attend an instructors meeting, teach a class, conduct an inspection, and . . . march the platoon. Sgt. Moss found himself struggling to ride that "new sergeant" bike again. Before he crashed, however, he installed a set of training wheels—me.

Sgt. Banks, our SOI troop handler, called out to Sgt. Moss, "Get that mob into the barracks to secure their gear!"

Sgt. Moss responded assertively, "Do you mind if I start breaking in our new guide?"

"No," Sgt. Banks encouraged him. "Go for it."

He went for it.

"Wee-ams . . . Front and center. . . ."

From that moment on I was the filter through which Sgt. Moss passed information and executed orders. He received the word from the SOI instructors, decided which parts of the orders he would carry out, and then delegated the rest to me. I welcomed the opportunity to assume the responsibilities of the guide. I liked being Sgt. Moss's right-hand man. It didn't take long for the others to appreciate his leadership as well.

The Marines under Sgt. Moss's charge led a charmed existence during the ten days of SOI. Lower-ranking Marines, like the corporal at the check-in counter, steered clear of him and us. Even the instructors, who would have otherwise micromanaged our training, deferred to his authority. Sgt. Moss milked it for all it was worth. We slept in late, finished early, and dodged as much work as possible in between.

We figured out just how lucky we were the following morning when our troop handler, Sgt. Banks, discussed the plan of the day with Sgt. Moss. The original plan required us to run three miles to a rappel tower, in full combat gear, along a dried riverbed. Sgt. Moss advocated on our behalf and nixed the combat gear. And after Dougherty suffered a twisted ankle on the riverbed, Sgt. Moss adapted our route accordingly.

We jogged in casually on the paved road that paralleled the riverbed, and arrived at the tower fifteen minutes late. The other three platoons had been broiling in the morning sun waiting for us. The riverbed had left them with bruised feet, twisted ankles, and battered knees. They stared at us with contempt as they sat in their platoon formations, soaked and exhausted from running with their helmets, flak jackets, and gas masks. We loitered about conspicuously wearing only our camouflage utilities and sunglasses.

That was classic Sgt. Moss.

Tension mounted as the tenth day of training drew near. The instructors reminded us daily of our shortcomings and warned that some of us weren't going to make the cut for LAV school. Half of infantry training was physical endurance. We either ran or humped everywhere we went. Dropping from either would put us in an unsatisfactory status. The other half of infantry training was demonstrating ability to safely and effectively operate the basic infantry weapons—the M16, the M203 grenade launcher, and the SAW machine gun. Failing to follow safety rules, or to hit targets, were sure ways to get removed from the LAV school roster.

The stress brought out the best in some and the worst in others. It brought out the best in Edsar and Frye.

They were our platoon's comedians, and they brought much-needed comic relief. Edsar was short and stocky, Frye was tall and lanky, and together they were larger than life. Perhaps it was because it was our first glimpse of them—or maybe it was simply the circumstance—but their first show made them instant celebrities in the barracks.

The usual calm just before lights-out that night was anything but quiet. Laughter echoed throughout the squad bay as Edsar and Frye took center stage, circled by Marines.

I found Dougherty and asked him what was going on. He was laughing so hard, I had trouble understanding him, "They—they call it . . . Kung Fu Theater!"

It didn't take me long to understand. Edsar and Frye were role-playing two kung fu warriors. Their skit captured the cheesiness of martial arts movies, satirizing the gratuitous fight scenes and the poorly dubbed English voice-overs.

It also didn't take me long to laugh. Edsar and Frye crouched and circled each other like kung fu warriors. They talked to each other in Chinese-speak, but their mouths moved out of sync with their words. Their timing was perfect.

Edsar overexaggerated a few karate chops and one sweeping kick at Frye. Then he added his out-of-sync dialogue: "Jarheaded one . . . you will not make it to da school of the LAV unless you survive da school of da 03-dum-dum."

He was calling 0311 infantry school "03-dum-dum" because Marines with low aptitude scores were limited to infantry MOSs. It was an unspoken understanding among Marines, and to hear it in that context was outrageously funny.

Frye complemented his partner with some of his own kicks, punches, and slow-motion maneuvers. "Oh, dog of the devil . . . I will wear da pack of da grunt . . . and a hundred pound of gear . . . and hump a thousand mile for dat honor!"

Then they exchanged a volley of blows and blocks, leading to a climax in which they both fell to the floor in a tangled mess of arms and legs as the rest of us fell to the floor from gut-wrenching laughter. Edsar and Frye were hysterically funny. They kept us laughing all summer, ironically, it turned out, considering the legacy they were destined to leave.

Dougherty was the closest thing I had to a "best friend" in the Corps. He embodied all that was good about the reserves. He was a college student and scholar whose intellectual perspectives paralleled my own. He was also an athlete whose physical fitness enabled him to carry his—in addition to others'—weight during the demands of infantry training. Most significantly, Dougherty was one of the most selfless people I had ever met. He was the reason I survived my first infantry hump up Mount Motherfucker. Anyone who thinks that is a crass name for a hill has never humped it. As we approached its base I realized that our first infantry hump was going to be memorable. The winding path before me stretched for miles upward along its face. It was the highest mountain within sight along the eight-mile trail, and I had serious doubts about my ability to make it to the top after only the second mile.

I was saturated with sweat under my thirty-pound pack. A dull ache had started across my shoulders under the compression of my flak jacket. My war belt had dropped and the caps from my canteens dug into my lower back, which rubbed two patches of raw skin that began burning like fire. My Kevlar helment felt like an oven that baked my brains. Worse, its sweat-soaked straps had stretched, so its rigid rim rammed the bridge of my nose with every other stride up-hill. I also felt a strange twinge on my back where my right pack strap crossed under my shoulder blade. But that was the least of my worries at the time—I was starting to feel nauseous.

Dougherty didn't look as fatigued as the rest of us. Unlike most reservists he had retained his boot-camp level of fitness. He jogged along the column, helping Marines along the way. We relied on our buddies to assist us, as most of our gear was on our backs and un-reachable. There were straps to adjust, canteen covers to fasten, and loose gear to secure. Those tasks were my responsibility as guide, but since I could barely take care of myself, Dougherty had assumed that role. I thought about asking him to hump beside me to help me along, but pride kept me silent.

The third mile of the hump was much more grueling than the first two. There were stretches of road so steep that I could reach out in front and touch asphalt. I thought back to how my short legs had managed to carry me through the ten-mile hump along the flatlands of Parris Island, but they were quickly failing me in the mountains of California. It wasn't a matter of motivation. I wanted desperately to get to the top of the mountain, but my body had other plans.

I was thinking about my experience during forming night when I felt the splash against my legs. I knew all too well what was happening. The vile heaving sounds from Pfc. Dean's guts behind me gave it away. My water had been trying to come up since mile one, and I had been fighting to keep it down. The polite thing to do was to stop, face outboard, and direct the trajectory of our body fluids away from the others. But we knew better. Infantry Marines did not just stop in the midst of a troop movement. Humps were not leisurely strolls. On the contrary, they were forced marches approached with life-and-death urgency. Even as students we understood that reality.

We knew in combat we could find ourselves humping to rescue fellow Marines under fire, to rendezvous at a strategic location, or to beat the enemy to a crucial objective. The hump needed to continue under any circumstance, and all Marines needed to keep pace. Any gap between Marines wider than an arm's length elicited barks from the troop handlers: "Close that gap! Tighten it up! Longer strides there, you!" Marines who failed to keep up received more aggressive incentives—slaps in the helmet, punches in the shoulder, and kicks in the ass.

The worst-case scenario was if a Marine fell out during the hump. Our leave-no-man-behind doctrine required the fallen Marine, and his gear, to be carried for the duration of the hump. We trained as if we were in combat, and in war we wouldn't call for an emergency transport until we arrived at our destination. Our instructors told us we were only as strong as our weakest link, and no Marine wanted the stigma of being the weakest link. Stopping was never a conscious option. And even those who passed out awoke ostracized as nonhackers. That is why I tolerated Dean's vomit spray from behind, and why I forwarded my own into Pfc. Bender in front. It was also why I ignored the throbbing pain on my back under my right pack strap.

By mile five I had fallen back to the end of our column to join the ranks of the weakest links. Dougherty positioned himself as the last Marine of our platoon and policed our pace. Anytime one of us slowed to the point where we touched him he pushed us forward, screaming all the while, "Suck it up! Move out! Get the fuck up there!"

By mile seven Dougherty and I were the taillights of the platoon. I trudged onward, forcing myself forward one painful step at a time, while Dougherty pushed and pulled me along. I heard the condescending threats approach from the rear. My lethargic pace had allowed the guide from the platoon behind us to close in. I understood that once he passed us I would be officially considered a nonhacker. Dougherty was determined to help me avoid that embarrassment, and he did. Ultimately he and I completed the hump with our platoon, but he damned near carried me for the last mile. His selflessness was unlike any I had ever experienced. Words cannot express how I felt toward Dougherty when we reached the top of the mountain. I was beside myself with humility, gratitude, and admiration.

The return hump down the mountain was not nearly as taxing as the ascent, and we arrived back at the squad bay with inflated egos from our accomplishment. My celebration, however, was short lived. As the adrenaline drained from my body the pain in my back became excruciating. I confided in Dougherty and called him over to my wall locker to check out my back. When I pulled off my skivvy shirt I heard the shock in his voice.

"Holy shit, Will . . . It looks like a baseball under your skin."

He didn't give me a chance to respond. He returned a few minutes later with Sgt. Moss and Sgt. Banks. Sgt. Banks took one look at the tumor splitting my skin and hustled me into his office. His urgency alarmed me. Before I had time to consider my options I found myself at the hospital, facedown on an operating table.

The local anesthetic numbed my back and shoulders, but not so much that I couldn't feel the sensation spread along my shoulders and neck as blood flowed freely around to my front. It pooled under my chin in bright red contrast to the white sheet. The sight of all that blood scared the hell out of me, but I lay silent and still until the cutting, poking, and pulling ceased.

Afterward the surgeon explained that the trauma of my pack strap during the hump had agitated a cyst that had existed unnoticed under my skin. He used a mirror to show me the golf-ball-size crater in my back just to the left of my right shoulder blade. What really bothered me, though, was what I learned next. I would need to keep twelve inches of gauze padding inside the wound to keep it open and permit healing from the inside out. There were two implications: I would have an open wound on my back for two weeks, and I would need the gauze changed twice daily.

I panicked, knowing that Sgt. Banks wouldn't let me miss all that training. I was sure when he found out I would be sent home. But thanks to Dougherty he never found out.

The first time Dougherty changed the packing in my back was the worst. It was painful to have a foot of cloth pulled from the inside of my body. It was even worse to have more reinserted. Then there was the blood, the puss, and the ungodly odor.

Dougherty handled himself with the professionalism of a true corpsman . . . and not just once. He repeated the procedure twice every day for the next two weeks of training. In all of my days, in the Marines or as a civilian, I have never experienced a more saint-like individual than Dougherty.

In contrast to Dougherty I had never experienced a seedier individual than Poole, who reflected the dark side of the reserves. Poole never fully bought into the concept of being a Marine. He was too busy being black to be a Marine. Most of us had learned in boot camp that being a Marine superceded all of our personal biases. Poole didn't get it, and few of us trusted him because of it. At his best he was a conflicted Marine. At his worst he was a militant, racist thug.

When in uniform he did what he had to do to get by—no more, no less. I always felt that was a shame because he had the potential to be a great Marine. Like Sgt. Moss, Poole demonstrated his potential more in the field than in garrison. He was amazingly accurate at firing small arms and, fortunately for me, highly skilled with demolitions.

Poole and I were paired during our first demolitions exercise, which required that we each insert a blasting cap into a detonation device. The blasting caps looked benign to me, like thin metal cigarettes. The instructor taught us how the relatively small explosion of a blasting cap detonated other more explosive material, like TNT or C-4. But the instructor also told us that "small explosion" was powerful enough to blow off our fingers if we mishandled them, which left me paralyzed with anxiety. My hands shook when I handled my blasting cap. Poole daringly played catch with his. It wasn't until the last step in the procedure that I realized I had inserted my blasting cap into the device backward. Poole looked the other way, leaving me no other option than to call the instructor over for help.

Marine instructors are not known for their therapeutic assistance.

"That's your problem, Crazy, not mine!" he said. "If you want to pass this station, I suggest you figure out how to unfuck that blasting cap . . . or shit a new one."

Poole felt sorry for me as I stood there fumbling tediously with the cap, ready for my fingers to blow off at any second. He snatched it out of my hands and pulled it free with one tug. He returned it with a disgusted look on his face. I was embarrassed, but grateful. Moments like that were few and far between, but nonetheless they showed his potential as a Marine—and a person. I wanted to like Poole, but he never gave me the chance.

To be Poole's buddy you had to trash-talk about drinking, drugging, packing, and pimping bitches. You had to call police officers "Five-O," and politicians "the Man," and idolize Malcolm X. And it helped to be dark green. But more importantly, you had to reject Sgt. Moss and his authority. Poole considered Sgt. Moss a buffoon, and openly disregarded his orders. He seldom used Sgt. Moss's rank when addressing him, preferring instead to call him "Moss." In the Marines, failing to use rank, especially when addressing a senior Marine, is considered disrespectful and grounds for disciplinary action. Fortunately for Poole, Sgt. Moss figured the best course of action was to ignore him.

I always wondered why he had enlisted in the Marine Corps. He wanted us to believe that the Corps provided him with an escape from the mean streets of Washington, D.C. I thought it was more likely that he had enlisted to gain leniency from a judge. He didn't talk about his personal life very much, at least not with us light-green Marines. He preferred to associate with the dark-green Marines—his boys. But some things were more important than the boys. Graduation from SOI was one of those things.

The second weekend marked the end of our ten-day SOI training. The four of us from Weapons Company, Sgt. Moss, Dougherty,

Poole, and me, had all earned slots in LAV school, and we planned
to celebrate together. Following the Friday formation Sgt. Moss
called us together to make plans. Sgt. Moss allowed Poole to decide
where we should go, as he had spent all last weekend checking out
the best places to party. Poole told us about a bar on a pier in a
nearby town called San Clemente. He explained how it was only a
short ride on the base shuttle bus, which dropped us off right in
front of the pier. It didn't take much to convince us.

"Beaches, bars, and broads!" Sgt. Moss concurred. "What more
could we want?"

I was committed to being faithful to Gina, but was more than
willing to indulge in the sand and the suds. We headed out to the
bus stop, anxious to get to the bar and drink ourselves into stupors.
It felt good to put aside our differences and celebrate our accomplishment. The four of us had not been together outside of training
since we arrived in California. It was a great moment of unity for
us. I felt a kinship among the Marines at the bus stop that I hadn't
felt before. We had endured ten days of hardship, and each of us
recognized we wouldn't have made it through without help from the
others.

While we waited for the shuttle we reminisced, sharing our favorite memories of the ten days past. Sgt. Moss bragged about how
he had saved us from all the bullshit the instructors had planned for
us. Dougherty boasted how he conquered Mt. Motherfucker, but
graciously left out the part of how it almost killed me. Poole listed
each of the weapons he had fired, and offered his commentary on
the merits of each. I reminded everyone about Kung Fu Theater,
and we all laughed until our insides hurt. Even Poole laughed, and
for a fleeting moment he was one of us. Then the car arrived.

The tinted window lowered on the driver's side and the dark-
green Marine inside called toward us, "Poole! C'mom, Dog. We got
to go!"

The Marines in the rental car were Poole's boys. Poole abandoned us and ran over to the car. He talked briefly through the window and then looked back at us in indecision.

We motioned for him to come back. The shuttle had arrived and we, too, were ready to go. Poole didn't look back a second time. He climbed in with his boys and sped away. I was disappointed in Poole. I wanted him to be one of us. But he wasn't then, and he would never be. If I knew then what I know now, I would have pushed him into the car myself. I might have even pushed him under the car.

We entered the classroom of LAV school at 0800 hours on Monday morning, after our big weekend in San Clemente, a bit overwhelmed and a bit hung over. On one side of the classroom there was a life-size replica of the driver's compartment. On the other side was a replica of the turret. The driver's compartment was littered with instrument panels, gauges, knobs, levers, and controls. The turret featured a gunner's station that was linked to a high-tech computer.

The assembled main gun rested ominously in a gun stand, while an adjacent table displayed dozens of parts from its unassembled counterpart. We cringed at the thought of learning all of the names for the parts, not to mention their function. We sat in silence, totally intimidated by the steepness of the learning curve before us. That is, until we heard it. Chinese-speak.

Edsar stood at the front of the class and role-played the instructor. "Is der a Wong in here? Where Marine named Wong?"

Frye displayed his signature slow-motion martial arts moves, as they used their mouths to make exaggerated sound effects, in addition to making their out-of-sync speaking gestures. Playing along, he stated his character's first name—"Sum Ting, Sir."

Edsar gave us his best puzzled expression. "Whut chu mean, sum-ting?"

Frye replied with the full name this time, "Sum Ting Wong."

Edsar pretended to misunderstand, "What wong?"

Frye stood and pointed to himself, "Sir, Sum Ting Wong."

Edsar pretended to lose his patience and ran over as if to confront a disrespectful student, "For da last time, what wong!"

Edsar's tone and timing were perfect. "And for da last time I tell you . . . Sum Ting Wong!"

It took some Marines longer than others to catch on. But once the anticipated fight started, laughter filled the room. Every Marine in our class was entertained by the show, except one—Cpl. Chin. But then again, not much humored Cpl. Chin. Perhaps he felt overshadowed by Sgt. Moss's authority. Perhaps he was bitter about being stuck in school with a bunch of reservists. Or maybe he just didn't appreciate a sophomoric satire of his culture. Whatever the reason, Cpl. Chin had distanced himself from everyone and remained a loner throughout LAV school.

Cpl. Chin studied, ate, and spent his free time in isolation. He reminded me of some of the Asian students I knew in school—serious, studious, and stoic. It had always bothered me that my Asian classmates outperformed me academically, especially in college. I wondered what they had that I didn't. The Marine Corps answered that for me—they had discipline. I began LAV school determined not to be outperformed—especially by Cpl. Chin.

Now that we were in an academic environment, I felt more confident and comfortable. But Sgt. Moss was like a fish out of water. His rank did little to help us with our studies. It was one thing to lighten our load for a combat run—preparing for exams was another. In fact, our roles had reversed. I had the power because I knew how to study.

I welcomed the opportunity to tutor Sgt. Moss and the others. In fact, I probably mastered the material because of all of the tutoring. By midcourse I had received kudos from the instructors for earning the highest class average. That was the impetus for my determination to graduate with the highest class average. My blinders were on. My sights were set. It would be a personal victory for me, as well as a symbolic victory for reservists.

I didn't consciously choose to race Cpl. Chin. But once I got into a study groove I worked like a monk in a monastery. I copied the chapters from our text into my notes over and over. I lay awake at night reciting all of the LAV nomenclature in my head. Sometimes I even stayed awake all night assembling and disassembling the main gun in the lab. My determination kept me buried in my books for the next four weeks . . . and on weekends. I resisted the temptation to go back into town with the boys. It was a lot more productive for me to stay behind and study.

My attitude changed on the sixth Friday of LAV school when I learned that I was one of the Marines scheduled to be promoted from the rank of private first class to lance corporal. Before the ceremony Sgt. Moss briefed Hunter and me on the close-order-drill procedures to be carried out by the promotion detail.

I couldn't believe it. Sgt. Moss was the last person I'd have thought capable of coaching us on how to conduct ourselves during a promotion ceremony. What I didn't know, however, was that Sgt. Moss had prepared. He had studied the close-order-drill manual so that he could keep me from embarrassing myself as he had a few months prior.

His instructions were perfect. When I finished leading the detail to the back of the platoon, after we received our promotions, he signaled me with a thumbs-up gesture. I don't know who was more proud—me for getting promoted, or he for teaching me how to perform in the ceremony. The pride of achievement was more powerful than my obsession with getting the best score in LAV class. So I succumbed to peer pressure and headed out for my second night on the town—this time in San Diego. We left with our heads held high. We returned with our heads in our hands . . . thanks to Lance Cpl. Hunter.

Hunter was an active-duty Marine who didn't mind associating with reservists. In fact, he fit into our group well. He was too mild mannered to care about such divisions. As far as he was concerned, we were all Marines. I liked that about him. Everyone liked Hunter—especially the women. His southern charm complemented his boyish good looks.

We stopped at the first bar we saw and wasted no time downing a few rounds of Coronas. We commiserated about the rigors of the past training, and discussed the challenges of the next two weeks to come. Then Hunter took over. He was a naturally funny person. He kept us in stitches with his hysterical impressions of the Marines in our class . . . and the instructors. Hunter was the life of the party.

During one of the lulls of laughter Sgt. Moss raised his bottle and offered a toast, "To Wee-ams and Hunter . . . the Corps's newest lance corporals. Let's have a night to remember!"

The toast prompted Hunter's slurred suggestion, "You wanna remember tonight . . . I saw a tattoo shop down the street!"

I had no inhibitions about tattoos. Both my father and brother had them, and I had always considered them rites of passage into adulthood. I didn't hesitate. We finished our sixth round of beers and headed down the street to Tiger Jimmy's tattoo studio. The waiting area was filled with Marines scanning the walls and books for that perfect tattoo.

I approached a Marine who was examining his new eagle, globe, and anchor emblem in the mirror. "Do you like it?"

He proudly shoved his upper arm in my face, offering the same slurred speech as Hunter. "This is the best place in San Diego to get a tattoo."

That was all I needed to hear. Two hours later I walked out of Tiger Jimmy's with a Marine bulldog on my right shoulder. I joined Sgt. Moss and the others who were still undecided about their commitment to tattoo that night. We decided to find another bar to continue the party, and walked the San Diego strip.

All of the bars had long lines of people waiting to enter. After we'd passed several, Hunter had his second brainstorm. "Let's go to TJ—I bet you don't have to wait to get into bars down there!"

The Mexican border was only a short drive south, and Tijuana not much farther. Marines thought of the border as the threshold into the promised land of sin. The word was that you could get drunk, high, and laid for twenty bucks. I had no doubt that was where Poole and his buddies were.

But Marine students were restricted from crossing the Mexican border. Sgt. Banks had warned us about TJ in his orientation speech before our first weekend liberty. He urged us to avoid Mexico, and to report any Marines who went. He scared us with horrific stories of abusive incarceration by Mexicali policemen, violent robberies and assaults, and deadly venereal diseases. Sgt. Banks's warning scared the hell out of me. But it incited Hunter.

Hunter continued unsuccessfully to try to convince us to go to Tijuana. Sgt. Moss reminded everyone that our platoon was scheduled for guard duty starting at 0600 reveille on Sunday morning, which was less than six hours away at this point. We considered it acceptable to get four hours sleep before duty, but Hunter didn't see it that way. He considered the goal to simply make it back to base before he was scheduled for duty. The alcohol clouded his judgment and made him angry.

As he headed away from the safety of our group he cursed us. "You're a bunch of pussies! A fucking bunch of pussies!"

It wasn't until noon the next day that anyone realized Lance Cpl. Hunter had not returned. Hunter was scheduled to relieve Wright for guard duty at 1200 hours, but never showed. Wright woke Sgt. Moss, who was sleeping off his hangover after his shift.

"Sgt. Moss, Lance Cpl. Hunter is UA! I can't find him anywhere. His rack is still made—We don't think he came back last night."

Sgt. Moss was worried. He called us together for a formation, which confirmed that Hunter was missing. Worse yet, Dean reported a rumor that a Marine had been jumped and robbed last night in San Diego. Bender confirmed the rumor. Sgt. Moss had heard enough. He organized a search team of Marines to head into San Diego to find Hunter and bring him back. At best he was stranded in town without money for the shuttle. At worst . . . well, we didn't want to consider the worst.

I remained on guard duty, monitored the phone, and waited for word. At approximately 1500 hours Sgt. Moss called to check in.

I reported, "No word here yet. The barracks is empty. . . ."

Sgt. Moss asked me again to confirm Hunter's suspected location. I replied, "Dean and Bender both heard San Diego. . . . They didn't say exactly where in San Diego."

Just then a disheveled Hunter walked into the quarterdeck area, brandishing a black eye, purple nose, and swollen lip. He moaned through the pain in his face, "Actually, it was Oceanside."

I looked up in disbelief, leaving Sgt. Moss in the silence of dead air.

Hunter continued past me and collapsed in his rack.

I put the handset back to my mouth, "Sgt. Moss, you're not going to believe this. . . ."

Hunter was a fortunate Marine. If he had been a cat he would have lost one of his lives that night. He would need the remaining eight for what fate had planned for him.

The last week of LAV school was spent preparing for three high-stakes evaluations—the written exam, the driver's test, and the final inspection. As I studied I could not help but recognize the chasm between the knowledge I had and the knowledge I believed I would need. I knew enough to function back at Camp Upshur, where the LAVs were used for little more than an armored transportation service. But I knew there was more to being an LAV crewman.

I might not have if it had not been for the live-fire demonstration we observed during our first week in LAV school. I was waiting anxiously to see the LAVs in action. We were informed by the voice on the loudspeaker that the active-duty LAV crewmen who operated the LAVs had returned from the recent combat in Panama. It showed.

The bleachers shook and our hearts skipped a beat as the main gun of the LAV fired its first burst of 25-mm rounds downrange. The LAV's engine screamed as it hit the hill before us, launching all eight wheels into the air. As the LAV made a U-turn back toward us, its turret traversed, keeping the barrel trained on the target vehicles in the distance. The vehicle slowed as the chain gun pumped high-explosive rounds into a truck, vaporizing it into a ball of flame. Then the barrel rose and thumped its next volley into a tank that was barely visible in the distance. I could make out the bright yellow and orange flashes as the armor-piercing rounds penetrated the hull.

On its third pass pop-up targets appeared, simulating an attack by enemy troops on foot. The vehicle commander mowed down the first row with his machine gun mounted atop the turret. Then the gunner's machine gun, mounted alongside the 25mm main gun, came to life. It sliced back and forth, leveling every target before it. While the last targets were being destroyed, smoke canisters ejected from both sides of the LAV.

The rear hatch opened and infantry scouts poured out under the concealment of billowing green smoke. Three dived to the ground on the port side, and three on the starboard side. They disappeared from sight and became one with the earth. Then we heard the familiar popping sounds of their M16 rifles as tracer rounds pierced the green haze. The streaks of red-orange tracers targeted a set of bunkers in front of the LAV. The scouts took turns rushing forward, firing their rifles, and dropping to the ground. More pop-up targets appeared. One of the Marines fired his machine gun, another assaulted with his grenade launcher, and a third sent a shoulder-fired missile into the bunker complex. Throughout the assault the LAV moved in unison with the scouts, supporting their fire and offering them a safe harbor for their regress. During the grand finale the LAV's guns joined the scouts' assault and the bunkers exploded into oblivion. The scouts reentered the hull as quickly as they had exited, and the LAV sped off into the distance.

The crowd applauded wildly. It had been an impressive demonstration. For some it was little more than a fireworks display, but for me it was a revelation. It showed me the combat potential of the LAV under the command of a well-trained, experienced crew. I watched the demonstration in awe of its capabilities. It was an impressively deadly machine . . . in the right hands. I looked forward to acquiring that level of expertise.

After eight weeks of instruction and cramming I could name just about every part on the LAV. I could also perform basic preventive maintenance, checks, and services on the diesel engine. And I could drive the LAV. Driving was emphasized so much, we joked that the course should have been called "LAV driver school."

With respect to driving the training was first class. I could confidently navigate the LAV through deep sand, up near-vertical inclines, over jumps, and along steep side slopes. I could use the winch to pull the LAV from the grips of a mud bog, the tow bar to pull a disabled vehicle to the Ramp, and the propellers to make amphibious entries into and exits out of the water. I felt highly trained in the driver's seat. In fact, there was only one part of the driver's test in which I faltered—the blind drive.

This test required me to drive while blindfolded, relying solely on the verbal guidance of the vehicle commander through my headset. It was extremely difficult to step on the accelerator and trust that the voice in my helmet would keep me from crashing. I completed the course, but my consistent hesitation cost me three points. Actually, those three points were the only points I failed to earn during the entire course. The blind drive was my Achilles' heel and nearly cost me victory over Cpl. Chin. In the end we both finished the course with 99.4 percent class averages and shared recognition as dual honor-graduates. I did not know at the time that my next blind drive would be in combat—only, then there would be more at stake than an academic honor.

I felt much less confident in my gunnery skills. The best thing I could say about LAV school gunnery training was that it prepared me to assemble and disassemble the main gun and the coaxial machine gun. To the untrained observer it appeared that we knew how to operate the main gun. But what happened inside the turret was far from mastery of gunnery skills.

The problem was rooted in a faulty curriculum. Despite the best intentions of the instructors there was simply not enough time in our training schedule to master gunnery skills. Of the eight weeks of LAV school we spent only two days on the firing range. The objective for the instructors was not to provide us with the basic skills we needed for combat. It was to get as many students qualified on the range as possible. The criterion set for qualification was absurdly easy to meet. We simply needed to land three rounds on selected targets identified by the instructor. Both the vehicle and the targets were stationary. All we did was aim and squeeze the trigger. Even at night the task offered less challenge than most video games. In an effort to get all of us qualified our instructors set up an assembly-line operation to force as many students through as possible. They completed all of the prep work needed to make the guns ready to fire. They did everything for us except pull the trigger, and in some cases they even did that. It was a highly effective way to get a maximum number of Marines through the minimal requirements. But it offered little preparation for war.

I left the range without ever opening an ammunition can. I didn't know how to unpack the rounds, inspect their alignment, feed the ammunition belt into the main gun chutes, or upload the rounds into the breach. I didn't know—and worse yet didn't care at the time—that these were critical steps in preventing jams. The instructors cleared our jams for us. Their expertise minimized the time the guns were down for repairs, which maximized the number of students cycling through their qualification stations. We figured the sooner we finished on the range the sooner we earned liberty. To say our priorities were not in order was an understatement.

During our final exams the inspecting officers asked us for feedback about training. I reported that I felt I needed more time to practice gunnery skills. The officer acknowledged that the school environment had its limitations. He added that LAV crewmen do not really develop combat proficiency until they train with their units under their respective master-gunner mentors. That might have been true for active-duty Marines, but it wouldn't be true for us reservists.

It was now August of 1990, and Uncle Sam would soon have other plans for us.

Our LAV instructors helped us celebrate our last evening in California with the traditional graduation party at the enlisted club on

base. It felt good to relax without the burden of passing exams.
There wasn't a lot to do in the club except drink. So we drank. And
we drank. Sgt. Moss and I shared a table and more than a few pitch-
ers. I was preoccupied with thoughts of home and wondered what
training would be like for us when we returned. He assured me that
he would try to get me transferred into his platoon. Then the conversation turned toward his promotion. I had broached the subject
with him in the past, but our conversation never progressed beyond
the comic banter about his promotion ceremony. Rank was a sensitive subject for Sgt. Moss, but his defenses were no match for the
alcohol and my incessant probes. I wanted to know how he had become a sergeant.

He explained that he was stationed at Quantico for most of his
four years of active duty, where he performed a variety of duties on
the rifle ranges at Officer Candidates School. He explained that he
liked the nine-to-five nature of the job, and that he was his own boss.
But the job didn't afford him the opportunity to develop his skills as
a noncommissioned officer. In fact, he told me how he was offered
the rank of corporal just as his contract was ending. Shortly after his
promotion he dropped to inactive ready reserve status and returned
to his civilian life.

Nearly two years later he surrendered to the urge to return to the
Corps by joining the reserves. Recruiters were looking for former
Marines like Sgt. Moss to fill NCO billets at the newly forming
Weapons Company. And not just NCO billets—platoon sergeant bil-
lets. He explained how Capt. Cruz offered to promote him to ser-
geant if he signed on for at least a year.

Practically speaking, Sergeant Moss was really Lance Cpl. Moss.
He didn't have any Marine Corps experience between his last days
as a lance corporal and his first as a sergeant. We both agreed it was
too much, too soon. Nonetheless, I thought he had the potential to
be a great leader. His disclosure, even though it was alcohol induced,
strengthened my resolve to be a part of his team. I couldn't think of
a better way to spend our last night in LAV school.

We stood proudly in our graduation formation on the sweltering
afternoon of 2 August 1990. The heat made it difficult to endure the

pomp and circumstance that was typical of Marine celebrations. The band played. The national anthem sounded. A dignitary lectured. And the base commander spoke. Only, it wasn't the kind of speech we'd been expecting. It wasn't the kind I'd heard at boot camp graduation and promotion ceremonies, the kind to be ignored. On the contrary I have never forgotten it.

The base commander began simply enough. "Today . . . Iraqi forces invaded the country of Kuwait."

That meant little to me. Few of us could have located either country on the globe that day, much less understood the geopolitical ramifications. But the CO spoke with passion and conviction. He told of how America would not let the Iraqi occupation stand. He shared the reports of atrocities committed by the Iraqi soldiers against the unsuspecting victims in Kuwait—men slain . . . women raped . . . children orphaned . . . communities pillaged.

Those were not things with which most of us could identify or even comprehend. It sounded horrific to me, but it was all a world away. I had read about these things in books, watched them on movie screens, and seen them on the evening news. I dismissed the concern as graduation rhetoric that was crafted to motivate the troops. I believed officers would tell us such things to validate all the time and effort we put into training.

Then the CO dropped the bomb.

"Effective immediately, all leave is suspended for active-duty personnel. You will have twenty-four hours to report to your units, where you will receive your orders."

I was relieved that I was not an active-duty Marine. After three months away from home I just wanted to get back to my friends, to school, and to Gina. I had thought, like many other reservists on August 2, that the Iraqi invasion of Kuwait wasn't my problem.

PART III

WARRIOR

SIX

THE WORLD WOULD BE DIFFERENT for me after 2 August, as it was for the ravaged people of Kuwait. Those fateful words from graduation stayed with me and tainted my homecoming. It seemed as if the rest of the world was still turning the way it had before I left, but I was out of sync—that is, the rest of the world except Camp Upshur. During my check-in following LAV school in August, Staff Sgt. Church confirmed for me what America was just figuring out. We were preparing to go to war.

The admin office was busier than ever preparing for a MORDT—Mobilization Operational Readiness Deployment Test. The staff sergeant explained that it assessed the unit's administrative readiness to support a mobilization. She added that our next drill would be an admin drill in which we rotated through processing stations, just as we would if we were mobilized for war.

Then she showed me one of the admin desks. "This is the 'legal' station."

One of the forms on the desk was titled "Power of Attorney," and the other read "Last Will and Testament."

"Last Will and Testament?" I asked.

My naïveté brought out her maternal instinct. She gently pulled the form from my hands and redirected me back to the office. "It's just an exercise, Pfc. . . . just an exercise."

But I knew better. And she did too.

★

Because so many Marines had returned from their MOS schools in August, the company reorganized again in September. Dougherty, Poole, and I were assigned to Sgt. Moss's platoon as LAV-25 crewmen. Our new titles as "crewmen" didn't help us get into the driver's or gunner's seats, though. The drill weekends during September, October, and November were all administrative, and the LAVs were kept locked and tarped on the Ramp.

We spent a lot of time in the big classroom, listening to intelligence briefs, and gearing up for the call. We knew we would be called, we just didn't know when. It felt like we were in purgatory. I tried to get in the right state of mind. After three months I thought I was ready. I wasn't.

The call came on 18 November 1990. It was a quiet Sunday evening, and I was sitting at the kitchen table writing lesson plans for my last week of student teaching, when the phone rang. I picked up the receiver, expecting to hear Gina's voice. We talked every evening before going to sleep.

Instead of Gina on the other end it was Sgt. Moss. He spoke slowly, with a solemn tone to his voice. "Wee-ams . . . this is the Big Ooh Rah. . . ."

And then there was just silence.

I didn't understand.

"Sgt. Moss?"

He answered with a sigh, "Yeah . . . I'm here."

More silence.

"What's up?"

"We've been activated," he said. "You need to report for formation this Friday at 0700."

At the end of the call I hung up the phone and stood paralyzed. I would only have four days to get my affairs in order. My mind fast-forwarded through the slide show of my life . . . my job . . . my students . . . my friends . . . my mother . . . Gina.

I'm not sure how long I stood in the kitchen staring at the wall.

At some point I sat down to finish the lesson plans for the next morning. Then I realized the futility of it all. I wasn't going to student-teach on Monday. I was going to say good-bye to my students and withdraw from Towson State University. As I worked through the implications, reality began to sink in.

My initial denial turned to anger, and then anger into rage. I cleared the dining room table with one aggressive swipe of my forearm. Then I stormed around the kitchen and paced like a caged animal.

Once the adrenaline subsided, I returned to the dining room to clean up my mess. My mother was due to return home shortly and I did not want to have to explain my rant. I wasn't sure if I was going to tell her at all. She had just married Pat the day before and was still in newlywed bliss. I couldn't imagine how to tell her that her only son was going to war, especially the day after her wedding. Such a severe emotional U-turn, I feared, could give her a heart attack.

While picking up the papers from my tantrum I found that I had broken, among other things, a photo frame. It held my favorite picture of Gina and me, happily reunited during my welcome home party from the past summer. As I walked back to my bedroom I recalled her toast, "To the last summer we will ever be apart!" I sat on the edge of my mattress, staring at the distorted images of us beneath the cracked glass, and engaged the phone in a silent showdown.

After an hour of thinking about the right words to tell Gina I had been activated, I realized there was no way to make it sound good.

"Hello," Gina answered.

"Gina Marie, it's Buzz." All I could muster was awkward silence.

"Is everything OK?"

"Do you think your parents would mind if I came over tonight?"

"Tonight?" She asked. "It's almost ten o'clock."

"I know, but it's real important," I said.

"OK," she agreed hesitantly. "I'm sure Mom and Dad won't mind."

It was clear she wanted me to tell her over the phone. I thought she must have realized that the news was about me being called to active duty. We had talked about my likely call-up frequently.

As I was walking out of the house to visit Gina, Mom and Pat were pulling into the driveway. Figuring that I'd have to tell her sooner or later, I headed back inside the house. Saying good-bye to my mother would not be as difficult as it should have been. My dislike of Pat had strained our relationship, and at the time we were barely speaking with each other.

"Mom. I won't be here when you get back from Florida."

"What do you mean, you won't be here?" She wasn't up to date on my pending activation, and she hadn't been expecting what I was about to say. "Where will you be?"

"Camp Lejeune, probably. Maybe Saudi Arabia." I wanted her to get emotional, and maybe even cry. Using my call-up to war was a hell of a way to get affection from my mother, but it had been months since I had felt any.

"We'll have to cancel the trip," Mom said, beginning to cry.

"No. No. No." I said. "I'm leaving Friday whether you go or not. What's the difference between saying good-bye tomorrow, or saying good-bye on Friday?"

She dwelled on that decision, which helped her to refocus and keep her composure. With some prompting from Pat, Mom decided to leave for her honeymoon on Monday as planned. It worked out for the best, because the farewell to Gina on Friday would be all I could handle.

After talking with my mother, I decided to call Gina instead of driving into the city to see her. It would have been after midnight when I arrived, and although her parents were understanding, a visit that late was pushing it. My fingers trembled as I dialed her number.

"Where are you?" she asked. "I thought you would be here by now."

"I was talking with Mom."

"Buzz—what's going on?" She asked impatiently.

"Sgt. Moss called me, Gina Marie—my company's been activated."

"That wasn't what I wanted to hear," she said quietly. "When do you leave?"

"Check-in is Friday morning, but—"

"Let me guess." She cut me off with a halfhearted joke. "You want to be there Thursday so you can stay up all night playing with your gear."

She knew me well.

Both Gina and my mother were stronger than I'd imagined. I was sure they feared the worst, as I did, but some things were better left unsaid. Dying in combat was one of them. There was plenty of dialogue going on inside me, though. My moral compass was now in overdrive, swinging violently between the polarities of bravery and cowardice.

I considered revisiting the hospital in Bethesda, thinking that my knee condition could keep me home, or at least stateside. I also considered evoking the protection afforded me as the sole surviving son. That meant I would still need to leave home, but as I understood it the provision would keep me from participating in combat. I even thought about declaring a conscientious objection to killing people. It was all too overwhelming to handle alone.

The next afternoon I would visit the memorial garden where my father and brother were buried, stare at the ground, and ask for help from beyond.

At the time I was not a religious person, but I felt I needed to be close to Lenny and Dad then. I had visited their graves from time to time and sometimes talked to them. For a while I yelled at my brother for having sent me the letters that got me interested in the Marines in the first place. It felt good to vent.

The serenity of the cemetery eventually cleared my mind and helped me focus on the moral principles that had guided me. I knew in my heart that anything less than deploying with my platoon would be dishonorable. In the end I decided that living with guilt would be more costly than dying in combat. But that realization wouldn't make saying good-bye any easier.

Gina and I spent as much time together as possible during my last four days at home. It was a painful time, but I look back on it as a defining moment for us. We had already made it through two summers apart—enduring separation had become a hallmark of our relationship. We convinced ourselves that the war was just another opportunity to prove our resolve to remain faithful to each other. It was the ultimate opportunity.

The night before I left I gave Gina a diamond ring. I had wanted it to be an engagement ring, but the possibility of dying overseas kept me from making it such. To her parents, and the rest of the world, it was a simple band with a single diamond stone. To Gina it was a precursor to engagement. To me it was a plea for her to wait and a promise for me to return.

The drive to Camp Upshur on Thursday, November 22 was awkward, to say the least. Gina's father was at the wheel and said barely a word. Her mother made polite conversation to mask her emotion. Gina sat next to me in the backseat and squeezed my hand tightly.

Gina didn't stay long once we arrived at the base. We had promised each other we would make our good-bye brief to minimize the misery, and we followed through. Gina's mother and father pulled my bags from the trunk, which gave us just enough time to hug. I was glad the windows in the car were tinted. I preferred my last memory of Gina to be the embrace instead of a tearful wave.

After the car drove off, thumping across the Upshur bridge, it dawned on me just how deserted the base was. Left alone in the barracks, it would have been easy to get melancholy. But my mind never idled long enough for sadness to creep in. Once the contents of my footlocker and wall locker were laid out on the deck, I began my usual predrill routine of inventorying and arranging my gear. But this was no ordinary drill weekend—and the routine I was about to begin was anything but usual.

On the floor lay the contents of two standard-issue seabags. Then it hit me—everything I would need to survive in the desert, and possibly combat, would need to fit into those two seabags. I sorted through all of it systematically, categorizing as I went: uniform items, field gear, and hygiene supplies. Then it was time to count everything, list the things that were missing, or short, and throw away the excess. When I was in my zone, there could only be even numbers of things, which is why my seventh pair of socks went into the trash.

I cursed the hygiene bag that had been issued to me at Parris Island because it wouldn't hold two of everything, and as I forced the zipper closed it tore at the seams, sending everything to the concrete floor. Now my toothbrushes were on the floor, soaked in cologne and shards of glass, and I wondered what I had been thinking bringing glass cologne bottles anyway. I heard the sound of a shaving cream can, rolling away and then coming to a stop under a rack across the squad bay. Then I shook the toothbrushes, crawled under the rack to retrieve the can, and congratulated myself on having a backup hygiene bag.

Uniforms were a no-brainer because the CO's letter listed the required clothing for deployment. I would need five green skivvy shirts, so I added a sixth, and folded them like Drill Instructor Sgt. Wagner had taught us. After failing to get them all folded into the same-size rectangles, I imagined his voice ordering me to dig on the quarterdeck. Finally I got the shirts folded and into the bottom of the seabag. But after the bag was filled, I saw an extra green skivvy shirt on the rack, which made me wonder whether all six had made it in. So I dumped the bag and started over.

After many unsuccessful attempts at getting all of my field gear into the seabags, I began to disassemble everything. I yanked, twisted, pushed, pulled, squeezed, and poked. Reluctantly, it all came apart: snaps, buttons, buckles, zippers, clips, flaps, and drawstrings. Then, like an intricate puzzle, I put all the pieces inside. After both bags were packed, I told myself it would be OK to go to bed after checking the CO's list once more.

That last check made my heart sink. How could I have missed it?

I read it over and over to be sure. We needed to fall into formation wearing our field gear the next morning at 0700. That gear was at the bottom of a seabag.

There would be no sleep this night.

23 NOVEMBER 1990

The 0700 formation was a zoo. Capt. Cruz called the formation to the position of attention as usual, but it was difficult to concentrate. The area around the formation was louder and more cluttered than I had ever seen it. Cars and trucks littered the field around the formation. Friends called to Marines from the distance, cheering and whooping. Mothers, wives, and girlfriends wept, hugged, and wept some more. Fathers shook hands, saluted, and snapped photos of their boys heading off to war, as many of them had done a generation before. And then there were the children—the little brothers and sisters who watched and waved, in all of their innocence, as their heroes became larger than life. I was sure many of them were hearing the yellow footprints call for the first time.

When I think back to that moment, I remember wishing I'd had a little brother. I wanted him to watch, and wave, and cheer. I wondered if he would have heard the call the way I had . . . and if so, I wondered if he would have answered. Like every generation before me I stood in that formation believing that our sacrifice would help to keep those children from having to go off to war when they grew up . . . that our effort would make the world a safer place. It didn't dawn on me that every generation before me had been wrong about that.

Even Capt. Cruz was distracted by Cpl. Keith's buxom girl-friend, who showed her support by lifting her shirt and flashing us from the passenger seat of his convertible. The formation was so chaotic, we could not differentiate the present Marines from the UA Marines. After consulting with a few platoon commanders, Capt. Cruz decided to move the formation to the big classroom.

Once we assembled in the quiet order of the big classroom, we were able to begin the business of processing for deployment. The first order of that business was determining unit strength, which meant counting the number of Marines that were present. I could tell by Capt. Cruz's agitated demeanor that we were not going to deploy at full strength. It was a real disappointment, given that our unit had scored 100 percent attendance during the last MORDT. But that had been practice. This was real.

Each platoon had at least one Marine who was considered UA, all of whom had hokey stories that justified their absence. The stories surrounding the UA Marines spread throughout the big classroom like wildfire. I suspected that most were phony, as every Marine in the unit had reported in ready, willing, and able during the previous month's MORDT. There was not enough time for lightning to strike that many Marines in that brief period of time. There was at least one Marine, though, who had a legitimate, albeit dishonorable, excuse for not reporting to duty. He was in the hospital recovering from an alleged hunting accident that had left him with one foot.

Most of us were appalled by the cowardly acts of the UA Marines. Some of the Marines who did show up carried ingenious, shameful ideas in the pockets of their minds like get-out-of-war cards. They were the traitorous sleepers of our company. A few Marines played their cards before we left Camp Upshur, requesting exemption for such bogus things as dying relatives and uncooperative employers. Others would hold them until we landed in Lejeune.

I was at peace, though, and card free. I had played my hand, made my decision, and pledged my commitment. That didn't make me any less afraid. It gave me the intestinal fortitude to swallow my fear. There was a lot of swallowing that day in the big classroom.

During the next sixteen hours we rotated through eleven stations, just as we had practiced during the MORDT. The tedium of it all was barely tolerable. Most of the time was spent waiting in lines. Fortunately for me, I went through the process with Sgt. Moss and Dougherty. Though part of me missed the structure that Sgt. Krause brought to his platoon, none of me missed Nagel, Draper, or Poole.

Our first stop was supply, where Staff Sgt. Bader made sure we had a complete issue of uniforms and field gear. After supply we moved on to medical stations for shots, physicals, and prescription lenses. Then there were forms, forms, and more forms. When I saw the Last Will and Testament form I hesitated and looked around for Staff Sgt. Church.

One of the admin sergeants hurried me along, "What's the matter there, Dorothy? Not in Kansas anymore?"

I cursed him under my breath. He was a member of the active-duty Inspector and Instructor staff who, by Marine Corps directive, remained at the reserve unit during and after mobilization. I found it absurd that the active-duty I & I Marines stayed back while we reservists deployed. They were the ones with all the experience. They were the self-proclaimed "real Marines." It didn't make sense to me, but there was nothing I could do about it. That was how the reserves worked.

Sunday began and ended on the Ramp. I was especially motivated because Dougherty and I were assigned to Sgt. Moss's vehicle. It felt good to be together again, even though we didn't see Sgt. Moss as much as we had during LAV school. He spent most of his time in platoon sergeant meetings and officer briefings. While we missed the extra hands and his sense of humor, Dougherty and I were more than capable of assuming all of the responsibilities for prepping the LAV. We immersed ourselves in the process and, as was common for crewmen, developed a sense of vehicle ownership. It did not take long for *the* LAV to become *our* LAV.

We spent sixteen hours prepping our LAV for the road march and, as best we could, for combat. First we unloaded, cleaned, and inventoried all of the internal and external gear. We went to excruciating lengths to beg and barter with our fellow crewmen to get a complete set of gear and tools for the LAV. Then we performed every preventive-maintenance check and service in the manual. We filled fluids, lubed the chassis, inflated the tires, replaced bulbs, and changed filters. Finally, we disassembled, cleaned, lubed, and reassembled the main gun and machine gun.

The procedure was backbreaking work, but it made us intimately familiar with the nuances of our vehicle. We knew that the engine leaked oil slowly and needed to be topped off during each fuel stop. We knew the cable connector that linked our radios to the power source was stripped, which made it the first thing to troubleshoot if we lost our communications. And we knew the HE chute for the main gun had bent pins and required insertion on a forty-five degree angle to properly install it. Knowledge of these quirks was critical to keeping the vehicle running, the radio working, and the weapons system operational. We knew that in combat, failure of any one of those systems could prove fatal. That was why Dougherty and I spent all day and most of the night checking and rechecking the vehicle. It wasn't until the first light showed on the horizon that we felt assured that our vehicle was prepared for the trip.

Our thirty-five-vehicle convoy lunged from Camp Upshur at 0700 hours on Monday, 26 November. We were motivated to get to Camp Lejeune and start training. The first seven hours of the trip went exactly as planned. Actually, they went better. None of us had counted on the overwhelming public support that we received from the people along the route. Passengers waved, drivers beeped, and pedestrians cheered. We felt like celebrities, and the attention we received kept our spirits high.

At approximately the halfway point, however, the vehicles started to have maintenance problems. We knew whenever there was a problem because Capt. Cruz called on the radio for all vehicles to pull off to the shoulder of the highway. It was a monumental task, as the column stretched for more than a mile. During the second half of our trip we stopped a dozen times to service disabled vehicles. Our mechanics made roadside repairs whenever it was practical. When repairs were too laborious, the vehicles were towed. By the time we arrived at Camp Lejeune, half of our column was towing the other half. The fourteen-hour journey taxed our crewmen, mechanics, and vehicles to their limits.

We limped onto our new ramp at Camp Lejeune at 2100 hours, barely moving. Our first priority was to park and the second was to sleep. Capt. Cruz held a brief formation to orient us to our new space, which had formerly been the home of the active-duty LAV unit known as 2nd Light Armored Infantry Battalion. At first it seemed intrusive to park on their ramp and sleep in their racks, but they no longer needed either. These Marines and their LAVs were already en route to Saudi Arabia.

The following morning brought several surprises. The first was the news that our LAVs were not available for training. The CO explained that the priority was to transport the vehicles to Saudi as soon as possible so they would be waiting for us when we arrived. After being serviced, they were locked, tarped, and staged for shipping.

The most serious implication was that our crews could not practice gun drills. Gun drill procedures would allow us to practice the skills that we had missed in LAV school, such as loading ammunition, simulating a jam, and clearing the jam. I was very concerned that we would not be able to work with the weapons systems. It meant that we would have to wait until we arrived in the desert to learn the skills we needed. I had no problem with on-the-job training, but I had a big problem with training under fire.

Sgt. Moss was concerned as well, but he was not able to help. He was no longer our platoon sergeant. This was because of another surprise—yet another reorganization of the company. Actually it was more than reorganization. It was a complete reconstitution that merged our company with Fox Company, an infantry rifle company from New York. Following the merger Weapons Company and Fox Company were no more. The newly consolidated unit was called Delta Company. We met as Delta Company for the first time on the grassy plot just outside our barracks. There was a lot of confusion and territorial tension. Delta Company needed only one commanding officer, one first sergeant, and one company gunny. Likewise, our platoons needed only one commander and one platoon sergeant each. Since our former companies already had these positions filled, our new company had two Marines vying for each leadership position.

When the dust of the consolidation settled, Capt. Cruz was still our company CO and First Sgt. Little was still our company first sergeant. Gunny Brandt wasn't so lucky. He lost the position of company gunny to Fox's Gunnery Sgt. Koffman. Gunny Brandt did not handle his perceived demotion well. He was openly critical of the decision and let everyone know how he felt. Gunny Koffman shared many of his company gunny responsibilities with Gunny Brandt in the spirit of collaboration. Gunny Brandt, however, considered them charity assignments and refused all of the offers. The only duties he performed were those assigned by Capt. Cruz, but even then he worked under protest.

One such duty was the distribution of mail. It allowed him to have daily contact with every Marine in the company, and a forum to appease his need for power. Gunny Brandt established two thirty-minute windows for mail call. One was to receive mail and the other to send. Although it was not a standard practice, he required us to perform tasks to be eligible to receive our mail. The tasks were functions of his mood on any given day. If he was in a good mood, we only needed to trap the letters between our hands, like clapping a mosquito, as he waved them around before us. If he was in a bad mood, he required us to beg for our mail. Sometimes he would simply send us away without our mail and without explanation. It wasn't only against Marine Corps policy—it was sadistic. Gunny Brandt had alienated most of the company before Gunny Koffman found out about his antics and fired him from the mail billet.

After the consolidation, I was assigned back in First Platoon under Sgt. Krause and a new platoon commander, Capt. Bounds. My reluctant return to First Platoon was tempered by the news that Sgt. Moss and Lance Cpl. Dougherty were reassigned with me. Sgt. Moss joined us as First Squad leader. Unlike Gunny Brandt he welcomed his demotion from platoon sergeant to squad leader because he was more comfortable with small-unit leadership.

Sgt. Moss, Dougherty, and I trained as a vehicle crew and formed an alliance. It was comforting to have a core group of Marines whom I liked and trusted. It helped me to navigate the stormy seas of the new tribal tension. The group dynamics of First Platoon had changed dramatically from the way I remembered them. Some members of the old tribe remained, like Nagel and Draper, who continued their subversive ways and butted heads with the newly trained crewmen. Poole, too, had joined us. It was no surprise to me that Sgt. Krause managed to fill his crewmen slots with school-trained Marines. Some of the other platoons, with less savvy platoon sergeants, were left with Marines in their driver's seats and turrets who hadn't been to LAV school. Even Capt. Bounds, our platoon commander, held a vehicle commander's billet without any formal LAV training. He, like many others, would need to settle for on-the-job training.

While much had changed, there was still one dynamic that remained since our days at Camp Upshur—the division between the crewmen and the scouts.

The scouts that joined us from Fox Company did not assimilate easily into the fabric of our company or our platoon. Their company was splintered into many more fragments than ours was. They resented the new chain of command, misunderstood their new mission, and mourned the loss of their buddies. I understood their adjustment difficulties because of my black-sheep experience from boot camp after being fast-forwarded. I worked hard to welcome the scouts and include them whenever possible, but it was difficult under Sgt. Krause's command. He referred to the scouts as attachments and treated them like second-string players. Even the training schedule he developed focused on the crewmen and neglected the needs of the scouts. His bias resulted in a divided platoon in which the scouts aligned with Sgt. Lopez, a former platoon sergeant from Fox Company, while the crewmen aligned with Sgt. Krause.

The division between us didn't last long, though. It faded in a matter of days as the absence of LAVs sank in. It was difficult, even for Sgt. Krause, to emphasize crewmen training without vehicles. Their absence did little for combat readiness, but it did a lot for platoon unity. So, too, did our march to breakfast the next morning.

Our first full day of training as the newly formed Delta Company at Camp Lejeune was Wednesday, 28 November. Despite Gunny Brandt's objections Gunny Koffman chose to march us to chow after the morning formation, as a company. Most of us shared Gunny Brandt's reservations. The active-duty Marines on base walked to the mess hall casually in pairs or small groups. We wanted to do the same, to blend in and fly under the social radar. Making us march was like making high school freshmen walk to the cafeteria in straight lines like kindergarten students.

Gunny Koffman didn't care. He wanted to flex his company gunny muscle. All six platoons snapped to the position of attention and pivoted on Gunny Koffman's command, "Riiight face!" Then more than one hundred Marines stepped off in unison. The gunny's voice reverberated between the barracks as we marched, "Ya left right . . . left right . . . left right left."

His cadence sounded like those of the drill instructors at Parris Island. The echo of his voice boomed loudly against the walls of the buildings that lined the route to the mess hall. The noise brought curious Marines out onto the balconies of their barracks to stare at us freshmen. I was mortified as they pointed and laughed.

Then the gunny unexpectedly stopped our forward movement. "Company, halt!" I glanced up to see that we were at an intersection waiting for the traffic signal to change from red to green. It was bad enough that we had to stop, but we stalled right in front of the active-duty hecklers. Their taunts were louder than ever without the sounds of our boots or the gunny's cadence. But one voice was recognizably louder than the rest. I had heard it before, but at first I could not place it with a face or a name.

At least, not until I heard the jeer, "Hey, everybody, the Green Machine must be broken. . . . Here come the spare parts!"

I recognized that voice, but couldn't believe it.

I looked up toward the balcony on my right and sure enough, there he was—Morrison. I would have recognized him anywhere.

The Marines in our company grew progressively agitated as the deluge of insults poured from the balcony and the crowd. Finally enough was enough. Poole was the first from our company to break ranks.

He walked right out of formation toward the crowd of Marines. "Step up, mu-fuckas! Say it to my face!"

One of the active-duty Marines accepted the challenge. Poole charged him like a nose guard, tackling him to the ground. Then some other parts of our formation broke off to join the fight, scouts and crewmen alike. I thought we were headed toward a full-blown riot.

Capt. Bounds stood between the potential melee and us and ordered our restraint.

"Stand fast! Stand fast!"

I stood fast.

Once our officers intervened, the fists and boots stopped flying. Fighting among enlisted Marines was one thing, but assaulting an officer was grounds for court-martial. The fight stopped as quickly as it had started.

Poole wasn't pleased with the officers' interference. He continued to scream insults at the active-duty Marines. Then he directed his anger toward the Marines who escorted him back into formation.

"We're getting ready to go to war, and you pussies are afraid to fight!"

Sgt. Krause jumped in Poole's face.

"Save it for the Iraqis!"

Gunny Brandt watched the whole episode with his arms folded and an I-told-you-so look on his face.

That was the last time we marched to the mess hall.

In the final analysis the fight served us well. It was the catalyst that started the bonding process within our platoon, especially between the scouts and the crewmen. It gave us a lot to talk about in the chow hall that morning. We put our differences aside and reveled in the bravado of Poole and the others who had joined him. Dark-green Marines sat with light-green Marines. Second-years shared tables with first-years. And scouts broke bread with crewmen. The integration was long overdue.

I sat with Dougherty and talked of my inauspicious reunion with Morrison. Dougherty pointed out that it was not quite a reunion, because he never saw me. During breakfast I bored Dougherty with all of the details about the rivalry between Morrison and me in boot camp. I carried on about his antireserve mentality, and our last meeting with Drill Instructor Sgt. Talley.

Dougherty was not nearly as taken aback by the encounter. All he could say about it was "It just shows you how small the Corps is."

Dougherty would be right about that. Fate wasn't finished with Morrison and me yet.

29 NOVEMBER 1990

We started our first training day crowded together elbow-to-elbow, in the bleachers that encircled the outdoor training area.

A strange captain took his place at the center of the circle and waited for our attention. "I am Captain Ricks, the officer in charge of your battalion-level training and preparation for Operation Desert Shield in Southwest Asia."

Some of us paid attention to him. Some Marines heard the standard welcome statement and quickly tuned him out. Capt. Ricks, however, was no standard instructor and this was no standard class.

He introduced the lesson with the generic statement "This is lesson one . . ." while he held a small metal canister, the size of a deodorant spray can, over his head. Then he pulled a tab and threw the canister on the ground in the center of the circle. We sat, stared, and waited for something to happen. There was no sound. There was no smoke. When I finally looked up at Capt. Ricks, he already had his mask on and was touching his shoulders with his hands, the universal signal for a gas attack. Capt. Ricks's assistants threw other canisters under our bleachers as their muffled voices shouted through the filters of their masks, "Gas! Gas! Gas!" By the time I figured out what was happening, it was too late.

The stinging sensation started inside my nostrils and under the lids of my eyes. I looked down through the blur of tears at the canvas bag strapped to my leg, and felt around to find the button that secured its flap. Inside was my gas mask . . . at least I hoped it was. It had not seen the light of day since it was issued to me. None of us had paid much attention to our gas masks. For that matter none of us had paid much attention to any of our nuclear-biological-chemical gear. Prior to the Gulf War we had perceived the threat of chemical or biological warfare to be negligible. The gear entered our consciousness only occasionally as an accessory to an exercise, but even then it was viewed by most as an obstacle that impeded the really important training. We joked that the initials, NBC, represented "No-Body-Cares," which reflected our indifference to its value.

Capt. Ricks's class was about to change that mindset for all of us, forever.

I had the wherewithal to keep my mouth shut but instinctively drew air in through my nose. The first whiff burned and I blew hard to get the air back out. Then, without thinking, I opened my mouth and inhaled.

It felt as if someone forced a flaming torch down my throat and singed my lungs. In an attempt to recover, I closed my eyes tightly and held my breath. I heard shouts and whoops as the Marines around me, too, wrestled with the bags on their hips. We poked and prodded each other with elbows and knees as we bumbled within the tight confines of the bleacher seats. Finally, with very little air left to support the effort, I managed to pull my gas mask from its carrier.

My fingers felt blindly along the unfamiliar shape of the mask. There was no metal cylinder like the ones we used in LAV school, only smooth rubber, hard plastic, and a tangle of elastic straps. I tried in vain to orient it, but couldn't tell the top from the bottom, or the inside from the outside. My eyes cracked open for a second, but the gas penetrated like acid and forced them back shut. I tugged, pulled, and stretched the straps like a madman, but still couldn't pull them over my head. It was difficult enough to fit the mask to my face under classroom conditions. It was impossible under the circumstances. I had no sight, no air, no time . . . and no chance. So, on the verge of blacking out, I threw the Hail Mary.

I frantically smashed the rubber to my face, straps and all, and sucked air in deeply. This time the torch in my throat was a flamethrower. Tears spurted from my eyes, while snot flowed uncontrollably from my nose, like water from a spigot. The slimy mixture covered the mask, my face, and my hands. Then the unavoidable happened—I dropped the mask.

I felt around feverishly at my feet until a muffled voice screamed over the mayhem into my ear, "It's too late . . . you're dead."

One of the instructors pulled me aside where the air was clear and I could begin to breathe again. I joined dozens of Marines, like me, who had failed to don their masks in time. When the gas cleared the training area, Capt. Ricks removed his mask and gave us the all-clear signal.

I retrieved my mask from under the bleachers and returned to my seat with my tail between my legs.

This time everyone paid attention when Capt. Ricks spoke.

"Do I have your attention, Marines?"

Marines wheezed, coughed, and gagged their affirmation. Capt. Ricks delivered the news gravely.

"Marines, I just returned from a base camp in Saudi Arabia. The NBC alarm sounds every day there. Sometimes it's practice—sometimes it's a False Alarm."

Capt. Ricks shook his head at Capt. Cruz. "You should be glad this wasn't the real deal, or you would have lost a quarter of your company."

Capt. Cruz acknowledged the grim evaluation with a nod.

"The good news here, Marines, is most of you reservists are smart . . . college types. You should pick things up quickly, and you'll need to. The bad news is that we do not have a lot of time to train. . . . Division gave your company twenty-eight days, to be exact. I call the training package: Twenty-Eight Days from Campus to Combat."

Capt. Ricks had our full attention after his demonstration and his speech. His warning was simple and clear. "You will likely be exposed to biological and chemical agents in the desert. If you pay attention and apply yourselves, I guarantee you'll survive. If you don't . . . based on the cluster-fuck I just saw, I guarantee you won't."

He and his staff worked with us all day providing immersion-style nuclear, biological, and chemical training. The experience gave me a newfound respect for my NBC gear, especially my gas mask. I no longer considered it a burden on my hip. It was a life raft on the *Titanic.*

Capt. Ricks hypnotized us with fear. We hung on to his every word, took copious notes, and participated actively in every exercise.

We repeatedly practiced inspecting, fitting, and donning our gas masks. We learned how to install and properly use the chemical protective hoods. And we helped each other into and out of our chemical protection suits.

His team explained all about the biological agents that we were likely to encounter, such as anthrax. They even showed us samples of the Cipro pills that we would be issued in Saudi to protect us against the deadly virus. It was like watching a science fiction movie—invisible germs . . . antidote pills . . . protective suits. But that wasn't even the worst of it. Capt. Cruz explained how another type of weapon made anthrax seem like the flu—nerve agents. The threat of anthrax concerned us, but the threat of nerve agents frightened us beyond words.

The instructors described several nerve agents used by the Iraqis, and shocked us with the graphic descriptions of how the slightest exposure, even a single drop, could shut down our central nervous systems and destroy us from within. They talked of bleeding from the inside out, melting organs, and complete incapacitation. Capt. Ricks tried to build our confidence by showing us the nerve-agent-protection pills that we would be issued in Saudi. He explained how the NAP pills helped us build resistance to the effects of some nerve agents.

Gunny Koffman asked the question in all of our minds. "And if the pills don't work?"

Capt. Ricks sighed for emphasis. "The last resort is atropine."

Capt. Ricks explained that atropine would slow the effects of nerve agent and extend our life for a few hours until we could receive medical treatment. But even then, he warned, our chances of survival would be minimal. He emphasized that atropine should only be given if we, or another Marine, were having a reaction to nerve agent—uncontrolled bleeding, convulsions, seizures, or paralysis. Then he showed us the tube that carried the atropine.

At first glance it looked like a tube of Crazy Glue, but it was actually a spring-loaded syringe encased in plastic. He simulated the act of thumping it into his thigh, which, in reality, would propel the syringe deeply into his muscle to deliver the atropine. I wasn't sure I would ever be able to thrust that injector into my leg.

Capt. Ricks finished our training by teaching us about an inconspicuous piece of gear called an NBC canteen cap. NBC caps looked like regular canteen caps, but had special valves that plugged into the gas-mask drinking tube. The tube allowed us to drink without removing our gas masks. Capt. Ricks had warned that we would need these to survive in the desert.

"You never want to have to choose between drinking and breathing," he said.

I examined my canteens after class. There were no NBC caps. Then I panicked. Other Marines panicked as well. Capt. Ricks's class had scared the hell out of all of us.

Sgt. Krause waved his arms to quell our rising anxiety, "At ease! At ease! We are scheduled to go to supply in the next few days and everyone will get his issue."

Capt. Ricks and his team of instructors were outstanding. I had hoped to get instructors with their level of expertise for all aspects of our training at Camp Lejeune, but that would only be wishful thinking. None of us knew that our first training day would be an anomaly. We expected twenty-seven more days of the same kick-ass instructors, hands-on experience, and real-life application. What we got was far less.

Company-level training in garrison was unbearably monotonous. In fact, it should have been called "company-level waiting." After we finished in one line we were hurried along to wait in another . . . then another . . . and another. We hurried and waited from breakfast through dinner.

What I recall most vividly about this period of our preparation was the number of shots we received. It seemed whenever there was a lull in our training schedule we were sent to the clinic to receive more shots. We received shots in the shoulders, in the arms, in the thigh, and the ass. Some were just under the skin and some were deep into the muscle. Some were to be massaged and some to be left alone. I felt like a human pincushion. One corpsman remarked as

we walked through a gauntlet of injections, "After all these inoculations you'll be able to swim in a cesspool and not catch a thing!"

On Sunday we experienced our first platoon-level training day.
Unlike company-level training, which included all six platoons of
our company, platoon-level training only included the four squads
within our platoon. At first I was relieved that Sgt. Krause would be
responsible for our platoon-level training schedule. I figured he had
the most infantry experience, which in my mind made him the most
qualified. Unfortunately, though, he spent a considerable amount of
time in meetings with the senior leadership of the company. His absence put the squad leaders, by default, in charge of our training.
Our squad leaders included Lance Cpl. Nagel, Cpl. Shane, Sgt.
Lopez, and Sgt. Moss.

Sgt. Moss and Lance Cpl. Nagel were school-trained crewmen.
They assumed responsibility for crewmen training. Sgt. Lopez and
Cpl. Shane were school-trained scout team leaders. They followed
Sgt. Krause's lead and segregated the scouts from the crewmen for
their training. The arrangement benefited the scouts more than it
did us. Sgt. Lopez and Cpl. Shane were highly skilled and respected
among the scout troops. Moreover, they did not need vehicles for
their training. The crewmen did.

Neither Sgt. Moss nor Lance Cpl. Nagel was qualified to lead
crewmen training. Sgt. Moss lacked the confidence. Nagel lacked
the patience. To make matters worse Sgt. Krause was not a school-
trained LAV crewmen, so he lacked the depth and breadth of experience to guide our ill-equipped leaders. The only resources to
support crewmen training were our guidebooks from LAV school.
The result was pathetic. We spent our fourth training day pretend-
ing our bodies were LAVs while we walked around the athletic field
and practiced movement formations. It would have been barely tolerable during a peacetime drill weekend. With only twenty-four
days left in our preparation for combat it was a criminal waste of
training time. I was disgusted.

Training day five, however, began with promise. During the
morning brief Sgt. Krause informed us that we were scheduled for
three rifle training days. That meant more battalion-level training–

useful training! I looked forward to getting back to the field, away from the stagnation of garrison. Moreover, I was excited by the prospect that Capt. Ricks might be in charge. My optimism was short lived. Capt. Ricks wasn't our instructor, and the rifle "training" days were anything but.

We spent the first rifle-training day in the armory. There was only one battalion armorer available to issue rifles, as all of the others were deployed. He was not thrilled to spend his day in the armory, and he let all of us know it with his wiseass attitude. I added the armory to the running tab of bad experiences with our active-duty counterparts, and to the tab of days spent waiting in line.

We started the next day with a ten-mile conditioning hump around Camp Lejeune that ended on the rifle range. For those of us who were only four months removed from the school of infantry, the hump was like a Sunday stroll. For many others it was a grueling marathon. The smokers wheezed, the alcoholics got dehydrated, and the couch potatoes fell out. We accommodated them with a snaillike pace and frequent rest breaks. Unlike the insuperable mountainous humps in California I had no trouble keeping up. The route was flat and I was in the best physical condition of my life. More importantly, I now knew how to adjust my clothing and equipment to protect my skin from the grind of the gear.

We arrived at the rifle range pumped for the type of training that Capt. Ricks provided, but when he was nowhere in sight it didn't take us long to deflate. The rifle training we received paled in comparison to the NBC training. Each of us was issued a scant forty-five rounds of ammunition. The first thirty rounds were fired hastily into stationary targets before the sun set. Then, after sunset, we fired the remaining fifteen rounds at the same targets under the light from illumination ordnance. It was another colossal waste of time as far as I was concerned. We barely fired enough to verify our rifle's accuracy. It was nowhere near enough to prepare us for the dynamic engagements we were likely to experience in the desert.

It bothered me that the only time I had ever fired my rifle was in a sterile rifle-range environment. My qualification as an expert did little to build my confidence as a warrior. The range was a highly structured environment, with stationary targets, and instructors who hovered over my shoulder. I knew that was not realistic combat training and I wanted more. I wanted to know how to use my sights without the aid of distance markers . . . to fire at moving targets . . . to exchange magazines on the move. My inexperience with my rifle was embarrassing.

Our third day of rifle training added insult to injury. It was actually not rifle training at all. It was rifle cleaning. It was supposed to be, anyway. Once we arrived and disassembled our rifles, however, we discovered that our rifles' butt stocks did not contain cleaning gear, as was normally the case. I was flabbergasted that we were not able to clean our rifles after firing them. Marines did not carry dirty rifles—it flew in the face of all that we had learned in boot camp and the school of infantry.

The next three days were scheduled as platoon-level training days. Despite my initial trepidation the quality of the crewmen training was much improved—thanks to Sgt. Krause. I knew he had heard plenty of complaints after our last experience on the athletic field. We were lucky that he listened. He used his sergeant clout to secure a battalion training classroom that featured a gunner's training simulator like the one at LAV school. It was the next best thing to having the LAVs. We eagerly took turns cycling through the gunner station in pairs. The drawback was that only two Marines could train at a time, which resulted in a lot of unproductive wait-time.

We took a break from gunnery training on our second Sunday to prepare for our deployment ceremony. Capt. Cruz touted it as one of the most significant events in the history of the Marine reserves. He explained that more than twenty thousand Marines would be massed in formation for review by the commandant of the Marine Corps. Then he put the numbers in perspective for us.

"Marines! That makes you part of the largest fighting force to assemble at Camp Lejeune since World War Two!"

The gravity of Operation Desert Shield and the looming war was unreal to me until I stood before the commandant, dressed for combat, bayonet fixed, among the twenty thousand other Marines poised and ready to fight.

The commandant's words were harrowing. "There is a lot of talk in the world and in the media about the reasons for this war . . . and how long it will last. I'm here today to clear that up for you . . ."

Both questions had kept me awake at night, so I was all ears. I expected politics. I anticipated motivational hype. I braced for Department of Defense rhetoric. What I got was classic Corps.

His words penetrated the armor of our flak jackets and thumped our hearts. "You're going because I tell you to go—and you'll stay as long as I tell you to stay."

His words awakened the conflict that lay dormant within me. I felt inspired, yet frightened. I wanted to take a hill . . . and hide behind it. I felt loyal, yet rebellious. I wanted to fight for the cause . . . and run for my life.

I recall leaving the parade grounds that afternoon convinced that the commandant was out of touch with the realities of the reservists. I felt that way because he spoke repeatedly about how well prepared and well equipped we were. His comments were either based in dishonesty, denial, or ignorance. I hoped it was the latter, as at least that provided hope for amends. It troubled me to hear our commandant talk of our undeniable readiness. I denied our readiness, and I was not alone—other Marines were just as concerned as I was. During evening dinner the chow hall buzzed with chatter about gear—more specifically, our lack of it.

I was focused on securing NBC caps and rifle-cleaning gear. Others talked about the need for compasses. They were number three on my list of priorities. The scuttlebutt from overseas was that Marines routinely got lost making head calls in the zero visibility of dark desert nights. Other Marines emphasized the need for tinted goggles and sunglasses to protect our eyes from grinding sandstorms and blinding sunlight. Still others focused on our uniforms, and for good reason. The green-and-black jungle patterns contrasted sharply with the brown desert landscape, making us highly visible targets for Iraqi soldiers. Our standard uniforms were anticamouflage.

It seemed as if we lacked the very things the Marine Corps told us we needed. Our survival would depend upon our ability to drink water, clean our rifles, navigate the terrain, see the enemy, and avoid being seen. Yet we lacked the gear and equipment to perform these tasks effectively, if at all. The commandant's speech was a wake-up call to all of us. It sounded the alarm that time was running out, and we forwarded the alarm to Sgt. Krause.

Sgt. Krause recognized our collective anxiety and made arrangements for us to visit battalion supply the very next day. We spent training day thirteen waiting anxiously in long lines in the voluminous warehouse, like hyperactive children in Santa Clause's workshop. Our zeal did not last long. The elves delivered their bad news over and over as we moved from one distribution point to another.

"All out in this bin . . . No more of those left. . . . All we have are these unserviceable ones."

At the end of the day we returned to our barracks with half-empty seabags filled with the leftovers from units past. Some of us received goggles with tinted day lenses, and some with clear night lenses. It was rare to have both. Some Marines had desert camouflage trousers, others had jackets, and some even had covers. Few of us had complete sets. None of us had desert boots. I considered our time at supply to be another wasted training day. So, too, did Sgt. Moss. But he had an answer to our questions about gear—Saigon Sam.

Saigon Sam was a military surplus shop just outside of Camp Lejeune that catered to Marines—especially Marines preparing for service in Southwest Asia. I should have looked to Sgt. Moss sooner. I had learned firsthand that he was a connoisseur of retail military gear during that snowy patrol last December. We headed out that night for our first assault on the shelves at Saigon Sam's store.

I didn't like that we needed to buy our own gear, but the items we sought were not luxuries as far as I was concerned. They were necessities, and Saigon Sam's manager knew it. There was a special aisle stocked with the items that our base supply lacked. I left with as much gear as my wallet allowed. Then I visited the bank, cleaned out my savings account, and returned to buy more. It was my first of many trips to Saigon Sam's store to feed my new obsession with survival gear.

Each week the list of accoutrements that I perceived to be necessary grew, and each weekend I stormed Saigon Sam's shop in an anxiety-induced buying frenzy. I wasn't alone. The news of Saigon Sam's bounty spread quickly. Marines swarmed the Desert Shield shelves like pirates around a treasure chest. Worse yet, we perpetuated each other's paranoia. No one wanted to be the Marine who missed out on that special piece of gear that everyone else had. The gear lust was the military equivalent of "keeping up with the Joneses."

Before leaving Camp Lejeune I would spend more than five hundred dollars purchasing combat paraphernalia. Among my most valued possessions from Saigon Sam's were my wraparound sunglasses, red-lens Mag-Lite flashlight, wrist compass, ass pack, and my Ka-Bar knife. Some thought Saigon Sam's store exploited our vulnerability. I didn't feel that way. I felt the ability to buy my own gear gave me power over my own fate, which had become a priceless commodity.

In retrospect I believe that it was money well spent. During my time in the desert I used everything I bought. In fact I would depend on my Saigon Sam gear more than my issued gear. Some of my purchases simply made desert life more bearable. Some would improve my ability to perform. And some of them may have even saved my life.

The same sort of gear lust was happening at the company and battalion levels as well. Gunny Brandt was upset that we had no water bulls assigned to our company. Water bulls were cylindrical water tanks that attached to the hitch of a truck. In remote desert locations, away from rear areas, they would be our only source of water to fill our canteens. Gunny Brandt was not content to wait until we arrived in Saudi Arabia to secure water bulls for our company. So he did what any gunny would do in that circumstance—he stole them. He described his action as "an unauthorized acquisition."

Gunny Brandt bragged that the two water bulls came from an active-duty admin unit that had more than they rated. Admin units were notorious for hoarding gear. We relished the acquisition as a victory for the infantry and for the reserves. Even Gunny Koffman was impressed with Gunny Brandt's resourcefulness.

Training days fourteen and fifteen were spent loading the LAVs onto a ship at the port in Wilmington. It was a bittersweet endeavor. It depressed us to separate from our vehicles. They defined us as Marines. Without them we were simply ground-pounding grunts. On the other hand, I recognized that we would need our LAVs in Saudi Arabia more than we needed them now in North Carolina. It was exciting to think forward about unloading and operating our vehicles in the Gulf. I hoped that they would be waiting for us when we arrived in Saudi. I had no idea then how unrealistic that was, and what the implications for us would be.

We started training day sixteen more motivated than ever when we saw that there were two LAVs parked on the athletic field. I had to rub my eyes to make sure they were real. Sgt. Krause explained that they were static displays only, and could not be driven. Ordinarily that would have agitated me, but under the circumstances two static vehicles were the equivalent of striking training-aid gold. The LAVs provided a much-needed reprieve from the humdrum nature of our prior platoon-level training. They afforded us opportunities to orient the scouts with its features and gear, as well as practice troop positioning and deployment. More importantly for us, they provided the opportunity to perform gun drills.

Lance Cpl. Nagel was more enthusiastic than I was about them. Effective gun drills required nonexplosive dummy rounds for uploading, downloading, and clearing jams. It was no shock to any of us that the LAVs did not come with dummy rounds. Without them our gun drills were limited to assembly and disassembly of the main gun. The partial gun drills were somewhat beneficial to the scouts, who had never worked with the LAV's weapons. For the crewmen, however, they offered little more than bloody knuckles and plucked nerves.

Nagel made the best of the situation, though. He broke up the monotony of the gun drills by officiating crew competitions. The task involved the complete disassembly and reassembly of the main gun. Some crews raced each other and some tried to beat their best time. The crew competitions were the highlight of training to that point. I still disliked Nagel, but I was impressed with his initiative. He could show leadership potential when he applied himself.

After two days of gun drills our proficiency plateaued and the novelty wore off. That was true for the other platoon-level training as well. We were thoroughly tired of and bored with hip-pocket classes. There was not a lot of variety. Our core classes included Armor Identification, Call for Fire, and Radio Communications. As we completed training day seventeen, our morale was at an all-time low.

Capt. Cruz and Gunny Koffman recognized our low morale, but also realized the limited resources with which we had to train. There was no other battalion-level training scheduled, no other inoculations to inject, no other gear to issue, and no other parades to attend. The hip-pocket classes were all that we had left, and we had exhausted their effectiveness. Our company was so depressed that Capt. Cruz met with his officers and senior NCOs to intervene. He announced his plan at the final formation on Sunday, 16 December. It was exactly what we needed.

Captain Cruz announced that he would evaluate our training over the next five days, which included more involvement of the platoon sergeants and platoon commanders. He told us that he accepted responsibility for improving the training schedule, but that in exchange he expected to see enthusiasm, initiative, and motivation. I was skeptical until he dangled the carrot—four days of liberty during the coming Christmas weekend.

Normally liberty was not such a powerful incentive, but those four days would not be just time off. They provided us with the totally unexpected opportunity to spend the holiday with our loved ones before we shipped out. The news sent a shock wave of enthusiasm through the company. The promise of time with our families rejuvenated our spirit. It carried us through the next five training days with ease.

Sgt. Krause and Capt. Bounds delivered what Capt. Cruz had promised. They supercharged the training schedule with hands-on learning and practical-application exercises. They presented the skills as if we were in combat, which shifted our training into high gear. Instead of reading call-for-fire commands from handouts, we called on radios, and blew up targets on a desert sand table. Instead of using our armor identification pictures like flash cards, we planted them at scaled distances and spied them through binoculars and gun sights. We even used the radios in the LAVs to practice our radio communications procedures. They were no longer the same old hip-pocket classes—they were hip-pocket classes on steroids. The five days flew by.

Our company was dismissed on Friday, 21 December, at 1800, which marked the completion of our twenty-third training day. I raced to the phone center to call Gina. She confirmed she would arrive at Camp Lejeune late Saturday, along with her father and my mother. I could not wait to see them. Gina and I talked about the visit as long as I could. There was a line of impatient Marines waiting to use the phones, and the last call for mail had just been sounded.

While I waited in line to receive my mail, I listened as Gunny Brandt and Gunny Koffman debated the merit of granting us liberty so close to our deployment. Gunny Koffman believed a weekend with our families would be good for morale. Gunny Brandt, however, believed that time with our families was a mistake. He argued that family visitation set us up for an emotional fall, and wasted four training days.

At the time I sided with Gunny Koffman. I could not see how time with loved ones could ever be a bad thing. I had forgotten the lesson I had learned in the phone booth on the rifle range.

I treasured the twenty-four hours with Gina and my mom as if it was the last time I would ever spend with them. For all I knew it could be. Sunday evening approached quicker than I would have liked. Their visit was a blur, and was over before I knew it. We choked back tears as we snapped our last photos. Then came the dreaded good-bye. This time the windows in the car weren't tinted, and I made the mistake of looking onward as the car pulled away. I watched Gina press her hand to the rear window and force a smile through her tears. I forced one as well until she was out of sight. I gushed with emotion as I turned and walked back to the barracks. I cursed the Corps for having made me say good-bye yet again, and prayed to God there would be another hello.

Gunny Brandt was right. The family visit had been a bad idea. It softened me just when I needed to be at my hardest. The visit was an emotional tease that I didn't need. None of us needed it. It started an avalanche of emotion that left many of us buried in depression. The avalanche worsened as we started training-day twenty-eight. During the morning formation Capt. Cruz made the announcement that we all knew was coming, but none wanted to hear—our transportation to the airport was confirmed for midnight. The announcement was devastating. But ready or not it was time to go. The calendar didn't lie—it had been twenty-eight days to the hour.

There was no denial that we had little to do but wait. The LAVs were aboard ship. Our bags were packed. And the buses were on their way. Gunny Koffman, however, did not believe in idle waiting. So in the absence of any meaningful training he released the company for liberty until 1800. Gunny Brandt challenged that decision as well. I heard him arguing with Gunny Koffman after the formation.

Gunny Brandt was adamant. "You can't tell these boys they're shipping out to war . . . and then cut them loose! A lot of shit can go down in ten hours!"

Gunny Koffman didn't get it. A lot of shit did go down in ten hours.

Neither Dougherty nor I paid much attention that our roommate, Poole, had been gone since the morning formation. Marines were scattered around the base taking care of last-minute details. Some made last calls to Saigon Sam's store, some called home, and some packed their gear. Dougherty and I loitered in Sgt. Moss's room and talked nervously about our departure. It was hard to believe that the time had come. Until the morning formation we had frequently used the expression "We are going to war . . ." but now we were literally *going*.

It was unsettling. For me the worst part was waiting—it allowed my mind to wander forward to combat and backward to home. Neither was very therapeutic. I was relieved when the call was forwarded to fall in for the 1800 formation. It forced me to focus on the present.

Once in formation, Sgt. Moss leaned forward to count the Marines in First Squad. The correct count was ten Marines. Sgt. Moss counted nine. Then he stepped forward to count again. Nine. Then he walked to the end of the squad and physically touched every Marine on the shoulder as he counted aloud. The count remained nine.

Sgt. Krause grew impatient. "Sgt. Moss, fall in and give your report!"

Sgt. Moss looked at me. "Williams . . . count the squad again."

Before I broke ranks Dougherty called out, "It's Poole . . . Poole's UA!"

Sgt. Moss bit his lip when he gave his report. "One UA."

Sgt. Krause snapped his head toward Sgt. Moss, who silently mouthed the name "Poole."

Sgt. Krause shook his head. So, too, did Gunny Brandt when he found out. Poole wasn't the only one absent from formation. The other platoon sergeants reported UA Marines as well. It was the third time that Gunny Brandt had earned I-told-you-so bragging rights.

After formation Dougherty and I returned to our barracks. Neither of us was surprised that Poole had left. Both of us were surprised when he returned. We knew it was Poole right away. We had heard enough of his drunken rambling to recognize him by voice alone. The echo rang out from the stairwell as he approached singing in slurred cadence, "If I die in a combat zone, box me up and ship me home. . . ."

He paused as his pickled mind searched the archives of classic cadences to remember the next verse.

Then he continued, "Pin my medals upon my chest and tell my mom I did my best. . . ."

Dougherty and I walked out to the balcony to survey the damage. Once he reached the top of the stairs his left foot continued upward as if to take another step up, where there was none. He landed in the push-up position, facedown on the concrete slab. Then he lumbered to his feet and proceeded to rebound between the railing and the building like a pinball against its bumpers.

He squinted through his beer goggles to see who was watching as he approached. Then he stopped short of us, wobbled around like a spinning top, and shook his finger at us. "I ain't gonna die in no combat zone, boys. . . . Uh-uh . . . not this nigga. Ain't gonna be no need to tell my momma a damned thing!"

He looked up at Dougherty and me as he crossed the threshold of the doorway into our room. "Ya know why?"

He drew patronizing stares from us as he mumbled on unintelligibly.

"I'll tell ya why. . . ."

He put his finger to his mouth to hush us and lowered his voice to a whisper. "Because I have a secret weapon."

He staggered backward, but managed to pull up his left trouser leg just enough to expose the knife strapped to his ankle. It was a special forces–type knife. It had a four-inch blade and was sheathed in a leather holder held to his leg by two Velcro straps.

We watched as he reached down, squinting and grasping at air. After the third swipe he grabbed the handle of the knife and ripped it from its sheath. The blade cut cleanly and deeply into his calf muscle on the way out, leaving a gash that exposed the pinkish white muscle. Poole didn't even flinch under the numbness of intoxication. Then the tip of the blade hooked his trouser leg. He fought angrily to free the knife, which sliced through the material and opened a slit in his trouser from his knee to his ankle.

Dougherty and I stared helplessly at the drunken spectacle. Poole paused momentarily, reconsidered his decision, and attempted to replace the knife in its sheath. The first attempt failed miserably, leaving another deep laceration parallel to the first. Then there was a third and a fourth. I cringed while the blood saturated the top of his sock and ran down the leather of his boot to puddle on the floor. Poole's failure to fit the knife in its sheath infuriated him. I moved toward him and held out my hand as a gesture to take the knife. It was a bad move. It placed me in the crosshairs of his anger. He looked up at me enraged, and before I could react I was pressed with my back against the wall with the knife to my throat.

Poole held the material of my camouflage jacket balled in his left hand against my collarbone. He wielded the knife tightly in his right hand, his knuckles pressed against my throat. I could feel the pulse of my carotid artery, just under the blade, throb from the pressure.

I stared at him as calmly as I could. Dougherty was frozen in place in the doorway. We were silent and still. Neither of us wanted to incite him further.

Poole panned back and fourth between Dougherty and me. We looked on as nonthreateningly as possible.

Then Poole focused his deranged eyes on mine. "Ain't this a bitch. . . . Ain't this a mu-fuckin bitch. . . ."

I thought anything I said might set him off, and there wasn't much margin for error on my part. So I continued to be silent.

Then he turned to address Dougherty, still in the doorway. "We leavin,' man. . . . I can't believe we leavin' out tonight. . . ."

As he spoke he continued to clutch my collar with his left hand, but waved the knife toward Dougherty for emphasis. "And ya know why I gotta go?"

No response from us. The knife returned to its place at my neck.

"Cause da black man always fight da white man's wars. . . ."

I tried hard not to show the panic rising within me. Then the knife waved again toward Dougherty. He recognized the pattern.

"Ain't that right, History Man?"

Dougherty didn't acknowledge the question. I braced for the knife's return.

"Goddamned slavery still alive and well . . . mu-fuckin' alive and well. . . ."

The next time Poole motioned the knife toward Dougherty, he was gone. Neither Poole nor I saw him leave. Even as I feared I'd been abandoned, I felt Poole's left hand tear away from my collar.

Dougherty had waited until Poole focused his attention on me, and then sneaked around to his blind side. Once Poole extended his arm to point the knife at the door, Dougherty intervened. He executed the knife removal maneuvers the way we practiced during close combat training. Dougherty was good. He grabbed Poole's knife-wielding wrist tightly with his left hand and then struck the back of Poole's hand sharply with his open palm. The force of the blow hyperflexed Poole's wrist and caused an involuntary extension of his fingers, which ejected the knife across the room.

Dougherty then forced Poole to the prone position, straddled his back, and jacked his arm upward behind him. Poole didn't know what had hit him and offered little resistance.

Once down, however, he began to yell. "Give me my knife! Give me my mu-fuckin' knife!"

I collected myself and showed a brave front for Dougherty's benefit, but I was rattled. Part of me wanted retribution. Poole's head was pressed to the floor but his mouth was still running. I considered kicking him in the face to shut him up.

"What do we do now?" Dougherty asked.

I grabbed the knife and locked it in my wall locker.

Once the knife was locked away, Dougherty released Poole. He wasn't much of a threat without a weapon.

Poole stormed out of the room and along the balcony, leaving a trail of blood behind. I figured he was headed for Scott's room. Scott was one of Poole's boys. I reasoned that Scott would calm Poole down. Dougherty did as well, so neither of us followed him. I headed to Sgt. Moss's room, while Dougherty reported to Sgt. Krause. We never figured Poole would double back to the room.

I returned to the room with Sgt. Moss just as Dougherty returned with Sgt. Krause. My wall locker was open and the knife was gone. A scarred bayonet lay at its base. We inferred, from the mangled metal edges, that the door had been pried open with the bayonet. We searched the room, but there was no Poole. There was, however, now a new trail of blood that led down the stairwell.

Sgt. Krause listened to our account of the story and decided to contact the military police. Once we left the room, however, we saw there was no need to make the call—there were already flashing blue lights everywhere. We looked at each other, puzzled, because neither of us had called the MPs yet. We were even more confused when one of the officers explained the call involved a bleeding victim. We were relieved, thinking the MPs had found Poole. But it wasn't Poole who was bleeding.

Sgt. Krause returned to us after meeting with the MPs in the room. He looked pale. "It's one of the corpsmen from Fox . . . they don't know what happened yet. They found him on the bathroom floor in a pool of blood."

Dougherty and I looked at each other in horror. We both thought Poole was responsible.

Sgt. Krause asked us to wait in our room until he returned with the captain, so we made our way back upstairs. We were so busy babbling about the drama that we didn't even see him when we opened the door. Poole! I couldn't believe it. He was sitting nonchalantly on the edge of his rack, fiddling with the new bandage on his calf. I glanced around the room, then to his leg, then to his gear. There was no knife.

Dougherty was poised for round two. I was poised for an exit.

Poole broke the ice. "Y'all can chill the fuck out. Doc Price hooked me up."

We looked at him intently and tried to put the pieces together. Poole calmly peeled back the bandage to peek at his wounds. He didn't look like he had just stabbed someone. I wondered why he had returned and why he was so at ease.

The truth was that Poole had been angry and afraid, but he was no murderer. We later learned that the Fox corpsman had slit his wrist. Poole had had nothing to do with it. In fact, he'd been getting first aid from Doc Price while we were looking for him. That didn't change my hostility and resentment toward Poole. Dougherty was a bit more understanding, but then again the knife hadn't been against his throat.

By the time Capt. Bounds arrived with Sgt. Krause, Poole was engaged in rational conversation about the ordeal. He was even remorseful. I, on the other hand, did not feel forgiveness was in order. I wanted justice. I expected Poole to at least be arrested so I could charge him with assault. Capt. Bounds and Sgt. Krause, however, were more influenced by his behavior after the assault than his actions during it. In the tranquility of the aftermath Poole didn't seem threatening. In fact he looked pitiful. In the end Capt. Bounds decided that going to war was worse punishment than going to jail. Poole boarded the bus to the airport with us in the early morning hours of 26 December.

As the wheels of the TWA airliner rolled to a stop, ending our twelve-hour journey, we heard the chipper voice of the flight attendant crackle over the intercom. "Welcome to Saudi Arabia, Marines. On behalf of the captain, crew, and all of America, we thank you for your service to our country. We wish you a safe tour of duty and a speedy return home."

Her voice was cheery and confident. It made me feel confident, too, like this was just the first leg of a round-trip flight. I watched her from the rear of the plane helping the forwardmost Marines to exit, and appreciated her upbeat attitude. The side window over the wing allowed me to watch them make their way down the stairs and onto the tarmac. The first Marines on the ground huddled around three mass-transit buses parked beside the plane. The buses looked the same as those back home in the States, except for the Arabic writing that stretched from the front wheels to the rear. They seemed very out of place in the desert—there were no streets. All that lay beyond the airport was an ocean of sand. It looked barren, desolate, and hot . . . a virtual wasteland. The visual prompted me to fill my canteens.

I filled them in the small kitchenette that separated coach from first class. That was where we kept several five-gallon jugs of water that helped us stay hydrated during the flight. I was anxious to fill up and get out, but the water jugs were near empty and the water had slowed to a trickle. I needed the water, so I held out for the last drop. As the last Marines made their way out of the plane the cabin quieted. That was when I heard it—the sound of a woman sobbing.

I turned the corner and looked forward beyond the first-class curtain to see the flight attendant—without her façade. She never saw me. She was focused on her reflection in her handheld mirror as she wiped the smudged eyeliner streaming from her tears. Her sudden emotion made the moment very real to me. I wondered how many men she had welcomed to war, and how many more were on the way. I wondered how many would return in the plush chairs of the comfortable cabin . . . and how many would return under flag-draped coffins in the cold cargo hold.

SEVEN

"**I** THOUGHT THE DESERT was supposed to be hot, Gunny!" I said.

The absence of humidity, combined with a strong breeze blowing across the tarmac, gave me the false sense that the desert would be tolerable.

Gunny Brandt put his arm around me as I reached the last step. "Do the words *any clime or place* mean anything to you, Lance Corporal?"

I recognized the words from "The Marines' Hymn—" "We have fought in every clime and place where we could take a gun"—and continued on my way with a halfhearted smile. By mid afternoon I'd experience the hottest day of my life to that point, not knowing that this was still considered the cool season by Saudi standards. Skin-blistering one-hundred-ten-degree days would be the norm in a matter of weeks.

As I continued past, Gunny Brandt kicked me in the ass. "That's for being last. Now get over there and start loading seabags!"

I dropped my carry-on bag next to the last bus in the column and marveled at the efficiency of the human chain of Marines that linked the belly of the plane to the undercarriage of the bus. Our seabags flowed along methodically, passed from one Marine to another, until they made it to the stack under the bus. I took my place in the camouflage conveyor belt next to Sgt. Krause.

"Are we going to pick up the LAVs right from here?"

More than a month had passed since we had loaded them on the ship.

Sgt. Krause kept the momentum of seabags flowing. "There's no word on the LAVs yet."

"So where are we headed?"

Sgt. Krause seemed annoyed by my curiosity. "We're going to a central staging area in Jubail . . . I'll give everyone in the platoon a brief when we get there."

As we waited to board the bus, I noticed that our driver was an Arab. He was dressed in traditional garb, including a long robe, sandals, and a black-and-white checkered wrap that draped over his head. He stood outside the bus doors and watched intently until all of the bags were loaded. Then he turned his attention to Gunny Brandt, whose MacArthur-like presence identified him as one of our unit leaders. He stared at the gunny and waited for him to issue the order to start boarding.

"What the fuck are you looking at?" Gunny Brandt said.

The Arab didn't need an interpreter to understand the insolence. He held the stare for an extra moment to save face, then acquiesced and took his position in the driver's seat. He remained at the wheel, eyes focused on the overhead mirror, as the long line of Marines formed at the door. I found Sgt. Moss and Dougherty at the end of the line and waited with them. Nagel and Draper waited just in front of us, entertaining each other with a show-and-tell exchange of comfort items in their carry-on bags. Nagel's *Playboy* magazines got the most attention, followed by Draper's boom box radio.

Draper high-fived Nagel. "Yeah, baby! These rag-head motherfuckers can kiss my ass!"

Draper was as politically uncouth as they came, but we all shared his resentment of the official ban on all things American. During our Culture and Customs brief we had learned the dos and the don'ts while serving in Saudi. The CO explained that we were expected to conform to the cultural norms when in public. Porn was a don't. Alcohol—another don't. So was rock music. And Christian symbols were a major don't. Few of us were familiar enough with Middle East politics to understand why.

We had no idea how rigid the Saudis were about such things. It didn't take long for us to figure it out.

The cheers rolled through the line like a wave as the first Marines to board unfurled Old Glory outside our bus, its top corners held by two center windows which were closed against the fabric.

I had never felt as loyal to the American flag as I did when I saw it hanging there. But I had never felt as protective of it as I did when the Arab stormed off of the bus and tried to pull it down. He would have succeeded if he hadn't been intercepted by Gunny Brandt.

The gunny stood between the Arab and our flag. "What's your problem?"

The driver pointed to the flag and mumbled something in Arabic.

Gunny Brandt didn't get it. He ordered the Arab back to his driver seat.

The Arab didn't budge.

Then a small, skinny Marine poked his head from the window of the bus and interpreted. "He says he will not drive if we fly the American flag. . . . He says it's against his government's wishes."

The lanky Marine was Lance Cpl. Haley. He was a former Fox Company scout who had studied Arabic in college.

Gunny Brandt looked at the Arab with disdain and pointed to the label US MARINES sewed onto his camouflage jacket. Condescendingly he said, "U . . . S . . . MARINES. The *US* stands for United States . . . as in America."

Gunny was a patriotic zealot, scorned.

"You know America, right? How about Desert Shield? We're the only reason your country wasn't annexed by Iraq! If it weren't for us you'd be Saddam's little bitch right now!"

The gunny worked himself, and us, into an anti-Saudi frenzy. We cheered him on as he faced off with the Arab driver.

"The flag stays!"

The driver turned and bolted to the next bus forward.

After a few minutes Capt. Cruz arrived and rained on our parade. He met privately with Gunny Brandt and laid down the law. The gunny returned to the bus defeated, pulled the colors down, and tucked them under his arm. He hated to lose.

Gunny Brandt got a running start and leapt from the ground onto the top step of bus. His approach startled the driver, who leaned away in a protective posture. He grabbed each of the poles at the front of the bus, leaned back, and roared an exaggerated "OOOHRAHHH!" Every Marine on the bus returned the same call to affirm our support. It shook the bus—and rattled the driver.

After his rabid display Gunny Brandt took his seat right behind the driver. I sat directly across the aisle and watched him, frothing at the mouth, stare at the Arab through the long rectangular mirror overhead.

The driver, ignoring the gunny's antagonism, honked the horn once to signal the first bus, and the engine rumbled to life. The buses in front kicked up massive clouds of dust as they moved off the tarmac and onto the unpaved desert road. As soon as the bus picked up speed, nervous chatter started. I sat backward in my seat and listened to the threads of conversation. Sgt. Krause reminisced with Sgt. Lopez about their days as infantrymen training in the Mojave Desert. Dougherty lectured a small group of Marines on the historical hostility between the Middle East and the West. Haley taught his fellow scouts some basic words in Arabic. And Nagel and Draper huddled behind their seatback and indulged in their goodies. Then the boom box came to life.

I recognized the long, drawn-out guitar note right away. So did many others, whose ears perked toward the back of the bus. Then came the crunchy guitar riff and telltale cymbal taps. Everyone in First Platoon recognized it: Black Sabbath's antiwar anthem—"War Pigs." It was a popular song among the Marines in Draper's headbanger clan. He had blared it routinely in his room back at Lejeune, while he and his buddies had sung along. They sang along on the bus, too, partly to express their objection to killing, but mostly to rebel against the Saudi ban of American culture.

The Marines' thundering chorus was so loud, it startled me, and I knew it was coming.

"Gen'rals gathered in their masses. Just like witches at black masses . . ."

The Arab's eyes snapped upward toward the mirror, where they met and locked with Gunny Brandt's stare.

Even more Marines joined in for the next lines.

"Evil minds that plot destruction. Sorcerers of death's construction . . ."

Suddenly there was nothing on the bus but the driving rhythm, the ear-piercing vocals, and the showdown in the mirror.

The crescendo continued to build with progressive intensity, like a volcano headed toward eruption.

"In the fields are bodies burning. As the war machine keeps turning . . ."

What had started as a spirited sing-along quickly became a cult-like incantation. The chant's synergy grew exponentially, and the Arab driver must have felt the rage directed against him on the back of his neck. His focus switched from the gunny to the possessed mob in the mirror. It looked like the front row of a rock concert. Heads bobbed back in forth in unison, fists punched upward toward the ceiling, and boots stomped violently on the floorboards.

Then came the most salient lyrics of the song.

"Death and hatred to mankind. Poisoning their brainwashed minds. Oh, Lord, yeah!"

I wasn't sure if the Arab was distracted, offended, or just plain afraid for his life. Whatever the reason, though, he had apparently had enough. We felt the forward jolt of deceleration as the bus swerved to the shoulder. The dust trails of the forward buses continued onward, without us. I glanced out the window at the nothingness that surrounded our bus and anxiety settled in. At best Draper could turn off his radio so the driver would drive on. At worst the driver could snap, pull out a gun, and start shooting. Or he could just abandon us in the middle of the desert, leaving us susceptible to attack or ambush. Anything was possible in the Middle East. But Gunny Brandt had an insurance policy.

The next time the Arab looked into the mirror he saw the barrel of a 9mm pistol pointed at his head. His eyes widened at the image in the mirror—black steel in a madman's fist . . . his finger on the trigger . . . and shit-eating grin. This time he didn't need Haley to translate.

As the steel pressed his temple, the driver closed his eyes and prayed. Fortunately, Allah's answer made it easy on us all.

Without further delay the bus reentered the road, and the pistol reentered its holster. As I resumed breathing I sat back and closed my eyes. I couldn't believe what had happened. I had never seen a gun pointed at anyone's head before.

I was relieved that the gunny had the balls to protect us if the shit had hit the fan. At the same time I was appalled by the thought of possibly killing another human being over a rock song. I played out the ambush scenario in my head, and considered how I might have reacted if the Arab had pulled a gun from his robe. At that moment I couldn't answer for sure whether I would have had the presence of mind to pick up my rifle, or to point it at him, or to pull the trigger. It was a reality I would have to face sooner or later.

The lines were already blurring: the lines that separated training from fighting . . . practicing from playing . . . killing from being killed. I opened my eyes and looked over at the gunny, poised at the edge of his seat. He nodded as if to say, *I won that one!* Then I sat back, closed my eyes again, and attempted to rest.

My mind took me back to Camp Upshur, and the comment by the wiseass admin clerk. We were definitely not in Kansas anymore.

"Where are the LAVs, sir?"

Capt. Bounds offered no more information than Sgt. Krause had. "At ease, Williams! We've been in-country five minutes. You know as much as I know right now."

Sgt. Krause heard me badgering the captain, so he assigned me to tent detail to busy my mind. It worked. Instead of worrying about the LAVs I spent the rest of the evening obsessing about the construction of our platoon tent. To call it a tent really understated its size. It was more like the circus than the camping variety, and would serve as home for me and the other twenty Marines in First Platoon. Our tent was one of eight that collectively formed our company area: six platoon tents, a staff NCO tent, and an officer tent.

Once our platoon tent was erected, Sgt. Krause released us to walk around and check out the area. The most impressive thing about our base at Jubail was the sheer acreage. Our eight tents formed a block that occupied about as much space as a football field. Each block was outlined with roads, which were actually nothing more than sand-covered paths, packed hard from vehicle traffic. About every quarter mile more prominent roads separated the blocks into communities. Each community had its own public works resources, like water tanks, outhouses, and electric stations, that served its member Marines. Some of the more established communities had leisure and recreational resources like volleyball nets, weight-lifting equipment, and video theaters. There were dozens of such communities that stretched for miles around, creating a sea of canvas as far as the eye could see. We called it Tent City.

We spent the last three days of 1990 becoming familiar with the amenities of Tent City. Beyond the creature comforts of our platoon tent there was not a lot to it. The two most prominent features were the chow hall and the heads. Although centrally located on the base the chow hall required a thirty-minute hike to get there. And because it was a shared facility, the line of Marines waiting for food stretched for hundreds of meters. Our wait lasted anywhere from thirty minutes to an hour. It was worth the wait, though. The chow hall was a social mecca, like an enlisted club without alcohol. Every visit was an adventure. There were farewell celebrations for units leaving and welcome-home parties for those returning. There were reunions of long-lost buddies and introductions of new-joins. There was talking, and laughing, and yelling, and brawling—and sometimes even eating.

Half of each day revolved around chow. Each meal consumed two to three hours, factoring in the walk to and from the chow hall plus the long lines. That didn't leave much time in between meals to train, so we usually didn't. Sometimes the only productive thing I did in between meals was visit the head to make room for more food.

The heads of Tent City were a phenomenon in and of themselves. I use the plural term, *heads,* because there were two. They were identical and impossible to tell apart from a distance, except for the crudely spray-painted labels on the outside walls—PISSER and SHITTER. But your nose was all that was necessary to differentiate one from the other upon closer inspection.

I had never once, in all of my twenty-two years of life, considered segregating the two processes. It didn't seem biologically normal, and was anything but practical, to piss in one structure, and then walk next door to shit. The explanation for such an absurd rule was that there were two different machines for sucking the waste from the holes in the ground—one for liquids and the other for solids. While there was no practical way to enforce the rule, most of us bought into the explanation. So we did our best to comply, believing that it somehow helped the poor bastard whose job it was to extract the excrement.

The pisser was no problem. I stood, popped a few buttons, emptied, refastened, and then left. It didn't matter to me who was coming in, standing behind, or going out. Shitting, on the other hand, was a whole different story.

For me, and many others like me, as I later discovered, the act of moving my bowels in front of another man was repulsive and way beyond the bounds of fraternal conduct. Yet there was only one shitter, three plywood holes, to serve our entire community—several companies of Marines. So the shitter was almost always occupied. Despite the odds I convinced myself that I could time my visits to the shitter such that I could be alone. All that I needed was a minute or two of privacy. Inevitably, though, no matter how much I pre-planned, I always wound up sharing the bench. Not even Parris Island had prepared me for this the first time it happened.

After thirty minutes of surveillance I finally recognized a window of opportunity. The shitter was vacant! And so, too, was the pisser.

Serendipity! I sprung into action and walked quickly to the small wooden structure. Before entering I gave one final 360-degree scan, and then pushed open the screen door. Once inside I carefully positioned my gas mask and rifle on the floor at my feet, and then raced the clock to drop my trousers. As soon as my bottom was bare I leaned back onto the sand covered plywood seat and . . . nothing.

Despite the fact that I had waited until my intestines were ready to burst, my bowels were now locked . . . a mental block. I tried rocking and bending and twisting and bearing down. Finally I resorted to self-talk. *No one is watching. It's completely private. Just relax.* Nothing worked. The clock was ticking and it was only a matter of time before the next patron visited. My anxiety grew with each second. *Relax, goddammit!*

Then my time expired. The screen door slammed open and in he came.

The crash of the door startled me and instinctively I looked up. He wasn't from my company, and I assumed by his disheveled appearance and rank odor that he was just returning from the field. He didn't look at me on his way in, and that was a good thing. Eye contact was taboo in the shitter. There were no words exchanged between us either. Talking was second only to eye contact as forbidden acts while on the pot. I considered my options as my constipation continued. He didn't have that problem, unfortunately.

He recklessly dropped his gas mask and rifle on the deck, plucked the buttons on his fly, and forced his pants to his ankles. As soon as he touched down a nuclear explosion detonated beneath him. Things didn't just fall, they shot out. There was a nauseating combination of gas and fluid and droppings that splattered, plopped, and splashed. The stench rose instantaneously. He moaned and groaned and pushed like a mother giving birth.

It was bad enough to have a bare-assed man sitting next to me within arm's reach, but it was horrific to have him there during the explosive throes of projectile diarrhea. I quickly considered my options: wait him out, or return to my reconnaissance position and standby for another moment of opportunity. At first I intended to wait him out, but then he broke rule number one. He was looking over at me!

Why in God's name is he looking at me! I thought. I considered telling him off . . . or reporting him. *Yeah, right.* Then I considered throwing a right hook. *But my pants are around my ankles.* His gawk was too much. It was burning a hole in my side. Enough was enough. I shot a pissed-off look his way, hiked my trousers, collected my gear, and absconded to my surveillance spot.

The Marine left the shitter after an ungodly interval, and this time I stared. I had never seen such a cruddy uniform, or such a filthy body, for that matter. He looked like walking death . . . so crude . . . so nasty. Where could he have been, and what could he have been doing, to get to that deplorable state? Would I ever go where he had been? Do the things he had done?

31 DECEMBER 1990

Sgt. Krause's evening brief marked the turning point for us at Jubail. Our first four days in Saudi had been threat free, and consequently carefree. But those days were the exception, not the norm. Our sense of security ended as soon as Sgt. Krause took center stage. He looked serious, somber, and pale. Sgt. Krause's brief was not actually a brief at all. It was a warning. It was a wake-up call. It was a very personal soliloquy laced with self-disclosure, and advice, and anxiety. But first came the warning.

Our intelligence officers had received word that Iraqi forces were preparing to launch long-range Scud missiles, fired from Iraq at American bases like ours in Jubail. Sgt. Krause explained that the Scud could deliver explosive ordnance, as well as biological or chemical weapons. Then he added the clincher—we expected an attack that night. When I heard the words, I reached down and pulled my gas mask carrier close to my side.

Sgt. Krause's demeanor was different than I had ever seen it before. I was used to seeing him present himself like Clint Eastwood's character in *Heartbreak Ridge*. What we got that night was Clint Eastwood in *The Bridges of Madison County*. Sgt. Krause was compassionate, sensitive, and thoughtful. This made me really uncomfortable. He reminded us of the importance of the buddy system, and being there for each other. He talked of how proud he was to be our leader, and how confident he was in our abilities. There were pats on the back for select individuals and generalized praise for the entire platoon. It was the first time I had ever experienced the warm and fuzzy Sgt. Krause. Before I had a chance to fully appreciate it, though, the speech took a morbid turn.

Sgt. Krause appeared especially grave when he spoke about the likelihood of casualties in the event Scuds hit our base. The dark reality prompted us to play out gruesome scenarios of death and destruction. We talked about the significance of each of the items stamped onto our ID tags—our name, rank, social security number, branch of service, gas mask size, blood type, and religion. I understood the purpose for everything but the religious denomination. Dougherty chimed in that it would help the chaplain give the appropriate last rights if we were killed. Then Sgt. Krause directed us to thread one of our ID tags onto our left bootlace, and keep the other one around our neck at all times. Again Dougherty offered up the rationale: The tags were kept apart to increase the odds that we could be identified if our bodies were blown apart. The one around our neck could be thrown and lost if we were decapitated, but the one in our boot would remain tied within the laces.

Draper broke the tension with his dark humor. "What if you lose the head and the leg?"

A few of his cronies chuckled, as Sgt. Krause removed his skivvy shirt and lifted his arm.

"That's why I have a meat tag."

I had never seen one. It was a tattoo on the skin over his rib cage with the same information contained on a metal ID tag. Everyone went gaga over it. I finished lacing my tag into my boot, and wished I had my own meat tag. Even after the brief I thought about it. It wasn't so much the physical attribute that fascinated me, as the

metaphysical implications of it. I imagined that the ink would provide a sort of supernatural life-insurance policy against being killed
in combat.

Logic wasn't a prerequisite for thinking at that point for me. I
was scared, and searching for some sense of security. Eventually I
found it. But not in a Bible, or a tattoo needle, or a bottle, or a pipe.
That night I found my security in a song.

I recognized it right away—"Unchained Melody," by the Righ-
teous Brothers. The ballad penetrated the canvas wall of our tent,
transporting me in spirit right back to Gina. It played on the sound-
track of the movie *Ghost,* which was the video we had watched during our last evening together. I ran across the road and into the tent
where the song was playing, sat next to the radio, and closed my
eyes. And for a brief moment I was back home, on the couch, holding Gina close. It moved me to tears. Right there in that tent I resolved to make it our wedding song. When it ended I made a
beeline back into my tent to write Gina a letter to tell her so.

As I began to write, I became overwhelmed with emotion. I
thought about the brief, and the Scuds, and the ID tags, and I
started to question whether I would make it through the night. The
thought of dying led me back to the idea of the meat tag. Then the
idea popped into my head. I would propose in a letter, then wait for
the response. *I couldn't die if I was waiting for her answer. And if she ac-
cepts, then I can't die, period.* That superstition was my security. That
was my guarantee for survival. At the time it made perfect sense to
me . . . absolute sense.

The lights never went out in our tent that night. Sgt. Krause's
speech, combined with the imminent threat of attack, left us all wide
awake. Nothing I had experienced in the Marines, to that point, had
been quite as intense as the tent's atmosphere. Few of us talked. Most
just focused on preparing our gear for whatever might happen that
night. I knelt beside my cot and worked on my gear like a surgeon
over an operating table—inventorying my supplies, inspecting my gas
mask, and cleaning my rifle. When I finished, I placed everything in
its place, as it would be when I slept. Then I pretended that the NBC
alarm had sounded and ran my own personal mock drill.

I lay in the cot on my back, completely dressed, rifle by my side, and at the position of attention. After I imagined that the alarm sounded, the first thing I did was hold my breath. Before even standing I pulled my gas mask from its carrier, fitted it over my head, blew the bad air out, and sucked in to seal it to my face. Then I slipped into my flak jacket, punched my arms through my H-harness, and snapped the buckle on my war belt. Lastly, I dumped my helmet on my head, snatched my rifle from the cot, and headed out the exit of the tent. The whole procedure took only seconds.

I repeated that mock drill dozens of times. Unlike the compulsive drill repetitions I had done during peacetime training, no one bothered to tease me now. They were too busy with their own affairs. Some prayed, some exercised, some read, and some tuned out the war with their Walkman headphones. Sgt. Moss did none of the above. He watched everyone else—especially me. He had seen me studying compulsively before at LAV school, but that was nothing compared to what he saw that night. He didn't interrupt me, not that it would have mattered. I was hell bent on getting the drill down to an exact science.

He, on the contrary, was more concerned with the challenge of falling asleep with the lights on. During one of my breaks between drills I noticed he had succeeded. In fact everyone else in the company had succeeded. They were all fast asleep. I sat on the edge of my cot and tried to convince myself sleep was a good idea. I had completed the series of steps countless times, and believed the process of waking would only add a few seconds onto my time. A few extra seconds seemed trivial when I looked over at Sgt. Moss, who was snoring away in the comfort of his boxers. I lay back, as I had during practice so many times before, and prayed that the next sound I would hear would be reveille instead of the alarm.

God wasn't answering prayers that New Year's Eve. The alarm sounded faintly in the distance, unlike the piercing whine I remembered from training. It was so faint that I second-guessed my ears and remained horizontal. By the time Sgt. Moss kicked my rack to jar me from my slumber he already had his trousers and boots on. Dougherty was already masked. That wasn't how it was supposed to happen. I was going to be the first awake . . . the first in my mask . . . the first out the door. I continued to lie, listening to the voices in my head send me deeper and deeper into a panicked funk.

Finally I sat up without thinking, without holding my breath, and without grabbing my mask. I watched, stupefied, as the gas mask carrier fell to the floor. I looked down but couldn't make my arms reach to pick it up. My arms seemed like they weighed a thousand pounds, and the bag morphed before my eyes. I rubbed my eyes, looked across the tent, and rubbed my eyes again. I hoped I was hallucinating. The alternative meant it was too late. The alarm seemed to grow louder.

Streaks of green canvas melted and ran like wax down a candlestick. Everyone around me moved in slow motion, like we were underwater. All the while the Marines' shouts blended with the siren, slowed in my ears, and distorted like a record playing on slow speed.

Then, just when I thought it was too late . . . the actual siren sounded, waking me from my nightmare.

There was no sleeping through the real siren. It ripped through our ears like a chainsaw. My plan worked just as I had practiced. It was nothing like my dream. I was breathing comfortably in my mask before my boots touched the floor. I stood up and surveyed the rest of the platoon. Most were in various states of undress. Dougherty was pulling his boots on. Nagel was fastening his flak. Cpl. Shane and Lance Cpl. Haley were using the buddy system to unroll their protective hoods. Sgt. Moss was in his mask . . . and in his underwear.

We helped each other mask and dress, and then headed out single file through the rear of the tent, into the dank night air, toward our hole. We walked with our hands on each other's shoulders to keep from separating. The blackout conditions, combined with the fog in our masks from the condensation of our breath, had left us virtually blind. When I felt Sgt. Moss's shoulders drop from my hands, I placed my feet together and jumped into the black hole below. I landed on Sgt. Moss's heels. Dougherty landed on mine. The sensation of cold and wet started at my knees and seeped down into my boots. It had rained the past two nights and there was a foot of water in the bottom of the pit. We picked up our boots from the suction of the muck, migrated toward the center of the hole, and made room for the others who had yet to take the plunge.

Once everyone was in, Capt. Bounds started a head count. He touched the Marine in front of him and said, "I'm one . . . you're two." Then that Marine touched another and repeated the count. "I'm two . . . you're three." It was difficult to speak and hear through the gas mask, especially with all the splashing and crashing in the icy water of the pit. When the last Marine was accounted for, Capt. Bounds offered muffled reassurance through the filters of his mask, "Ooh rah, First Platoon! Everyone made it."

It seemed like we waited for an eternity in the hole—shivering and shaking, cursing and complaining, hoping and praying. Until that point all of my focus had been on preparing to enter the hole. Once inside I realized why we were there. We were waiting to hear the whistle of an incoming missile. To feel the ground shake from impact. To see the sky light up from an explosion. To smell anything other than the stink of our own breath inside the rubber of our masks. We were waiting to see if we would live or die.

Finally, after ten minutes, the long-anticipated call ended our suspense.

"All clear. . . . All clear . . . All clear!"

The Marine in front of me didn't wait to remove his mask. He pulled it off as soon as the all-clear sounded. I removed my mask, too, and turned my face upward to the sky to feel the cool fresh air.

Then he leaned in close to my face and inquired, "Is that you, Williams?"

I could tell it was Capt. Bounds. "Yes, sir."

He laughed relief as he put his arm around my neck, "Happy fucking New Year, Williams."

I leaned in and completed the hug, "Happy fucking New Year, sir."

★

We found ourselves shivering within the sandy walls of the bomb shelter hole several times over the next two days and nights. We shivered partly from the cold rainwater that pooled at its base, but mostly from the terror we felt, wondering if a gas-laden Scud would come crashing down on us. Despite the fact that no Scuds had actually landed in Tent City, the alarm reminded us it was possible.

Our imaginations made it probable. Every time the alarm blasted its warning and I leapt into the hole, I hallucinated about the invisible gas working its way under the rubber seal of my mask. Other Marines, too, talked of their hallucinations in the hole. It was a horrible test of our mental strength, and it quickly took its toll on morale. Finally, after six days at Tent City, Capt. Cruz reached his threshold of tolerance playing the waiting game. The status quo was no longer a viable option. Word spread around camp that Capt. Cruz planned to move us out of Jubail as soon as possible.

The evening formation on 2 January was highly anticipated. During the day rumors began to spread that our vehicles had arrived in-country. One of the admin Marines from the headquarters tent overheard the officers planning a major troop movement for our company. Our supply Marines reported that a pallet of MREs had arrived, and a five-ton truck was staged on the road adjacent to our company area. The evidence around the company area was compelling—we began to be convinced that the LAVs had finally arrived.

As we stood in formation waiting for the CO to make the news official, I imagined how different life was going to be with our LAVs. The most important thing to me was that we have a few days of training time before the 15 January deadline that President Bush had identified as Saddam's last opportunity to withdraw his troops from Kuwait. The general consensus was he would not withdraw, and that we would quickly switch gears from the defensive mode of Desert Shield to an offensive mode. I knew we had a lot of work to do before we would be ready to launch an offensive attack. None of our crews had even half the proficiency that I had observed during the live-fire demonstration by the Panama veterans in LAV school. Our most experienced crewmen, like Nagel and Draper, only had a few weekends of LAV driving and firing experience. The majority of our crewmen, like myself, had no experience with them outside of LAV school. But the Fox scouts were most disadvantaged. They had never even heard the engine run. I worked hard to put those thoughts behind me and look forward to tomorrow's opportunities—training, purpose, and an end to the waiting.

Capt. Cruz called the company to attention and shared his news.

"Marines, as many of you know, tonight will be our last night in the rear."

Sgt. Krause interjected a motivational "Ooh rah."

The rest of the company echoed their approval and returned with a collective "Ooh rah!"

Capt. Cruz continued, "I didn't bring you men halfway around the world to wait around for Scuds to drop on us—"

The company interrupted again with more ooh-rah accolades, as if the CO were delivering his very own State of the Union speech.

"So we're headed out to the field tomorrow to train . . ."

Busy anticipating, I nearly missed what he actually said.

I turned to Dougherty. "Did he just say *without our LAVs?*"

Dougherty closed his eyes in disbelief and nodded yes.

Then the CO lowered the boom. "The vehicles are still at sea, and we don't know when they will arrive. . . ."

Sgt. Krause asked the most poignant question in the exchange that followed, "What will our mission be after the deadline without the LAVs?"

Capt. Cruz's response was predictable. "As of now we are a rifle company, and we'll train as a rifle company. . . . If the LAVs arrive, we'll train as an LAV company."

It was that simple. That quick. We were no longer LAV crewmen. We were 0311 grunts. That meant humping instead of riding. It meant a return to those loathsome days of drill before LAV school. It meant we would relive those brutal days in the mountains of Camp Pendleton. It meant enduring extreme weather, sleep deprivation, digging holes, holes, and more goddamned holes . . . and humping.

To my knowledge, in any other branch of the service, the loss of a company's vehicles would have been a showstopper. That was not the case in the Marine Corps. As soon as we landed on the yellow footprints, we learned that every Marine is first and foremost a rifleman. That meant a pilot without a plane became a rifleman. The engineer whose bulldozer finished dozing was a rifleman. We were all riflemen. Military policemen. Mechanics. Air-traffic controllers. Electricians. Radiomen. Even the admin pogues—all riflemen.

To say that we were crushed was an understatement. I couldn't even fathom the implications.

Capt. Cruz understood that we were upset, and he ordered the platoon commanders to give us the night off to come to grips with our new lots in life.

"Give your Marines a night to rest," he said. "They'll need it for the hump tomorrow—all eighteen miles of it."

We were livid. I spent the better part of the night participating in the platoon tantrum that followed the formation.

The next morning I stood crunched over with fifty pounds of gear on my back, stuffed from the crow that I had eaten for breakfast, prepared to take the first step of our eighteen-mile excursion. I was still raging inside. We were all raging. Then the infantry gods descended on us and blessed us with good news.

Gunny Koffman shocked us with his order. "Platoon sergeants! Ground those packs and get them loaded on the truck!"

Then the news got even better. We learned that the gunny planned to use the truck as a troop transport shuttle to relay back and forth between our field position and our hump position. We loaded the packs on the truck in record time, determined to send it on its way before the gunny changed his mind, or before the CO changed it for him.

As the truck disappeared into the dusty distance, we made the final adjustments on our clothing and gear. Even though I had embarked upon dozens of humps in the Marines, this one was like no other. We weren't just filling time on a training schedule. We weren't just building stamina. We weren't just trying to get to class in a remote location. We were preparing to march off into combat. It felt like it, smelled like it, sounded like it, and looked like it. The scene reminded me of the barren wastelands in the movie *Road Warrior*.

The Marines in Second Platoon plodded away alongside us, in full combat gear, amid gigantic clouds of white dust that swirled around them like a miniature nebula. They trudged through ankle-deep sand as the earthy powder worked its way upward, covering their boots and trousers above the knee. Some carried rifles, but most wore them slung across their backs. In either instance the rifles were dirt encrusted from barrel to stock—so much that I doubted they would even fire without being punched with a rifle bore. That's what our eyes, ears, nose, and mouth would have looked like if they had not been completely covered.

Each of us wore a tan wrap draped over our heads, ears, and necks, much like the Saudi headdress, with tan bandannas around our faces like the cowboys in old Western movies, pulled over our noses and tied behind our heads. Both the wraps and bandannas were held in place by oversized tinted goggles. Our apparel had nothing to do with fashion or style, as it often had during training back in the States. It now had everything to do with survival. Without the wraps our ears would cake with sand and our necks would blister. Without the bandanna it was impossible to breathe. Without the goggles it was impossible to see. We were living testimonials to the message scribbled on the wall back at Staff Sgt. Bader's issue point, WITHOUT SUPPLY YOU WILL DIE.

Six miles into the hump, the truck returned to load me and the other Marines of First Platoon for transport to the forward area. It was a slow, arduous, bumpy ride in the back of the truck, but no one dared to complain. The truck was a godsend. I thought about the other platoons back in the sand as we slowed to a halt. We had been on the road for nearly an hour. They were still humping. Poor bastards.

When I arrived I saw a pile of packs, a squad of Marines, and brown flatlands as far as the eye could see. That was it. That was our forward area. There were no trails. There were no identifiable land features. It was like floating in the middle of the ocean, only surrounded by sand instead of water. Even after our entire company arrived, we would occupy no more than a speck on the map. It didn't seem there was anything productive we could do in the area. There was nothing to attack, or protect from attack. I had a queasy feeling nothing good would come from it.

Sgt. Krause gathered us together as we landed. Our mission was to occupy a defensive position and forward any information about enemy activity up the chain of command for submission to battalion intelligence. Translated, that meant we were going to dig holes, get inside, and wait. Day One was bearable because of the novelty of our new mission and tolerance for the sand. Both faded quickly.

Sunrise of Day Two started with the unwelcome command, "Reveille!" I popped the first button on my sleeping bag and poked my head out. My chin scraped along the frozen dew from the icy night air. After sampling what was waiting for me, I quickly drew back inside my toasty bag. Reluctantly, I reached down to the pocket of space at my feet to collect my uniform. Everything I needed to wear remained with me inside my sleeping bag, which kept it warm, dry, and scorpion free. Once I had my trousers and blouse on, I stepped out into the freezing air. The frozen layer of moisture atop the sand crunched under my boots as I took a few steps, stretched, and then returned to my bag for my field jacket.

In the distance I could hear Lance Cpl. Haley's raspy Long Island accent approaching as he made his way from sleeping bag to sleeping bag, kicking the still ones to wake the heavy sleepers, and yelling into the moving ones to speed up the slow dressers. "Thirty minutes to fall in!"

Waking in the field was nothing new to me. During our training in the woods I had developed a routine. The first order of business was the head call. Afterward I'd use a canteen cup of water to shave and brush my teeth, then baby wipes to wash the critical areas. If all went according to schedule, I would have a few minutes to eat an MRE. Well, that was my routine in the woods, anyway. I had never awakened in a desert before, with the sandman as my mate. It didn't take long for the romance between us to end.

He clung to my genitals as I straddled the piss trench for the first mission of the day, itching and grinding against me as I made my way back to my pack. He slithered about in the shaving cream, which dulled my razor and chafed my face. He hitchhiked onto the bristles of my toothbrush for a tour between my teeth and under my gums. He embedded himself into the fabric of the wipes, making its once-soft texture feel like pumice. He swam in the stagnant water inside my canteen, and sank in the quicksand mush of my MRE breakfast. There was no escape from the sandman, in either time or space, and I hated him for it.

The second and third days in the defensive position were identical. We lived in the confines of our four-by-eight fighting holes, waiting for something to happen that was worthy enough to report, and battled the sand. Day four, however, ended the mind-numbing monotony of standing watch at the defensive perimeter. During the morning formation we were excited to hear the scuttlebutt that we were headed back to Tent City. As primitive as it was, it seemed like the Hilton compared to the field.

When the call to saddle up came, I was very relieved. After three days I felt as if we had reached our threshold of tolerance for the misery of the field. All of the telltale signs were present—thin patience and thick heads, short fuses and long stares, shallow talk and deep depression. I had no idea that those measly days in the field had not even scratched the surface of the depths of misery that we were to experience.

We were all shocked to learn that the scuttlebutt had been wrong. We weren't withdrawing . . . we weren't boarding the truck. We weren't returning to our cots at Tent City. We were advancing!

6 JANUARY 1991

When the front of our column halted at the overhead camouflage netting, the end of the column was still a mile away. The five-mile stretch of deep, loose, virgin sand between our defensive position and our new training area was unforgiving. But it was not nearly as unforgiving as the battalion officers and NCOs who waited for us under the shade of the netting.

The terms *instructors* and *training* were not even fair labels. They didn't just teach. They abducted and dragged us, kicking and screaming, into the fiery depths of hell. They were the men on the recruiting posters who paddled stealthily down rivers, and rappelled down cliffs, and parachuted behind enemy lines. They were the heirs to swashbuckling leathernecks who protected our shores and thrashed the enemies of our fledgling country in the late 1700s. To the raging Devil Dogs of the First World War who charged into Belleau Wood, and who scared the piss out of the German soldiers during World War Two. To the legends of the Frozen Chosin in Korea, the rice paddies of Vietnam, and the rubble in Beirut. I wanted to be like them. I needed to be like them.

Staff Sgt. Rodriguez stood at the entrance to the E-shaped trench and narrated for us as his instructors demonstrated the procedure for clearing the trenches. A four-man fire team of Marines crouched below ground level and waited for the team leader's signal. Each was armed with a grenade and two magazines loaded with blank rounds. Then the point man stalked forward into the bottom leg of the E, followed by the other three. When he reached the first right turn he pulled a grenade from his belt and threw it around the corner. Staff Sgt. Rodriguez, acting as the trench official, yelled out, "Blast!" to signal the grenade explosion. Then the team leader turned the corner and sprayed the trench with several three round bursts from his M16. The next two riflemen followed with their muzzles pointed down and outboard. The last man kept his muzzle pointed toward the rear to watch for enemies approaching from behind.

The team then huddled close by the middle leg of the E, just before the next right turn. Again a grenade led the charge, and again the staff sergeant called out, "Blast!" Then the first two entered the trench while the last two covered the lane from the front and rear. This time the staff sergeant tossed a smoke grenade into the trench and called out, "Gas!" In addition to officiating he controlled the obstacles and challenges that the Marines in the trench encountered along the way—in this case the obstacle was a simulated gas attack. The Marines instinctively donned their masks, and then vanished in the green haze. When the smoke lifted I heard the team leader spray more fire, and the pair advanced to the dead-end path. After the staff sergeant called out, "Clear!" the pair doubled back to the main leg of the trench and resumed the lead to the final leg of the trench.

Before they arrived the staff sergeant screamed, "Enemy from the rear!" The last man turned and fired into the trench behind until he heard the call, "Clear behind!" Once the team leader reached the top leg of the E, he pulled a grenade from his belt and waited at the final right turn of the trench. A fortified bunker, surrounded by sandbags, lay just around the corner. The second man waited for the signal from his team leader and lobbed the grenade into the bunker. Once the staff sergeant announced the blast, the team infiltrated the bunker and assumed firing positions at all four corners.

"That's how it's done!" Staff Sgt. Rodriguez screamed to us. "Who wants to get some?"

I did. This was by far the most realistic training I had ever witnessed, and I didn't hesitate to volunteer to be part of the first four-man team tasked with clearing the trench. The team leader assigned me to the rear position and signaled to the instructors that we were ready. They were positioned strategically around the top of the trench. Staff Sgt. Rodriguez waved and the team leader's rifle popped. The three in front crouched and stumbled through the trench. Midway to the corner I remembered to turn and cover the rear. So I pivoted around and started to creep backward, just as I had observed during the demonstration. But during the demonstration the team leader didn't trip and the other two didn't land on top of him, as was the case for our team. As soon as my boots hit the pile of twisted bodies I, too, fell backward onto the pile. I lay there for a moment until I heard the call, "Abort!" and I stood up. Then I felt the crushing blow of a two-by-four board to my helmet, which drove me downward onto my face.

A voice from above yelled, "You're dead, motherfucker! Lay down! Dead men don't walk!"

I lay facedown in the sand, trying to spit my mouth clear of the crystals and wondering what had gone wrong. It wasn't long before the next wave of Marines entered the trench. I saw their boots hesitate when they reached us—dead bodies littering the path.

"Move out!" The instructor commanded. "If you can't step over 'em or around 'em, then step on 'em! They're dead. They can't feel it!"

I felt it. The first boot landed across my shoulders. The second hit at the small of my back. Then the stampede ensued and the so did the pain . . . a smashed ass cheek . . . a pulverized hamstring . . . a crushed kidney . . . a squashed testicle. . . .

We were reincarnated eventually, but not before the physical and psychological damage was done. The challenge of the trench pushed some Marines away to other training areas. It lured me back for more.

Playing dead wasn't just a minor humiliation, as it may have been intended. It was total annihilation of my civilian self, and the rejuvenation of my warrior ego. The warrior ego was something I had first discovered at Parris Island. I had rediscovered it in the mountains of Camp Pendleton. And here, in the trenches of Saudi Arabia, the beast was awakened again. I resolved then and there, facedown in the sand, that I would conquer that trench. And I had five days of opportunities to follow through.

Our trench-warfare training was only one of many stations we rotated through. There was very little waiting, because multiple training areas operated simultaneously. The desert provided unlimited space to move and fire. At the Breach station we inched along on our bellies and stabbed our Ka-Bar knives into the sand to locate mines. At the Assault Course we rushed forward with our teams, firing in concert at the metal drums, tires, and MRE boxes that littered the course. At the Call-for-Fire area we called in mortars and watched in awe as they annihilated the earth on impact. At the Enemy Prisoner of War area we intercepted, captured, and incarcerated each other. The battalion instructors knew exactly what would be expected, and they held us to task—sixteen hours every day.

At the end of each day we migrated back to our defensive positions, where we bailed out the sand that had refilled our fighting holes, ate the last meal of the day, and attempted to sleep between intermittent fire-watch duties and simulated chemical attacks. The first day of our precombat training was tolerable. We were fueled by eight hours of sleep and three square meals per day, which was all that any infantryman needed to keep on top of his game. Unfortunately, as the days wore on, both commodities became progressively scarcer.

We entered into the second training day with only four hours sleep and two incomplete meals. We depleted our MRE supply and were forced to rely on the battalion field cooks to prepare our food. The food they cooked was good. There just wasn't enough of it, so it was rationed. Breakfast was little more than a ladle of scrambled eggs and a slice of stale bread. I didn't even bother to cover my food from the blowing sand, figuring that it would at least add bulk. The hunger in my gut, however, was nothing compared to the hunger that drove me back into the trench.

The second time in I was more assertive. I joined the team of scouts who were part of our old vehicle crew—Cpl. Shane, Haley, and Dougherty. We preplanned our strategy and selected our positions. Again I was in the rear and more determined than ever to learn from my mistakes. Rifle in hand, I stepped off with the group, spun to the rear, and stepped backward carefully, turning forward to check the progress of those in front. I gasped when the instructor affirmed our progress: "Blast!" Cpl. Shane turned the corner into the main leg and lit up the trench with a steady stream of fire. Haley followed, then Dougherty, and then I. Once we reached the second corner, my mind started to blank. At some point Cpl. Shane and Haley were going to advance, leaving us to cover. Only, I couldn't recall who or what to cover—a type of lapse that gets Marines killed.

Permission came from above—"Blast!"—then Cpl. Shane's rifle paved the way into the middle leg of the trench. Dougherty leapt forward through the intersection and covered us from the front. I thought he then followed Haley into the trench, so I went in, too, leaving our rear exposed to enemy fire. Again the two-by-four dropped. I was again pondering my shortcomings facedown in the sand. But I had made it to the second leg. I was halfway there. And I couldn't wait to get back in and try again.

We limped to the ranges during day three, a little more tired and a lot hungrier. The hours of sleep seemed to shrink proportionately with the amount of food available. During breakfast I looked over at the entrance to the trench and mumbled to myself that today was my day. Then I stretched a nonthreatening yawn, looked down disappointedly at the morsels on my Styrofoam plate, and ran through the trench-clearing steps in my head.

The first leg progressed as planned. There was the blast, the spray, the forward press, and cover to the rear. The middle leg, too, went exactly as planned, except for the noticeable omission of gas. The instructors always switched the variables to ensure that we were ready for the unexpected. The unexpected was what we got . . . and we were not ready. Instead of calling, "Gas!" the instructor yelled, "Enemy troops from the rear!"

I flicked my thumb against the select lever of my rifle and flipped it to the fire position. Even though my magazines were loaded with blanks, I was hesitant to fire in the confines of the trench. I was conditioned for safety, not for combat. But I didn't want to feel the concussion of the board split my helmet again, so I squeezed. The rifle popped a three round burst, driving the stock into my shoulder. The burst felt different from the single shots required on the rifle range. It felt good. I aimed at the far wall and squeezed off another burst.

Staff Sgt. Rodriguez screamed down to me from the ledge above, "Get some! Get some! Kill those rag-head motherfuckers!"

I fired again and he cheered again. It felt damned good. Then I emptied my magazine into the imaginary bodies that piled up at the end of the trench. While I switched magazines, the omnipotent voice called down to save my life, "All clear in the rear!"

With so much adrenaline, I could have charged the enemies and ripped their limbs apart with my bare hands, had they not been fictitious. Firing was addictive, and I wanted more. By now the group had advanced about twenty yards ahead. I crouched low and sprinted forward, banging and clanging against the trench walls. I was in a zone and didn't even realize that my gas mask had fallen out of its carrier along the way.

Staff Sgt. Rodriguez saw it, though, which explained why he threw the gas canister at my feet. As the green smoke filled the trench I reached confidently into my carrier, prepared to mask like I had so many times before. The horror of feeling the emptiness in my gas mask carrier was inexplicable. My mind flashed immediately to the bleachers . . . and Capt. Ricks . . . and the horrendous sensation of fire inside my face. As the green smog engulfed me I felt the two-by-four yet again . . . another blow to the head . . . another self-inflicted funeral.

Staff Sgt. Rodriguez had seen that I had become fixated on making it through the trench, so he had committed to making the journey as rigorous as possible. Each time I drew closer to the top leg, he would fabricate some cockamamie scenario that ended with me getting clubbed in the helmet. By the time we formed to hump back to our night positions, I was thoroughly pissed off. My frustrations, fatigue, hunger, and aches had formed a bomb inside me, ready to blow. On the way back to our night position I found the match that lit my fuse.

The evening hump was always more debilitating than the morning hump, as our reservoirs of energy and patience were drained. The only saving grace was that it was slightly downhill. That allowed us to build momentum, as long as we were able to keep a steady pace and take long strides. Neither was possible in my position behind Draper. About halfway through the hike he started whining, as usual, like a broken record.

He began by bellyaching about the long hump back, and questioned why we couldn't just spend the night at the ranges. Then he moved on to the hunger, the thirst, the sand, the wind, and the fatigue. But mostly he complained about being on foot instead of on wheels. The quicker his mouth ran, the slower his boots did, and I found myself slowing down to keep from crashing into him. Slowing down required both energy to apply the brakes and then more energy to accelerate again. During all the preceding days I had had the endurance in reserve to muddle through. That day I did not. My patience wore thinner with every gripe. My jaw clenched tighter every time my front crashed into his back. Bitch . . . crash. Complain . . . collide. Cry . . . crash. Finally I snapped. I took a giant stride forward until I was in striking distance, reared back with all of my might, and drove my fist into the back of his neck just under his helmet.

Draper had the temperament of a toddler, but the body of a tank. My punch didn't pack nearly enough power to take him down. Instead of falling he absorbed the blow and ran forward a few steps. Then he turned around and squared his shoulders. I squatted just before impact and then launched into him, shooting my open palms into his chest. He landed on his back, kicking and flailing like a turtle on his shell. I pounced on top and strangled him. He pulled up hard against my hands to save his throat from my grip. Then I freed my right hand and cocked it way back. I wanted to shatter his teeth, crush the bones in his nose, gouge his eyes—I wanted to kill him.

Before either of us had the chance to do any real damage, we were pried apart and ordered to opposite ends of the column.

Draper was confused. He rubbed his neck and squawked through his squashed larynx, "What is your problem, asshole?"

Sgt. Krause turned me away from him and pushed me along, so I held my tongue and rushed forward to join the faster Marines in front. Nagel wouldn't even make eye contact with me as I approached. I wanted him to. That was all it would have taken for me to pummel him as well. I was fed up with both of them. I found my place at the front of our platoon just behind Dougherty, and coasted the remainder of the way under the influence of my testosterone rush. When we returned to our holes, Sgt. Krause scolded me for the fisticuffs, but there was no real punishment as there would have been during peacetime. Under the current circumstances fighting was par for the course.

We awoke on 10 January, the fifth day of training, with our batteries drained. Capt. Cruz's morning brief, however, jump-started our engines. We had only one more trip to the ranges to endure, after which we were scheduled for two days rest and relaxation back at Tent City. The promise of food, and sleep, and showers was exactly the motivation we needed. I could hardly wait to take on the trench.

The group for my last trip into the trench included my buddies on the dream team—Cpl. Shane, Dougherty, and Haley. Cpl. Shane assigned me to the rear position, as it was the role I had the most practice with. Then, on the staff sergeant's signal, we forged into the bottom leg of the trench. Like clockwork Cpl. Shane tossed the grenade, waited for the blast, turned the corner, and showered the openness with rounds. I covered the rear and rejoined the team at the middle leg.

Again we executed the clear-procedure flawlessly. The green fog moved in and we masked. The enemies sneaked up from behind and I fired. They rushed from the front and Dougherty fired. They hid around corners and we lobbed our grenades. As we worked through the top leg of the E toward the bunker, Staff Sgt. Rodriguez pulled out all the stops and sent in enemy troops from three sides. We weren't fazed. Dougherty emptied his magazine into the trench to his front. Cpl. Shane and Haley both landed grenades in the bunker. And I pumped a steady stream of rounds into the embankment to our rear. After my rifle quieted I took a knee, aimed at the ground, and waited for the next curveball.

The sweat that pooled in my mask sloshed against my chin and lower lip. My heart raced under the compression of my flak. My elbows and knees burned from the crawling and bumping and sliding and slamming. My forearms still vibrated from the recoil of my rifle, and my finger trembled near the trigger with anticipation. But there was no need to continue firing. The last pitch had been thrown. Finally, over my pounding heartbeat and heaving breaths, through my ringing ears and the rubber covering them, I finally heard it—the all-clear signal.

I stood up cautiously and squinted into the glare of the sunlight through my fogged lenses. Up above, on the ledge of the trench, Staff Sgt. Rodriguez waved us back to the entrance. As I slid my thumb under the bottom of my mask, the briny fluid drained down my neck and chest, making room for my first breaths of fresh air. I swaggered back toward the staff sergeant, still wearing my armor.

Of all my accomplishments in the Marine Corps to that day, none compared to the unparalleled honor of Staff Sgt. Rodriguez's handshake at the trench. I had finally become a warrior. Not a boot camp warrior, or weekend warrior, or spare part warrior—a *warrior*.

The truck ride back to Tent City the next day provided plenty of time to reflect on my time in the field. In the grand scheme of things it had merely been nine days of training. But it was nine days of realistic training—active-duty training. Our time with Staff Sgt. Rodriguez and his instructors had closed the gap between the reservists in us and the active-duty infantrymen in us. It was a metamorphosis in terms of attitude and appearance. We had left Tent City as naive anxious college kids with scrubbed bodies and laundered uniforms. We returned cocky, confident grunts with battered bodies and salt-stained uniforms.

As soon as the truck stopped, I jumped out and headed straight for the shitter. Like most of the Marines in the company I had been working through a vicious case of diarrhea. Doc Price, our platoon medic, figured that we hadn't washed our hands properly after wiping our asses in the field, so that fecal matter had ultimately found its way back into our mouths when we handled our food. All I knew was that when my bowels started rumbling I only had minutes to release, which was a lot easier in the desert than it was in the bed of the truck. I had been holding back the dam in my guts for the last thirty minutes of the ride. As soon as the wheels stopped rolling I bailed out of the back and hit the head.

I slammed open the door to the shitter and stormed inside. A wide-eyed private jumped from his seat when he heard my raucous approach. I recklessly dropped my gas mask and rifle on the deck, plucked the buttons on my fly, and forced my pants to my ankles. As soon as I touched down the nuclear explosion detonated beneath me. Things didn't just fall, they shot out. There was a noxious combination of gas and fluid and droppings that splattered, plopped, and splashed. The stench rose instantaneously. I moaned and groaned and pushed like a mother giving birth.

After the first wave of cramps passed I looked over at the Marine next to me, who looked like he had just stepped off the bus. He had an awkward, embarrassed look on his face. His uniform was clean, his boots polished, and he smelled of soap and shampoo. I stared at him blatantly because, quite frankly, he was an anomaly. His face wasn't sunburned. His lips were not chapped. There were no bags under his eyes, or goggle rings around his eyes, or sand trapped in his eyes—or caked in his ears, or nose, or mouth, for that matter. His hands were not cracked, or blistered, or bleeding. . . . I didn't see a single scab. His boots were black, and his skin was white, and his uniform did not smell of sweat, gunpowder, and shit. He was quite a sight.

As he rushed to finish he glanced over as if to question my stare, but he left without an explanation from me. It was just as well, because I didn't know if I could have explained it anyway. I sat for the longest time, in that grotesque head, thinking back to how I had acted, looked, and smelled just days before when I stepped off the bus. It seemed like such a long time ago.

Sgt. Krause understood that rest and relaxation were just what we needed. We were afforded seventy-two hours of uninterrupted personal time before the basewide stand-to order on 14 January—the eve of the UN deadline for Iraqi troops to evacuate Kuwait. We slept through most of the twelfth. I probably would have slept through all of it if Sgt. Moss hadn't waked me to make our phone calls home.

The three-mile hike to the phone center provided plenty of time to banter. I rambled nonstop about the proposal letter. I burned Sgt. Moss's ear all the way to the phones, worrying and wondering whether Gina had received it, and if she had, whether she would accept. All the worry was for naught. When I got through on the phone to her, she told me she had received it. And she did accept.

It was exactly the news that I needed. With the deadline

approaching quickly, there was no doubt in my mind that we would participate in the offensive. All that anyone talked about back at camp was the pending gloom and doom on the horizon. The hottest topics included the casualty rates among the infantry troops on the ground, the likelihood that Saddam would use chemical and biological weapons on us, and the overwhelming numbers of Iraqi troops and armor that waited across the border.

The climate was somber and morbid, to say the least. But Gina's acceptance buffered the pessimism, and shielded my consciousness from considering the unthinkable. That was priceless peace of mind.

The 15 January deadline came and passed peacefully. The sixteenth did as well. But peace ended at 0300 on 17 January when we heard the first sorties thunder overhead. We lay awake until sunrise listening to the hum up above and preparing mentally for our roles down below. As anticipated, Capt. Cruz called us to formation at 0600 and delivered the news. Operation Desert Storm had begun. The offensive was under way. And so were we.

We repeated the routine from our first departure for the field. It was a lot easier the second time around. We loaded our packs on the five-ton truck and formed two columns that lined the dusty road leading out of Tent City. I guessed that we were humping back out to our dreaded defensive positions. Although we started on the same familiar road, a few hundred meters into the hump we turned and headed in a different direction. No one challenged the deviation. One location in the desert sucked just as much as the next. It just didn't matter.

Then without warning we stopped. We stood in place and watched as the CO continued forward to the crest of a sand dune up ahead. Capt. Cruz looked pleased with what he saw, and soon the platoon commanders joined him on the top of the hill. Sgt. Krause followed the other platoon sergeants as well. They stood and pointed and scanned with their binoculars. Then they stood and pointed some more. Our curiosity was thoroughly piqued by the time Capt. Bounds and Sgt. Krause rejoined us, but they wouldn't tell what they had seen. They wanted us to see for ourselves, so they led us up the dune.

The first Marines to reach the top stopped and looked too. Then they disappeared over the top of the dune. Then other Marines followed quickly to see for themselves. The column continued to move faster and faster as Marines disappeared over the crest, until we had all broken into a run.

When I hit the top of the dune I couldn't believe my eyes. I thought it was a mirage. Our company was scattered along the downward slope. There in the flatlands below was the greatest sight any infantryman could ever see. Wheels. And LAVs were attached to the wheels . . . Six platoons' worth of LAVs, to be exact.

EIGHT

THE UNCHARACTERISTIC RADIO CHATTER blasted inside my helmet and roused me enough that I sat up in the cramped driver's compartment, sure that I had missed the cue to start our engine. We started the engine every four hours, for thirty minutes, to keep the batteries charged. The glow from my wristwatch showed only 2200, which meant we had two more hours to sleep before our start-up.

As I lay back down atop my flak-jacket mattress, I keyed the microphone on my helmet and called to Dougherty, who was monitoring the radio traffic on fire watch. "What the fuck is all the noise about, Dougherty?"

He snapped, "Get off the intercom, Will! I think we're about to stand to . . ."

Before he even finished I was asleep, but not for long.

The next thing I heard was Dougherty's call inside the hull. "Stand to! Stand to! Take a NAP pill and go to MOPP Level Four!"

Stand to meant engagement with the enemy was likely, which was scary enough. But the call for a Nerve Agent Protection pill, combined with MOPP Level Four was terrifying. Going into the Mission-Oriented Protective Posture meant we were under imminent threat of attack by biological or chemical weapons. The NAP pill meant the threat included exposure to nerve gas.

Practice was over. It was game time.

I held my breath while I pushed a NAP pill through the foil lining of the plastic strip and popped it in my mouth. In a matter of seconds my mask was on and my canteen was plugged into the drinking tube. But the mask and the pill offered little guarantee of survival. The gas mask was only MOPP Level One. MOPP Level Four required special boots, gloves, trousers, and jacket. The first and last time I wore the whole suit had been during Capt. Ricks's class back at Lejeune. There was no time to think about his class, or review notes, or to discuss the steps with a partner, or any of the luxuries afforded during training. It was time to act.

I reached back behind my head and pulled the plastic bundle that held my MOPP gear onto my lap. Then I shoved it up through the driver's hatch onto the top of the LAV engine compartment. As I pulled myself up and out of the hatch, I gripped the plastic tightly, careful not to let it slip from my hands into the pitch-black void beyond our vehicle. Once topside I glanced around to see what was happening outside the LAV. Dougherty was climbing out of the gunner's hatch with his bag in hand. Cpl. Shane and Haley assembled on the port side of the LAV. Doc Price was wriggling inside his sleeping bag like a caterpillar struggling to break free from its cocoon.

Nagel was spazzing inside the turret. "Where's my goddamned MOPP suit? It was right here! Who took my fucking MOPP suit?"

Shaking my head, I climbed down the side of the hull to link up with Cpl. Shane, my designated MOPP buddy. Once I hit the sand, Nagel emerged from his hatch, suit in one hand, gas mask in the other. He panicked when he looked down at the seven of us wearing our masks. He was still sucking unfiltered air. It would have been funny had it been training. Under life-and-death circumstances it was just pathetic.

To show my composure I pulled my Ka-Bar knife from its sheath and carefully sliced my way through the protective bag that held Cpl. Shane's MOPP suit, just the way Capt. Ricks had taught us. Just as I started lacing my protective boots over my regular boots I looked up to see Nagel tugging furiously at both ends of his MOPP suit bag. It soon burst, sending the pieces of his suit everywhere.

Some were on top of the LAV, some under the LAV, and some landed in Dougherty's pile. Nagel was so frantic that he started a tug of war with Dougherty over a protective boot.

Fortunately Dougherty was strong enough to pull Nagel onto his face. Then in true Dougherty fashion he stopped dressing until he found Nagel's missing boot. Dougherty was a far better man than I. Had Nagel been my MOPP buddy I would have let him low-crawl through the sand to find his own gear.

Once dressed we boarded the LAV, pulled our helmets over our hooded heads, and listened to instructions. Black Six, the radio designation for Capt. Cruz's vehicle, called all crewmen to stand by for a short count. That was the audio countdown—three, two, one—which synchronized our start-up. The procedure was designed so enemy troops within listening range could not count individual engine starts, and consequently identify the number of vehicles in our unit.

After the short count I yelled, "Fire in the hole!" and flicked the switch that brought the engine to life. The engine and radio chatter left me virtually deaf to Nagel's calls from above. It was difficult to hear anything recessed down inside the driver's compartment. The thump on my helmet got my attention, though. Nagel crouched down and yelled into my face as I stood on my seat.

"I didn't tell you to start the engine! Why did you start the engine?"

"Black Six ordered a short count!"

Nagel clenched his jaw and ran back to check with Dougherty, who confirmed the short count.

Then Nagel stormed back to yell some more. "Take your NAP pill!"

I was annoyed. My shit was together. "I already took it!"

His order caught me off guard. "I said take it now . . . I have to see you take it."

That was bullshit—another Nagel power trip! With no idea about the effect of a double dose I shook my head no and repeated, "I already took it!"

My refusal sent Nagel over the edge and he called me out of the LAV. Pissed that I had to leave the radio to deal with Nagel's nonsense, I removed my helmet, threw it onto the open hatch, and pressed myself up onto the engine compartment. Just as I gained my balance I looked up into the barrel of Nagel's M16. *Unbelievable.*

He ordered me again, this time at rifle point. "Take your NAP pill! Now!"

His absolute insanity infuriated me. I knew that he was a piss-poor leader, but under the stress of combat he had become a certifiable lunatic. My reaction was just as idiotic.

I charged forward, ramming my chest into the barrel, screaming, "Go ahead and shoot me, motherfucker! Go ahead and shoot!"

My charge drove him back a step. Then I used my forearm to knock his rifle out of the way.

I grabbed the material at his collar with both fists and bellowed as loud as I could, "I told you I took the pill! Do you hear me? I took the fucking pill!"

Completely flabbergasted with his breakdown, I released him, turned my back on his rifle, and returned to the sanctity of my driver's compartment. Once in the confines of my hole I had my own conniption, pounding the steering wheel, stomping the deck, and raging inside my mask. I cursed Sgt. Krause for separating me from Sgt. Moss and forcing me under Nagel's thumb.

He stuck it to me every chance he got. The latest, in a litany of beefs I had with him, was my assignment as driver. Dougherty had complained that he was too tall to fit comfortably in the driver's tunnel, so Nagel switched us, even though I was the better gunner.

Between rants I heard Capt. Cruz over the radio, which diverted my attention back to driving. Iraqi armor was rolling our way, and at least one active-duty LAV company was engaging them. Engines raced by as LAVs advanced. Our moment of truth had finally arrived. Dougherty fumbled with the ratchet to upload rounds. Nagel slapped a belt of ammunition onto the feeder of the machine gun. Cpl. Shane briefed the scouts and issued ammunition. Black Six's frazzled commands faded in and out of my helmet. My heart raced,

my chest heaved, and I repeated my silent prayer into my mask—
God help us all.

LAVs roared on our left and right as Nagel's overanxious voice
blasted into my helmet. "Move out! Let's go!"

My foot remained on the brake as I called back to Cpl. Shane on
the intercom, "Are the scouts aboard?"

Cpl. Shane called back, "Wait one! Doc is looking for his sleeping bag!"

Nagel cut in, "Goddammit! Get him the fuck in here! Now!
We're pulling out!"

Doc Price was the thorn in the foot of our crew. He was dead
weight, a complainer, and a pussy through and through. What
pissed me off most about him was that he never assimilated into our
grunt world. Most navy corpsmen fit in so well, it was difficult to tell
them apart from the Marine infantrymen, but not Doc Price. He
was a prima donna. Doc refused to dig his own fighting holes or to
serve fire watch. He argued that he was supposed to be kept from
harm's way. It was a fight we let him win for the sake of our safety.
None of us was confident that he could keep watch for enemy contact or fire. Doc's ineptitude always bit us in the ass. Now the rest of
the company was rolling off into a firefight as he was crawling
around looking for his sleeping bag.

Nagel was no longer screaming about Doc. He had turned his attention to Dougherty, who was having radio comm problems.

Dougherty was screaming into his microphone that his comm
was down, that he couldn't hear anything. Nagel was screaming just
as loud into his mike, "Dougherty, can you hear me? Dougherty?
Dougherty!"

Finally, after removing and reinstalling the comm cables,
Dougherty was back on-line.

That gave Cpl. Shane enough time to drag Doc and his bag inside. "Troops are in!"

Next I heard Dougherty's voice in my helmet for the first time.
"Permission to cycle the ghost round?"

"Cycle!" Nagel replied.

Cycling the ghost round was the procedure that involved firing the main gun once to move the empty link through the feeder and place a live round in the chamber. If performed properly, there was no risk of misfiring. But I knew Nagel was too impatient to read through the gunner's checklist to assist Dougherty. The checklist was to be read by the VC and gunner before firing, like a copilot and pilot before takeoff. Nagel should have called out, "Turret powered up?" After which Dougherty should have responded, "Check!"

Instead I heard Dougherty's frustrated curses as he banged and clanked his way through the power-up procedures. There was only so much I could do to help from the driver's tunnel. The most I could do was reach into the tangle of metal and wires to double-check the switches were in the right positions, the chutes were fastened properly, and the rounds were loaded correctly.

There was little time for a thorough check. As I slithered back into the driver's seat I called over the intercom to Dougherty, "Make sure you're on single shot." Dougherty appreciated reminders.

Nagel didn't. "Unkey the mike, Williams! You worry about driving, we'll worry about shooting."

That was a typical response from Nagel, but the stakes were too high to remain quiet. If the weapon were configured for any setting other than single shot, then the ghost round would fire along with the live rounds that followed. And they would continue firing until Dougherty released the trigger. Preventing Dougherty from shooting the vehicle in front was worth Nagel's grief.

Once my helmet was back on my head, I heard Capt. Bounds call for all red elements to fall in. First Platoon's vehicles were designated Red. There were four vehicles in all. Our vehicle was Red Two and Capt. Bounds's was Red One. Sgt. Krause's and Staff Sgt. Sanders's were Red Three and Red Four, respectively.

The whir of hydraulics whined as the driver's seat raised my head up into the opaque night above. To my left I could see a dark hulk moving in front of us, and assumed it was Capt. Bounds. On my right was the menacing barrel of the main gun, its muzzle resting only inches from my head. During training I would have never even been permitted to have my hatch open with the main gun loaded. Not only was my hatch open, my seat was raised. There was no other choice. If I lowered myself into the hull I would have to drive blind. There was not enough visibility to allow me to see through my vision blocks, and there was no time to install my night sight. Hopefully it would be installed before we needed to fire. The way things looked, that could be anytime.

With my head outside the LAV I heard dull crashes and thuds like rolling thunder in the distance. I could feel the ground quake as impacting rounds vibrated the hull. It was difficult to tell if the rounds were incoming or outgoing, artillery shells or mortars, tanks or air support, friendly or enemy. None of that mattered, anyway. What mattered was driving, the one thing I could control.

Nagel's high-pitched cry wailed inside my helmet. "Get this pig moving!"

Once I found the shadow of Red One in front, I stepped on the accelerator and we rolled into the column. We crept along at five miles per hour for about fifteen minutes, after which Black Six called the company to a stop. Then he called all vehicle commanders to rally at his vehicle for a brief. That was a relief. It meant that we were not under imminent threat of engagement. Not by the enemy, anyway.

Shortly after Nagel trotted off into the blackness, the signature *thump, thump, thump,* of a LAV's 25mm main gun exploded from behind. Simultaneously the ear-shattering blasts thundered past my head.

It took a few seconds for the reality to settle in. "Dougherty! What the fuck was that?"

Dougherty called back over the intercom, "We're taking fire from the rear!"

He was right, but it was not just fire. It was LAV fire. Friendly fire. It had come from Lance Cpl. Bates's LAV. His was the last vehicle in our column, and he was the last gunner to have cycled his ghost round—only, he'd done it on rapid fire. Bates's error had sent three armor-piercing rounds just two feet above the turrets of our column. Had the vehicle commanders been standing upright in their usual positions, exposed from the waist up, many would have been gutted. The lack of training and experience had finally caught up with us. And the cluster-fuck had only just begun.

The unexpected overhead fire sent crews into a panicked frenzy. One driver up ahead stepped onto the accelerator and rammed into the LAV in front, starting a chain reaction of collisions. In another vehicle a scout accidentally fired his rifle in the crowded troop compartment, sending the round up and out of the troop hatches. All the while the radio buzzed with erroneous reports of enemy fire that sent our VCs scrambling back into their turrets.

Once the company regained its composure, we learned what was happening off in the distance. While we'd been waking up, suiting up, and fucking up, an active-duty LAV company was engaging in a battle with Iraqi tanks off to our flank. That was all the information we received before the next order came to move out.

We never would take enemy fire that night. We never even fired at the enemy. We might have, if we hadn't missed the turnoff . . . or if the middle of our column hadn't broken off after a few miles and doubled back to find it . . . or if we'd had some semblance of organization and order. By midnight our company of LAVs had become a discombobulated mess.

I know now that organization and order are not prerequisites for battle. We had experienced the same combat chaos that U.S. Marines have experienced for two hundred years, spanning dozens of generations, battles, and landscapes. It is something all Marines have to experience personally before they can function fully within that environment. We were fortunate to have had the time and space to gain that experience in the absence of casualties. Our active duty counterparts were not so lucky.

Several days later we learned some of what happened that night. We learned that the active-duty LAV company suffered two friendly fire hits during their skirmish. One TOW variant mistook a LAV for an enemy tank and fired on it, killing all four Marines aboard. During a separate incident an A-10 Warthog airplane fired a Maverick missile into the topside of a LAV-25, killing seven of the eight Marines aboard. The word was that the driver had been blasted upward through his driver's hatch, and although badly cut and burned, he had survived. When I heard who the driver was I was floored—it was Hunter, the party animal who was jumped in Oceanside during LAV school.

He was lucky, as far as I was concerned. He knew his fate. He knew he was going home.

8 FEBRUARY 1991

We moved around quite a bit during the first days of February, with plenty of action all around. But until this night the action had been little more than radio drama for us. Our new position had moved us closer to the action than we had ever been. During the past few days we had heard reports of nearby units engaging Iraqi tanks, intercepting convoys, and apprehending surrendering soldiers. It was only a matter of time before our company would cross paths with the enemy.

I was doing fire watch at dawn, scanning for enemy troops with my forehead resting on the rubber pad just above the gunner's sights. It required a conscious effort to keep it in place. The position made it impossible to doze off for any period, because once I relaxed my neck muscles my head would slide to one side or the other, driving my eye socket into the protruding lens. It worked well. There was a welt under my right eye to prove it. The green glow of the sights, the methodical rotation of the hand wheel, and the constant hum of the radio combined to put me into a trancelike state—just one notch away from sleep.

To describe our current condition as fatigue would be an understatement. We were all pushing our limits. The only thing keeping my eyes open, and my hand on the wheel, was the constant threat of attack. The fear of Iraqi soldiers sneaking into our perimeter haunted me every second of my watch. If that happened, they could do to us what our scouts practiced doing to them. Taking a rocket in the hull, or a grenade down the hatch, or any similar circumstance, would send us all to hell in a flaming fireball. Perhaps the worst threat of all, though, was the possibility of living through an attack that I could have prevented, living with the guilt that others died because I fell asleep.

My left hand cranked the wheel, which moved the turret and the gun sights mounted to it from left to right and back again. The sights allowed me to see a few hundred meters into the desert, from the nine o'clock position to the three o'clock position. Our vehicle was positioned strategically along a convex arch of LAVs such that my sector of responsibility overlapped with that of Red One to my left and Red Three to my right. Each vehicle was positioned approximately a hundred meters apart from its neighbor. Our company's defensive perimeter stretched for nearly a mile. Inside the hub of the arch were the three vehicles of Headquarters Platoon—Capt. Cruz's vehicle (Black Six), the logistics vehicle (Black Three), and the command-and-control communications vehicle (Black One). They formed the nerve center of our company, and protecting them from attack was paramount.

There was no reason to believe the morning would be any different from any other morning. Cold. Quiet. Boring. The first sign of light was looming on the horizon, and I had almost finished my watch. The first time I saw the small shape in my sights I thought my mind was playing tricks on me. After three checks I still wasn't sure. The distant blob grew as it moved closer, until finally I could see . . . it was a truck.

Before I had the wherewithal to call in my sighting, the radio erupted. "Black One! Black One! Enemy vehicle approaching from the front!"

And another, "Black One! Black One! Truck en route with a machine gun mounted and manned!"

And another, "Enemy vehicle headed toward Second Platoon!"

Then Capt. Cruz interrupted. "All rainbow elements move forward and intercept!"

I reached across and shook Nagel, who was sleeping in the VC seat with his head against his sights. "Truck . . . armed and headed our way . . . a thousand meters out!"

Nagel didn't need to hear it a second time. He had his helmet on and binoculars up in seconds.

Dougherty heard my call and already had the engines fired up. Cpl. Shane didn't waste time reporting that our troops were inside.

After blasting through my prefire checklist I wrapped my fingers around the joystick and pulled right, searching for the truck in my sights. Dougherty stepped on the gas, thrusting me backward into my seatback. We bounced and shook and swayed from left to right as we maneuvered toward the truck. My head, too, bobbed around wildly, and I had to force it into the rubber headrest to maintain visual contact. Finally, I locked the truck into the kill zone. The ammo select switch was set to the high-explosive type, and the rate of fire was set to two hundred rounds per minute. All I needed to hear was Nagel's order to fire.

I wanted to fire. I wanted to make them pay. So I looked through the sight, and held on to the gun control, and prayed for the order to fire. After all, it was their fault I was there. It was their fault I stared through the sights with a cold heart. It was their fault that Gina sat at home with a heavy heart . . . and that Doc trembled in the hull with a chicken heart . . . and that Hunter lay in a hospital bed with a purple heart . . . and that eleven mothers cried at caskets with broken hearts.

My enthusiasm to fire was curbed, however, as the truck drew closer. The gun mounted on top was turned backward, and a white flag hung from its muzzle. There was a white flag in the passenger's hand, and another in the driver's. There were several more being waved by people in the back.

Capt. Bounds called over the radio for us to hold our fire and hold our positions. As our vehicle rolled to a stop, Nagel told me to keep my eyes in the sights in case the order changed. The truck headed straight into Second Platoon's formation, white flags flying. That was Sgt. Moss's platoon. Scanning the column of vehicles off to our left flank, I saw one, two, three vehicles in position . . . but no fourth. Even after double-checking, there were still only three. Then I saw the fourth, back five hundred meters! It hadn't moved from our night position. We had moved out and left it behind. That was a problem. A big problem. The vehicle's absence left a giant gap in Second Platoon's formation, which provided a window of opportunity for the truck to infiltrate our line.

As the truck rolled closer to our line of vehicles, I kept it in my sights. It rolled up to our line, then through our line, and then directly into the cluster of headquarters vehicles—Capt. Cruz's vehicle, our comm vehicle . . . our nerve center! None of us could fire. Our guns were turned such that we could only shoot each other, or the headquarters vehicles. All we could do was watch.

The truck slowed for a moment, as if to show respect for our command post, but then continued on through our ranks. We continued to watch through our sights as an army unit off to our flank stopped the truck and apprehended the Iraqis. The radio was jumping from its base with Capt. Cruz's rant. He wanted the VCs to report to his vehicle. He wanted an investigation. He wanted answers, and he wanted them immediately.

We returned our LAV back into our original positions just in time to watch the drama unfolding. Capt. Cruz ran up to the LAV and banged his fist on the hull. There was no answer. No movement. Nothing. Capt. Cruz continued to bang, and shout, and curse, until finally the VC hatch opened. And there before the entire company emerged Sgt. Moss, oblivious to the world outside his LAV, stretching and yawning like a bear leaving hibernation.

Capt. Cruz went berserk. He was out of his mind with anger, incensed with fury, and overcome with madness. He cursed and spat and spewed up at Sgt. Moss like he wanted to kill him. Sgt. Moss stood atop the turret, a deer in the headlights, completely clueless that he had missed a vehicle movement, unaware that he had allowed our first prisoners to escape, and ignorant of the fact that he had jeopardized the life of our company commander, and even worse—embarrassed him. Helplessly, I watched the train wreck that was about to take place before my eyes. Sgt. Moss climbed down from the turret slowly, and prepared for the impact of the runaway locomotive.

Capt. Cruz ripped Sgt. Moss's chevrons from his collar and stomped them into the sand. Sgt. Moss recoiled against the LAV as Capt. Cruz yelled, and pointed, and yelled some more. It was like watching a major league baseball coach going head-to-head with an umpire. But Sgt. Moss did not fight back. He bowed his head in shame and took it. It was difficult to watch. Sgt. Moss didn't have the kind of inner armor to handle such a personal attack. He kept his head down as Gunny Koffman led him away—away from his vehicle, men, and honor. All I could do was sit and watch.

That was the last I saw of Sgt. Moss until 21 February, when our LAV cycled back to the rear for maintenance. While at the battalion area we were left to our own devices, and my personal mission was to get as far away from Nagel as possible. My curiosity led me to our enemy prisoner camp, and right to the Marine in charge of the prisoners—Sgt. Moss!

"Hey, Colonel Klink!" I called to him.

"Wee-ams!"

After a handshake he gave me a phony chuckle. "Yeah . . . well . . . Here I am"—rubbing his fingers over the holes in his collar where his chevrons had been.

"So where have you been? What have you been doing?"

"Right here. Doing this." He stretched out his arms and turned around in a circle. "This is all mine, brother. I might be a private, but I'm the HMFIC of this prison camp."

He got a puzzled stare from me.

"Head Mother Fucker In Charge," he explained. "C'mon, I'll show you around."

"So did you really get busted all the way to private?" I asked.

"Who the fuck knows," he said. "I'm supposed to meet with Capt. Cruz the next time he rotates back to the rear. I guess I'll find out then."

I thought it best to address him as Sgt. Moss until the CO decided otherwise.

Sgt. Moss led me to the back of his truck, where six Iraqi prisoners lay side by side, facedown on a canvas tarp, their wrists bound behind their backs with plastic zip-strip fasteners. It was a sight.

"Watch this. . . ." Sgt. Moss cued.

He walked around to their heads, stooped over, and uttered a few strange sounds. The prisoners wriggled themselves to their knees.

He speaks Arabic? I thought.

He showed his pistol to them and called out sternly, "Don't any of you get crazy on me. . . . I'll blow your fucking head off."

And in the same breath he handed his canteen over to one, and an MRE meal to another, and adjusted the head wrap on a third to keep the sun from burning him.

They appeared so grateful—bowing, and smiling, and thanking him in Arabic. *"Salaam aleikum. . . . Salaam aleikum. . . ."*

Sgt. Moss clearly enjoyed his role. *"Lekum salam."* He smiled back.

It was a perfect fit. He needed power. They needed compassion. And they got it—at least they did once they arrived at Sgt. Moss's camp.

He pulled one of the prisoners to his feet and asked me to step around in front so the others could see.

Before I could say no, his pistol was in my hand and I was being introduced. "Now, listen up! I'm gonna help you boys out here, but if you try to fight"—he faked a punch—"or run"—he jogged in place—"then this Marine will shoot!"—he mimed a shot to the head with his finger.

None flinched. Sgt. Moss held the prisoner by the arm and cut the zip strip from his bloody wrists.

"As if these boys haven't been through enough shit," he said, "they have to put up with the gunny and his henchmen. . . . They tightened these zips down to the bone."

As soon as the plastic dropped, the prisoner bowed his head and prayed. Then Sgt. Moss wrapped gauze around the raw flesh and fastened a looser zip. He did the same for all of them. They were lucky to have Sgt. Moss in charge. His loss in rank and stature was their gain.

We spent the day reminiscing about drill, and LAV school, and Lejeune. It felt good to remember life before the war, and the day flew by.

It was difficult to leave Sgt. Moss that evening. The next day we were staging for the ground assault, and my anxiety was beginning to build. How had I gotten to this point? To the brink of the ground assault? To the edge of the berm?

Beyond the berm there were minefields and booby traps, trenches and bunkers, mortars and artillery, rifles and machine guns, grenades and flamethrowers, tanks and armored vehicles, and God knows what else. . . . I felt as if I had been abducted by the monster of war. It didn't matter that I wasn't ready. I was going right into the fiery hell beyond that berm. And I would be going without Sgt. Moss.

22 FEBRUARY 1991

Our LAVs were staged in a circle like wagons in the Wild West. At the center we gathered for the evening brief. The sun had set and already rounds were exploding just beyond the berm. A loud thump thundered overhead. A burst of antiaircraft fire streamed into the sky. A barrage of allied bombs crunched the earth. What was going on beyond that mound of sand?

The questions started from the back of the formation.

"Are those rounds incoming?"

"Can their arty hit us from here?"

"Who's watching the berm?"

That was just it. We were responsible for the berm. So when Black Six got the word Iraqi forces were headed toward the berm—our berm—all hell broke loose.

"Mount up! Prepare for contact at the berm! Power up your turrets!"

I ran as fast as I could to our LAV, climbed aboard, and dropped inside the driver's hatch. No sooner had I started installing my night sight then Nagel's spastic voice crackled in my helmet. "Move out! Move out!"

Move out? I couldn't even see. Instead of answering I kept both hands on the sight.

Again the wired voice jarred my headset. "Williams! Williams! Fire up this beast! What are you doing down there?"

Frustrated, I held the sight with one hand and flipped my comm switch with the other. "I am putting the fucking night sight in so I can fucking see. . . . Give me a fucking minute!"

I slammed the sight back into the cavity and started winding the wing nuts, feverishly.

My helmet buzzed a third time. Startled, I dropped one of the wing nuts onto the deck. "Williams! If I don't hear this engine fire up in one second I'll make you a scout for the rest of this goddamned war!"

The smoke from the oil wells, combined with nightfall, left zero visibility. The instrument panel was only inches from my face and I couldn't see the controls.

On touch alone I flipped the ignition switch. "Fire in the hole!"

"Forward! Go!"

My foot was still on the brake. "Are you fucking deaf? I can't see shit out there! Give me thirty seconds!"

Nagel didn't quit. He wanted to be the first to the berm. He wanted the glory of engaging, capturing, or killing—at any cost.

"Drive by my commands! I can see!"

I didn't respond. If I couldn't drive blind in LAV school with instructors I trusted, I wasn't going to begin now.

As I reached below for the lost wing nut, Nagel's voice boomed over the intercom.

"Cpl. Shane! You're our new driver! Switch with Williams!"

I didn't give Cpl. Shane the chance to open the rear hatch.

"Hold tight, Cpl. Shane! We're on the move!"

With all my weight I mashed the accelerator to the floor, hoping to jar Nagel right out of the turret. No such luck.

Nagel's voice was still in my ear. "Dougherty! Is the gun up? Dougherty?"

Dougherty's comm was down again. *No comm . . . no fire. . . . .*

Nagel knew he needed to be able to speak with Dougherty to

issue the fire commands. But he didn't need to speak to Dougherty more than he needed to guide me. He should have waited to help Dougherty. He should never have ducked inside the turret to fix those fucking cables. He should never have removed his eyes from his night vision goggles.

Without Nagel's voice to guide me I was left alone to navigate. I picked up a faint visual of tracks, so I followed them, figuring they would lead us to the berm. They might have if they had been LAV tracks, but they weren't. They were tank tracks—tank tracks that led directly into a tank ditch. A ditch big enough to swallow an entire tank below the surface of the earth, to shield it from fire. By the time I saw the dark mass in front, it was too late. My swerve left us straddling the crater, with our left side grounded and the right side suspended in midair.

The right four wheels dipped into the hole and the front of the vehicle smashed head-on into the far wall of the ditch. The force threw me into the steel rim of the hatch and knocked the wind out of me. We hung suspended for a moment before the inevitable rollover. My knees caught the underside of the steering wheel as we flipped, which was the only thing keeping me inside the hull. Had I fallen out I would have been crushed beneath the fifteen-ton mass of the LAV. As the vehicle turned bottom-up, my knees gave way and I dropped through the hatch onto my head. The steel hatch broke loose from the weight of the vehicle, swung down, and bashed my helmet. That was the first thing I remembered after the roll. Then screaming. A lot of screaming.

Upside down, I lay disoriented and trapped in the two-foot space created by the height of the turret. Then I smelled it . . . felt it . . . and tasted it—fuel. It kick-started my senses enough that I managed to wriggle my way back into the driver's compartment. Once inside I crawled toward the rear of the vehicle. At least I tried to. Down was up, and left was right, and I was so disoriented I didn't know if I was coming or going. Then I remembered the red-lens Mag-Lite tied to my flak. First I flashed it toward the VC side, as it was the most accessible route to the back hatches. But Nagel's body blocked the path—twisted, contorted, and upside down.

His arms were pinned beneath him, disappearing after the elbows. For all I knew his forearms lay outside the vehicle, crushed flat, or maybe even severed. And for all I cared they could have been. I hoped they were! He wasn't getting any help from me. As I maneuvered past him on the gunner's side of the turret, Nagel screamed, and flailed, and begged for mercy.

The gunner's side was also impassible. Doc lay there unconscious, beneath a pile of hundred-pound ammo boxes. One lay on his head, torqueing his neck perpendicular to his body. He was much worse off than Nagel. At least Nagel was well enough to scream. The sight of Doc's limp body turned me back toward the driver's hatch.

Nagel's bloodcurdling screams were relentless. It sounded like he was being murdered inside the turret. The others might have been screaming, too, but I didn't hear them. Maybe they were less injured than Nagel. . . . Maybe they were more. . . . Either way I needed to get out to get some help.

The crawl space outside of the driver's hatch was a dead end. All around, sand. After a quick scan I determined the only way to free myself was to tunnel out. The sand was so soft, I moved it with my bare hands, reaching above my head, scooping, and sweeping it downward toward my boots. It was like swimming upward, after a dive to the bottom of a pool, toward the surface of the water. But I was swimming in sand, and the pool walls were closing in. My body slid upward, inches at a time, pinched between the sandy wall and the hull steel. The dig lasted only minutes, but they were long and tense. I feared the vehicle would shift as I tunneled, and crush me. When my head popped out of the sand I traded Nagel's screams for Dougherty's distant call.

"Will? Nagel? Anybody?"

"Dougherty! Over here! Can you hear me?"

No response. My legs quivered from shock and buckled under my weight the first time I tried to stand. I crawled along the edge of the ditch to the back of the LAV. It looked so strange upside down, wheels up. The vehicle rested on the turret, with the front angling downward, jacking the rear into the air. Once around back I saw Cpl. Shane suspended from the left troop hatch, tangled in a web of straps and camouflage netting. As I made my way closer he kicked open the rear hatch and Nagel's screams poured out.

It was difficult to yell over Nagel's agony. "Cpl. Shane! You hurt?"

"No! Just tangled. Can you pull my rifle out?"

His rifle had slung across his back during the rollover, and caught the underside of the hatch, preventing him from falling out. Amazingly, my knife was still in the sheath strapped to my leg. Cpl. Shane used it to cut himself free. After he dropped to the ground, he reached back inside to pull Haley out.

By that time Dougherty had made his way to the rear as well.

"Didn't you hear me calling?" he asked. "I thought you were all trapped inside!"

Dougherty hadn't held on to the inside of the turret, like Nagel, when the vehicle pitched. He was catapulted across the desert. So far, in fact, that he hadn't initially been able to see the vehicle from where he landed.

Dougherty worried even more after he heard Nagel's screams up close. "What's the headcount?"

Cpl. Shane reached out and touched us one by one. "You and Will are out. Nagel's stuck in the turret. Haley and I made it out. That leaves. . . . Doc."

"Doc's bad," I said. "He's real fucking bad."

Until I spoke the words, I had kept myself together. It was all I could do to keep from crying. "Jesus Christ, Dougherty. . . . I think Doc's dead."

My mind raced through the options. *Crawl back in and call on the radio. Shoot a flare. Start CPR. Stick him with morphine. Run for help. That's it. Run for help.*

"Cpl. Shane! I'm going to follow our tracks back to our rally point. . . ."

Before he had a chance to respond, I was running off into the darkness, staring down at the tracks. We had only driven about a half mile, but in zero visibility it seemed like a thousand miles. After a hundred meters my legs seemed like lead, my adrenaline gone, and I slowed to a walk. Then the sky lit up. *An illumination round! But is it ours, or theirs?* My mortar days during weekend reserve training had taught me enough to know that illum meant take cover. There was no cover to take, but the adrenaline surge allowed me to start running again.

The night was so dark, I nearly ran headlong into one of the LAVs back at the rally point. As I ran I shouted for help. "Corpsman up! Corpsman up! Corpsman up!"

Sgt. Pitts was the first to stop me. He grabbed me by the shoulders and held me still. "Calm down! What happened?"

"Our vehicle rolled about a half mile out. . . . Nagel's trapped . . . and Doc's hurt bad. . . . He might be dead. . . ."

Sgt. Pitts mobilized a pair of vehicles and drove us out to the crash site. When we arrived, I ran to the rear hatches. Nagel's screams had faded to a whimper, and Doc was still limp. Another illumination round lit the sky, and the crash scene. The LAV looked horrific upside down. The flickering light from the sky made it creepier still. Moments after the illumination popped, rounds started impacting. One fell in the distance. Then another fell closer.

Sgt. Pitts called out to the rescuers, "Let's hurry the fuck up! Those rounds are walking in on us!"

I was spent. It was just too much—the roll, the run, and now artillery and mortars exploding beyond the berm. I sat down, buried my head in my hands, and fought to keep from breaking down crying. It was all I could do. My legs wouldn't carry me farther. Sgt. Pitts understood. He scooped me up and carried me over the berm, where two sand dunes provided cover.

For some time that night I lay awake thinking . . . second-guessing . . . crying . . . and praying. Back at the ditch the recovery vehicle's winches whined as Red Two righted, and the chopper blades thumped as they flew Doc and Nagel out. The ground vibrated soothingly as bombs exploded far away, and shook violently as rounds impacted closer to the berm. They didn't matter. Nothing mattered to me at that point—unless, of course, one should fall in between my dunes. But even that, as long as it was quick and painless, wouldn't have mattered. At times that night I would even have welcomed it.

The first morning light showed the shambles that our crew had become. Our gear and personal effects were strewn across the desert. Some were between the berms, some back at the ditch. During most of the morning I worked like a zombie, painstakingly collecting, inventorying, and organizing my gear. The most difficult thing was revisiting the hole. Our LAV was gone. The tracks were haunting.

Dougherty knew me well enough to wait until I was finished with my gear-organizing compulsions before he visited. He didn't seem nearly as rattled as I was about the rollover. Neither were Cpl. Shane or Haley. They knew I was taking it hard. I felt responsible, but was playing a hell of a blame game inside my head. Interviewed for the after-action report I was adamant that Nagel was responsible. He and his quest to be first to the berm, to be the hero of the war, to be anything but the whining, sniveling, immature fuck that he was. That was my story, and I stuck to it.

Nagel should have let me install the night sight. Nagel should have stayed topside with his night vision goggles on. Nagel should have waited for Dougherty to fix his own cables. Nagel. Nagel. Nagel. But deep inside I felt responsible. All my reports about Nagel were true, but they were beside the point. I was behind the wheel, succumbing to Nagel's asinine tantrum, deciding to drive instead of switch with Cpl. Shane, following the tank tracks, and swerving too late. The guilt was paralyzing.

The morning later brought two pieces of good news. Most important, Doc and Nagel were alive at the time they were evacuated, though we had no news on their present condition. The second scoop was that our LAV was returning around noon. Vehicles had been rolling over all across the desert, and battalion maintenance had become experts at getting them back into service. Having our LAV back was bittersweet. Sweet that we would be able to participate in the ground offensive as LAV crewmen instead of trench-clearing grunts. Bitter because I was gun shy about getting back inside, sitting behind the wheel, in the turret, in the rear . . . I knew it would all come back to haunt me. And who would replace Nagel?

We watched as our LAV approached in the distance, blurred and wavy on the horizon under the radiating heat of the afternoon sun. The engine's roar grew louder as it approached, full speed, from the distance. We stood at the ridge of the berm, waiting for its arrival. When it was about a few hundred meters out we could see a body, exposed from the waist up, in the VC position. He was waving his arms in a jumping-jacks motion, and yelling so loudly we could hear him over the engine. Cpl. Shane used his binoculars to identify our new VC. His mouth dropped when he saw who it was.

"You're not going to believe this, Will!

He was right. I couldn't believe it. It was Sgt. Moss! Not the depressed Moss, or the awkward Moss, or the embarrassed Moss . . . the John Wayne Moss. When the LAV skidded to a halt, he pulled off his helmet, flipped up his collar to show off his sergeant chevrons, and stood atop the turret like Moses on the mountain.

He leaned back to fill his lungs and then wailed, "Yahhh-hooo! Yeahhh, boys! Climb aboard. . . . It's time to go make history!"

It was one of those few times in my life when I actually believed in the power of prayer. If I had to climb back into the crypt, suit up in MOPP gear, drive over the berm, fire and kill, and maybe die in the process . . . I was glad it was going to be with Sgt. Moss.

24 FEBRUARY 1991

The smog from the burning oil wells blanketed the sky, hanging just below black rain clouds, making even the night sight ineffective during midday. That left me driving with my head popped just above the safety of the armor, straining my eyes to avoid the hazards of the battlefield and keep us on the path into Kuwait City. When the rain clouds passed and the smog thinned out, we could see two hundred meters. Most of this day, though, we couldn't see our hand in front of our faces.

Dougherty and Sgt. Moss were talking constantly on the intercom, scanning for enemy tanks, bunkers, trenches, mines, and
troops. Cpl. Shane stood up through the top hatch in back of the
vehicle to cover our rear. Haley and our new scouts, Lance Cpl.
Bennett and Lance Cpl. Wells, prepped their trench-clearing weapons
in the rear of the LAV.

Although I wanted to be in the gunner's seat, Sgt. Moss convinced me to remain the driver. Regardless of the initial proficiency
we had when we first picked up our LAVs, I now had logged the
most time behind the wheel, and Dougherty behind the gun. Sgt.
Moss explained that he needed the most experienced driver to keep
us from hitting land mines, which threatened our lives as much as
hostile fire.

That was true. The path through the breach was laced on both
sides with engineer tape and tags marking mines. We rolled through
the minefield breach for about an hour before entering the battlefield and opening our formation. Much of the Iraqi armor we encountered was in flames, already destroyed by the wave of M1
Abrams tanks that had rolled in ahead of us. We were to engage
anything and everything that the tanks left behind. Dougherty
pumped armor-piercing rounds into any tank that appeared intact,
to be sure there were no Iraqis inside waiting to fire on us. It seemed
more like target practice than combat.

The biggest threat during the first hours of the ground war was
the hidden bunkers and trenches that harbored Iraqi infantrymen.
Unlike the unknown danger of the stationary tanks the trenches
were manned, and assumed to be hostile. Our first encounter with
trench warfare was nothing like what we had practiced with Staff
Sgt. Rodriguez. Not for us crewmen, anyway. Sgt. Moss was the first
to identify the thin dark line, about a hundred meters to our front.
We could see enemy soldiers moving in and around the trenches as
we halted and called in our report. At first we followed procedure,
and called to ask permission to engage the target. But there were so
many targets, and so many requests to engage, the radio was
jammed with traffic.

". . . armed infantry in the open . . ."

". . . troops hiding in a bunker . . ."

". . . manned fighting holes to our front . . ."

As the sound of LAVs started firing around us, Sgt. Moss took the initiative to issue his fire commands.

"Gunner! HE! Troops in a trench! One hundred meters! On my position!"

Sgt. Moss, looking above the turret, reached down to his gun control and slewed the barrel to the general area of the trench. I ducked down into the hull and stared through the vision blocks.

Dougherty's voice followed. "Identified!"

"Fire!"

The first three-round burst thumped into the center of the trench. Three bright explosions lit the earth on impact, sending Iraqi soldiers running for their lives. Then Sgt. Moss ordered machine-gun fire.

"Gunner! Coax [denoting machine-gun rounds]! Troops in the open!" he said.

"Identified!" Dougherty called back.

"Fire!"

The spray zigzagged, blasting holes into the desert floor way short of the trenches. Dougherty adjusted and sprayed again, this time chasing the soldiers back into the trench to take cover. The main gun forced them out of the trench, and the machine gun forced them back in. Other crews in the company were experiencing the same frustration, but some had actually managed to take prisoners—and the prisoners talked. The Iraqis told how they had wanted to surrender, but had feared being shot if they came out of hiding. When we heard that over the radio, it changed our strategy completely. We still fired into the trenches with our main gun, but we did so at one end of the trench. Once the Iraqis exited the trench, we stopped firing, and sent our scouts to intercept them.

The strategy worked. Iraqi soldiers poured from their underground hiding places in droves. In a matter of hours our entire position was overrun with surrendering Iraqis. They walked right up to our vehicle with their hands on their heads, rifles slung upside down, and giant smiles on their faces. Haley, our lone Arab speaker, was invaluable in securing the prisoners. Many spoke English.

"We love George Bush!"

"USA! USA! USA!"

"America is great!"

When a wave of surrendering Iraqis moved past us, we fired on the trenches to clear them of any remaining Iraqis, and then moved on. God help the soldiers that had remained in hiding. Our firepower was devastating, and if they had not left when the others did, they would never get the chance.

I wanted them to live. With their famished frames, bloody feet, tattered uniforms, weathered skin, and pitiful expressions—they were pathetic. After looking into their eyes it was difficult to hate them. They were no longer evil, soulless killers. They were sons, and brothers, and husbands, and fathers. They didn't want to kill us any more than we wanted to kill them.

That was how most of our sweep into Kuwait City went until the next afternoon. Until then our rounds had been lost in the hulls of abandoned tanks, sandy trenches, and plywood bunkers. Until then any killing had been masked by steel, earth, and wood.

Until then I had never seen death.

25 FEBRUARY

All four LAV platoons were on-line and stationary in our usual convex arc formation when the radio report came in.

"Truck approaching from ten o'clock!"

Then a flurry of radio banter from second platoon followed. "Black Six . . . this is Blue One. . . . We have a civilian truck headed our way. . . . Advise, over. . . ."

"Blue One . . . this is Black Six. . . . confirm or deny surrender, over."

Through my left vision block I could see it moving toward our column. A brown truck, filled with people, but no white flag. Blue One saw the same.

"Black Six . . . this is Blue One. . . . No surrender, over. . . . I say again . . . no surrender, over!"

"Blue One . . . this is Black Six. . . . Are you taking fire?"

That was the last radio call I heard before gunfire erupted.

My forehead was pressed into the glass vision block, so I could see what was happening. The truck had veered away and headed parallel to our column. Then there was more fire, and bright flashes coming from the side of the truck.

They were firing on us!

I flipped the switch on my helmet to key the radio. "Black Six . . . this is Red Two. . . . Muzzle flashes from the truck. . . . Muzzle flashes from the truck. . . . They're firing on us, over!"

Sgt. Moss called the fire commands like the eight other crews in First and Second platoons.

"Gunner! HE! Truck in the open!"

"Identified!"

"Fire!"

What I should have heard was a burst of thumps from the main gun. Instead I heard *ka-chink . . . ka-chink . . . ka-chink . . .* and then Dougherty yelling, "Fuck!"

A jam!

My eyes were glued to the vision blocks, focused on the truck, and the men inside. Blue One wasn't jammed. Its gun blasted burst after burst into the truck. The first rounds stopped the truck in its tracks, exploding on impact, and blowing the two near passengers out into the sand. The next burst incinerated the truck into a ball of flames and flying shrapnel. The explosion was followed by silence. The two bodies in the sand rolled and writhed for a few moments, maybe by reflex, but I doubt it. More likely it was their last gasps at life, a feeble attempt to escape the rounds that pierced them, the shrapnel that ripped them, and the flames that melted their flesh. Eventually they lay still. It was a horrific end.

My eyes were still fixed on the gruesome scene as our officers rushed to investigate. They combed the area, compared notes, and interviewed crewmen.

It would take hours before they figured out what had happened—hours of sitting, and staring, and reliving the massacre over and over again, hours of flashbacks to the bus ride on our first day in the desert. All the while the words of the song "War Pigs" haunted me:

> *Now in darkness world stops turning*
> *Ashes where the bodies burning*
> *No more war pigs have the power*
> *Hand of God has struck the hour . . .* ©

Eventually Capt. Bounds returned to his vehicle and reported the official findings to us over the radio. The news was unsettling. The occupants wore Iraqi uniforms, and in fact were officers—officers delivering pay and mail to their troops. That was all the truck had been carrying . . . bags of money and mail. They had pistols, but all were in their holsters. And even if they had been stupid enough to fire at a company of armored vehicles with pistols, their guns would not have registered muzzle flashes like I had seen.

That was because what I had seen had not been muzzle flashes. They were rounds ricocheting from the body of the vehicle. Rounds fired *at* the truck . . . not *from* the truck.

In the fog of war some things are left to interpretation. In the case of the mail truck Uncle Sam would exonerate us. That did little to ease my guilt. Maybe no one had heard the report I called in, and maybe there were so many others who saw the flashes that the order to fire was inevitable. But maybe Blue One was undecided, and my call had made the difference. That burden weighed on my conscience, as I sat solemn and still. I've carried it ever since that day, when the fog of war crept in, clouded my judgment, and claimed four lives.

As the call to mount up came across the radio I fired the engines and looked back once more at the smoking truck, and the charred bodies. And as we rolled on toward Kuwait City, I knew there would be more.

The song played on in my head.

> *Day of judgement, God is calling*
> *On their knees the war pigs crawling*
> *Begging mercies for their sins*
> *Satan, laughing, spreads his wings. . . .*

NINE

THEY HID INSIDE BURNED-OUT buildings, behind abandoned vehicles, and even underground, within giant craters carved by our B-52 bombers. They waited until our convoy was close, stopped, and vulnerable. Then they rushed from every direction, yelling, banging, and climbing onto our vehicles.

They were not enemy soldiers. They were children. Children desperate for water, food, attention, and assurance that the bad guys were gone.

We welcomed the rush. As soon as we stopped rolling, our hatches flew open and Marines poured out to assure them the good guys had arrived. As driver I was supposed to remain ready for the call to mount up and resume our road march. But the call to comfort the kids was too much.

"Sgt. Moss, can I go?" I asked.

"I wondered what took you so long to ask," he said. "Go ahead . . . but stay close!"

The children swarmed to get my water, MREs, and sunflower seeds. The tall ones hugged my arms and the short ones clung to my legs. An older boy, maybe ten years old, rescued me from the siege. He organized the children into a group and distributed the water and food. They ripped the packages open and smashed the food into their faces like wild animals. My visit was brief.

"Back inside!" Sgt. Moss called. "Mount up!"

Before I left, the older boy handed me a paper Kuwaiti flag. "Thank you. . . . Thank you, *jundee* (soldier). Come back. . . ."

I told him I would. It was a promise I couldn't keep.

They stood along the side of the road smiling, waving, and cheering as I climbed into the driver's hatch.

"Good luck!" I yelled to them.

My words were lost in the pandemonium that followed as a car broke through our column, headed for the children, still eating, drinking, and frolicking. They scattered just in time as the car raced over the spot where they'd been sitting. Had the car lost control?

No. It was no accident. We watched in horror as the car reversed, then accelerated again, intentionally aiming for the children. The older boy called for them to run for cover, guiding them through a break in the fence and over a guardrail separating the highway from their hiding places. One by one he pushed them through as the car circled around for a third pass. He barely made it through before it rammed the guardrail, the only thing stopping it from crushing him and the others. Then the car pulled back and, surprisingly, double-parked next to our column. Two civilian Arabs, carrying AK-47 rifles, got out and started yelling.

Haley interpreted. "They want our leader. They want to speak with the CO."

The vehicle in front had already deployed its scouts, holding the Arabs at gunpoint until Capt. Cruz arrived.

After a brief exchange, Capt. Cruz shook hands with them, sent them on their way, and called all VCs to his vehicle.

It wasn't what they did or said that earned the handshake. It was who they were. They were Kuwaitis—the *good* guys. The children were Palestinians—the *bad* guys.

Dougherty filled us in on the political implications over the intercom as we drove to our next position. He explained the historical hostility between the Palestinians and other established Arab groups. During peacetime Palestinians were outcasts among the people of Kuwait, second-class citizens who were little better than slave laborers. As retribution many provided aid and comfort to the Iraqi invaders terrorizing the people of Kuwait, and Yassir Arafat had spoken out in favor of Saddam Hussein's invasion. Although we had forced the Iraqi soldiers out of the city, many Palestinians remained behind. The conflict between returning Kuwaitis and traitorous Palestinians made the city a hotbed of civil unrest. And we were rolling right into the middle of it.

4 MARCH 1991

At the sound of rifle fire I woke enough to check my wristwatch. It was only 0300, an hour before my fire-watch shift. Poking my head from our makeshift tent I looked around for trouble. The LAV was thirty meters away. Sgt. Moss was calmly checking with Wells, in the turret on radio watch.

"Any word about those rounds?" he asked.

"Nope. Radios are quiet."

The sound of distant rifle fire was commonplace, so I lay down and began to drift off. Until the sudden snap and pop of rounds grew too close to ignore. Now these rounds were slapping the wall behind our position, and thumping the dirt beside Sgt. Moss's feet. The only time rounds had ever whizzed that close to my head before had been while I was pulling targets on the rifle range at Parris Island.

"Wake up, boys!" Sgt. Moss called. "Those rounds have our names on them!"

Stepping into my boots, I reached over blindly to shake Cpl. Shane awake. He screamed as my index finger jabbed his eye.

"Cpl. Shane! Wake up! We're taking fire!"

Outside the tent the rounds were louder than ever, zinging past my ears, peppering the landscape. Dropping for cover, I surveyed the situation. Most of my gear was inside the LAV—my helmet, flak, and gas mask. Grabbing my rifle, I crawled toward the rear of the LAV. Sgt. Moss opened the rear hatches.

"Let's go!" he wailed. "Mount up! Get the fuck inside!"

That was easier said than done. There was a lot of ground, churning from bullet impacts, between the LAV and me. I took another quick survey. There were steel construction pipes stacked off to my right . . . farther than the LAV, but away from the bullets. Five seconds later I was tucked inside one of the tubes, rifle pointed out, finger on the trigger.

Cpl. Shane ran for the LAV in between bursts of fire, and made it in safely. That made me last. Every time I saw an opportunity to run, though, more rounds would hit. There were no muzzle flashes, troops, or vehicles. Only ricochets zipping all around. My fuse ran short after a few minutes trapped inside the tube.

"Fire those motherfuckers up! How about some fucking cover fire?"

Sgt. Moss was in the back of the LAV. Wells was in the gunner's seat. No one was in the VC seat, or on the pintle-mounted machine gun atop the turret. That infuriated me.

"Wells! Get on the pintle mount!" I called. "Sgt. Moss! Get somebody on the machine gun!"

Wells transferred to the VC position and pulled rounds into the feeder of the machine gun.

"Yeah, Wells! Yeah! Get some! Get some!"

Nothing. Not a single round fired. Not one.

Thinking no one knew how to operate the weapons, I made a mad dash and dived headfirst into the troop compartment of the LAV. My momentum carried me into the steel cage that separated the troop compartment from the turret, gashing my left brow. The adrenaline masked the pain but didn't stop the blood. It ran through my left eye, into my mouth, and down my neck. My sleeve served as a pressure bandage while I got the word from Sgt. Moss.

"Dougherty's on the main gun . . . he doesn't see muzzle flashes. Neither does Wells!"

"Fuck the muzzle flashes! Just start firing! Sweep the whole fucking front!"

That was shit talk and Sgt. Moss knew it, but Dougherty and Wells could hear me shouting in the hull. Moss wasn't taking any chances on botching this one.

"At ease! We're not firing until we see who the fuck is firing at us. Got it?"

More questions from me.

"Who's on the radio? Does Black Six know? And where is Red Four?"

Dougherty had tried repeatedly to raise them on the radio, but they had yet to respond.

Sgt. Moss raised his head through the troop hatch and quickly lowered it.

We were still taking fire.

"Dougherty!" he called. "How about those muzzle flashes?"

"Nothing!"

"How about Red Four?"

"No answer!"

What was going on around us? Our radio signals didn't travel as far in the city, but we had had contact with Red Four all day. Maybe that was it. Shit was going down at their post too. Maybe Red Four was under fire! But they would be on the radio, unless there was no one to call . . . or no radio . . . or no Red Four. Sgt. Moss made a command decision.

"Who's in the driver's seat?"

"Bennett!"

"Fire in the hole, Bennett! Get us to Red Four!"

Dougherty spun the turret back and forth with his finger on the trigger. Sgt. Moss stood in the VC hatch, scanning with his night vision goggles, his finger also ready on the pintle-mount machine gun. Cpl. Shane and Haley stood upright through the rear troop hatches, sighting in with their M16s. An entire city block was one flicker of light from being decimated.

Sitting idly in the darkness of the hull I waited and wondered, a bloody sleeve to my head. After five minutes of bobbing and weaving our way along the dirt mounds that lined the route to Red Four, we finally arrived. Sgt. Moss ordered Cpl. Shane and the scouts to secure the area around Red Four. While the scouts took positions outside, I climbed back into the driver's seat and waited. Through the sight I could tell Red Four's hatches were closed. There was no one outside either. Cpl. Shane gave the all-clear signal and rapped the hull with his rifle butt. Nothing. Then a second rap, and third. Finally the VC hatch opened, and out came Sgt. Krause, groggy.

Rat bastard! He was asleep!

"Sgt. Moss!" I said. "You thinking what I'm thinking?"

He was already on his way to confront Krause.

"Your fucking radios up?" Moss said, angrily.

Krause knew he was caught. "What are you doing here? Why did you leave your post?"

Sgt. Moss stood for a moment, stared at the ground, and shook his head in disbelief.

"I left my post because we were under fire and couldn't identify the shooters! And because I couldn't raise you on the radio . . . couldn't maneuver to take cover . . . and didn't want to take a rocket up the ass! But mostly because I thought you needed us more than we needed you! Why else wouldn't you answer our calls for help?"

Inside the driver's compartment I was cheering. *Let that cocky sonofabitch have it!*

"So again. Radios up, Platoon Sergeant?"

Krause knew he was fucked, but tried to save himself.

"You abandoned your post under fire! Why did you abandon your post under fire?"

"I'm asking the fucking questions," Sgt. Moss replied. "We both know what happened here tonight. Do you really want to point fingers?"

"It's your word against mine! And your word doesn't hold a lot of weight—"

"No," I said stepping forward. "It's your word against ours."

The rest of our crew rallied behind Sgt. Moss.

We waited on full alert at Red Four's position until first light, when Capt. Cruz began his investigation. After several hours of searching, questioning, and consulting with local authorities, the CO returned with his findings. One of the buildings to our front was a Kuwaiti jail, holding Palestinian prisoners of war. Overnight,

Palestinian guerrillas had attempted a rescue, engaging the Kuwaiti police in an intense firefight. According to the report we had simply been in the wrong place at the wrong time—caught in the crossfire.

I balked at the theory. There were too many rounds impacting around us to be accidental. Besides, rounds fired from the police station would have shown muzzle flashes. We'd had three sets of night vision goggles looking for bursts of light.

Sgt. Moss stifled my criticism of the theory, and he was right. Regardless of the origin of fire we had made it through the incident without casualties. Moss reveled as Capt. Cruz offered congratulations.

"No muzzle flashes . . . no comm . . . and under fire," Capt. Cruz said. "I would have gotten the hell out of Dodge too!"

Although Sgt. Moss's after-action report omitted any mention of Sgt. Krause or his crew falling asleep on watch, he reported the incident to Capt. Bounds the next morning. Nothing would come of it in the way of disciplinary action against Sgt. Krause, but Sgt. Moss had expected that.

Sgt. Moss was finally at peace with himself. His decisions had saved a city block from annihilation, prevented countless civilian casualties, and brought the entire crew through safely. Most importantly, though, he rose above Sgt. Krause in performance, integrity, and honor before his fellow Marines. It would carry him valiantly through the last days of the war.

5 MARCH

We returned to our original position after the investigation, with new respect for our circumstances. Although the ground war was over, we were still in danger. Operation Desert Storm had ended, but our post-ground-war mission had just begun. Our LAVs provided the mobility, speed, armor, and firepower to keep the peace during the civil unrest that followed the Iraqi retreat. Our journey home would be seven weeks away.

What we needed was information about our surroundings. Dougherty figured the best way to learn the landscape was from a minaret a thousand meters to our right. The narrow concrete tower was used to broadcast Muslim prayers throughout the community. Five times per day the unintelligible rambling, chanting, and singing blasted. It was the only structure left untouched by allied bombers. Every building around it was destroyed.

After the minaret speakers fell silent, Dougherty and I humped twenty flights to the top. Clear skies provided a panoramic view, ten miles around—it was an awesome perspective. The LAV looked like a matchbox. Delta Company's LAVs were positioned around a semicircular stretch of highway. We covered an entire community from the nine o'clock position to three o'clock, with our LAV at nine. At twelve o'clock a six-foot chain-link fence separated us from the highway. The far side was lined with buildings, including the jail. Our company's position was a sniper's dream, with hundreds of places from which to fire. We were vulnerable to attack from the right and back as well.

There was a construction site that stretched several hundred meters to our right, well past Sgt. Krause's position. That explained the stockpile of steel pipes that had provided cover the night before. Farther behind the pipes was a residential community with several blocks of row homes, but no people. It was a ghost town.

To our left was an industrial plant, which was the only asset within our sector of responsibility that might have been a target for attack besides us. A twelve-foot concrete wall encircled the plant, except for the guard shack at the entrance. Cars traveled in and out of the plant, and people milled about the guard shack. That was the only sign of life in our area, and it was our next stop after the tower.

Sgt. Moss and I teamed for the visit to the guard shack, while Dougherty assumed fire-watch duty. Inside the shack we met a jolly Kuwaiti named Jabul. He identified himself as the manager of the plant, which was a water treatment facility.

"Come in! Come in, my friends. You sit and drink tea," he said.

Sgt. Moss took the lead. "You speak English well."

"Not as well as I want, but I try. Now you sit."

We sat, and drank, and listened to Jabul's broken English. During the first thirty minutes he thanked us, praised us, and prayed for us in the name of Allah. I thought it was overkill, until Jabul started telling stories about life under Iraqi rule. He started with the invasion of the second of August. It was the day we graduated from LAV school, when the CO talked about those atrocities I couldn't relate to, which I hadn't cared about or understood.

"The tanks rolled right down the street. . . ." He stood and pointed to the road in front of us. "Trucks too. Big trucks that hold the men. . . ." He walked outside and pointed to the homes behind our position. "The soldiers come and take them. All the men gone."

"What do you mean, gone?" I asked.

Jabul held his hands up. "Some give up and go into truck." Then he pretended to shoot an imaginary rifle. "Some run and the soldiers shoot them."

"What happened to you, Jabul?" I asked.

"I am old man. . . . They leave me to work. . . . They need water." Jabul pointed to the community in ruins behind our position. "This is where the soldiers stay . . . seven months they stay."

Jabul's tears let us know the worst was yet to come.

"The women they keep. . . ." He pointed again to the houses. "The children they send away. They take all this. They steal it all. The big trucks come back to load, and go back to Iraq. Then they come back for more."

Sgt. Moss was aghast. "Motherfuckers rolled through here like the Third Reich."

Jabul grabbed my arm and pointed onward. "You come. I will show you. . . ."

Sgt. Moss declined for both of us. "We need to stay here. We're protecting you, Jabul!"

Sgt. Moss had no intention of going into the houses behind us. "Way too fucking creepy," he said later. "Not for me."

But Jabul had opened Pandora's box, and the monotony of standing guard, day after day, intensified my curiosity. Eventually I wore Sgt. Moss down and he allowed me to search the houses, as long as I took a rifle and a buddy. Cpl. Shane was as restless as I, and up for the adventure, so in we went.

Sgt. Moss paced nervously as we walked off. "You've got thirty minutes! And if you hear the engine start, get your asses back here!"

We turned into a dead-end alley where the backyards lined each side. The concrete drives were littered with trash, clothes, broken appliances, disabled cars, and broken glass—a ghetto. Most of the windows were shattered, the doors ripped from their hinges.

Then I saw something move. Cpl. Shane looked at me strangely when I tilted my rifle his way to emphasize clicking the safety off.

"Why aren't we talking, Will? You know something I don't?"

My rifle led the way through the back door, finger on the trigger. Beads of sweat rolled down my face. *Don't be a chickenshit*, I thought. *You're a Marine, for Christ's sake.* Once inside, a shadow darted in front of me. Immediately I dropped to one knee, sighted in, and scanned the front.

"What the fuck was that?" I said.

Cpl. Shane was amused. "It was only a dog, Will. Better let me go first before you shoot the whole place up."

Not that it mattered. The place was a pigsty. Food-encrusted plates filled the sink, spilling onto the counters and floor. Flies buzzed, maggots crawled, and mounds of shit steamed on the tile in the sun's rays. The funk forced us into the living room. Beautifully decorated, the walls were outlined with ornamental crown molding and fancy wallpaper borders. A single couch remained against the far wall, contrasting against carpet matted with shit, mud, and blood. On one of the cushions lay the Koran. Cpl. Shane snapped a photo of me holding it.

"Remind me to take this on the way out, for Jabul."

Cpl. Shane disappeared down the hall while I flipped through the pages.

"Hey, Will. Take a look at this."

"Bedroom?"

"No. Rape room."

It didn't sink in right away . . . a mattress on the floor . . . bloody undergarments strewn about . . . lengths of rope for binding hands and feet . . . kerchief gags for muffling screams. It was a nightmare.

"Jesus Christ!"

"Yeah," Cpl. Shane replied. "Savage bastards."

As I walked back toward the living room, a toilet caught my attention. What I wanted was to take a leak, but even the bathroom wasn't what it seemed. Electrical wires from a chandelier ran along the ceiling, with bare ends dangling into the bathtub. Next to the tub was a homemade device fashioned with batteries and wires. And more rope. A torture chamber for electrocution! The pain and suffering the prisoners had endured was sickening.

"Cpl. Shane, let's get back to the LAV. I've seen enough."

But Cpl. Shane was entranced. He detoured into a small room off the kitchen. The washer and dryer showed it had once been a laundry room. The blood splash on the wall, though, showed that it had been used for executions. The walls and floor were sticky with innards—blood and guts and brains. The grisly scene drove me out into the alley gagging on the stench of death, spitting to rid my mouth of the taste, and blowing to lose the smell.

Even the unflappable Cpl. Shane was shaken. "Un-fucking-believable!"

"You got the Koran?"

"Oh, shit . . ." Cpl. Shane stopped in his tracks.

"You going back in?"

"Fuck, no." he said.

That was the first and last time I ventured into the houses. The scenes played as vivid nightmares for many nights after. Jabul's description hadn't done the suffering of those people justice. Nor had the description that the CO had given us on graduation day. The people of Kuwait had endured much more than I could ever imagine. Seven months of torture, rape, and murder. Did anyone back in the States really understand?

No one back home feared tanks rolling down Main Street, blasting holes into the local church, bank, and school. Husbands and fathers and brothers didn't worry about being dragged away from the dinner table to be taken prisoner or shot. Children had no fear of being discarded, locked outside, left to pound windows and claw doors while their mothers and sisters screamed inside. Women did not have to fear the hell of being tied, beaten, and raped to death. Back home parents worked, children played, and life went on.

Thank God they didn't understand.

12 MARCH

After a week of twiddling our thumbs and ducking bullets, we said good-bye to Jabul, leaving him and his plant in the hands of the Kuwaiti police. Their return allowed us to move into desert positions on the outskirts of the city, where the soft sand made it easy to dig holes for cover. Our new positions, however, would provide even greater dangers than the firefights in the city.

We occupied a position in our former battlefield, just outside the city limits. Although the Iraqis were gone, the landscape was still very much alive—and just as deadly. Tanks and mines—bunkers and trenches—grenades and rifles. But we were different. We were no longer afraid. For some the abandoned battlefield was a playground. For others it was a museum. And for the misguided, like me, it was a wasteland of combat trophies. Tanks with all their gear, supplies, and rounds. Bunkers with all their rocket launchers, grenades, mortars, rifles, and uniforms. All free to anyone brave enough, or stupid enough, to go inside and claim their prize.

The desire to get trophies was irrational. Everyone wanted to get his share. Worse yet, there was competition to get the best souvenir. That often meant going into harm's way. But harm's way didn't seem very daunting this time through. There were no Iraqis in the turrets, under the bunkers, or inside the trenches. There was no thunder or lightning. The storm had passed. We thought the cease-fire had granted us immunity from death.

Sgt. Moss had enough sense not to stray far from the vehicle. He wanted an AK-47 to hang in his den as much as the rest of us, but he was disciplined. Not me, though. I walked right out into the minefields, climbed up into the tanks, jumped down into the bunkers, and crawled through the trenches. Many of us did. Our balls were bigger than our brains. Day after day the trophies got bigger, and so did the risks.

Then one night Sgt. Moss called our crew together for the evening brief. "Have a seat, boys. . . . Got some word to pass."

He was more subdued than usual.

"This afternoon a Marine from Bravo Company was killed by a grenade, and another was wounded. Word is they were trophy hunting . . ."

No one spoke.

"They were pulling grenades and ammo belts out of an Iraqi armored vehicle. One of the rounds caught the grenade pin and pulled it out. . . . His flak jacket was open. . . . He didn't have a chance. The CO issued an order to stop all scavenging immediately." Sgt. Moss continued. "All the shit we've been collecting must be turned in—all of it."

We grimaced.

"You have a one-hour immunity to turn in your shit. Then Capt. Bounds and Sgt. Krause are going to inspect."

My desire to collect vanished immediately. Reaching over to my sleeping bag, fastened to the outside of the vehicle, I found the strings that kept it rolled. With one tug the bag opened and all of my trophies dropped to the sand. My most prized possessions lay on top—two AK-47 assault rifles with folding stocks. Beneath was an Iraqi helmet, diary, canteen, shoulder patches, and dozens of coins, round casings, and other trinkets—weeks of hunting, buying, and trading.

Sgt. Moss had no idea I had half of it. Rubbing his hand back and fourth over his head he lamented, "Goddammit, Wee-ams! How's this gonna look?"

"I thought you said we had immunity," I answered.

"I'm pretty sure that doesn't apply to me. Did you forget about Krause?"

Dougherty cut in. "Bury it."

That's it! Bury it!

While the others dumped their stuff onto the pile, Sgt. Moss and I dug the hole. By the time Sgt. Krause made it to our vehicle, we were clean.

"So where is it?"

Sgt. Moss acted aloof. "Where's what?"

"I've seen your boys snooping in the field, Moss. Don't fuck with me."

"I have a look-no-touch policy," Sgt. Moss replied. "There's nothing here that Uncle Sam didn't issue."

Pissing Sgt. Krause off provided some temporary entertainment. The next morning, however, we were buried in depression after attending our first field funeral. Bravo's position was a few miles from ours, an easy hump. Their base camp, like ours, had abandoned tanks, armored vehicles, bunkers, and trenches. One armored vehicle, though, had a group of Marines clustered around it. Odd, I thought, until I realized it was not just a vehicle. It was *the* vehicle where the grenade had exploded, and the Marine died. It looked like so many others that I had crawled through.

We slowed to pay our respects. There were still grenades and belts of ammunition inside. The back hatch was charred black from the blast. Hallowed ground. A few hundred meters ahead Marines formed for the funeral. Along the way I spotted a shiny object in the sand. It looked like a foil wrapper from an MRE, and I nearly dismissed it as trash. Far from trash, it was the mangled ID tag of the dead Marine. I picked it up and found the information was barely readable. The bottom was missing, and the center had a jagged hole punched through. There was just enough tag to make out the last name—EDSAR.

"Sgt. Moss!" I called, showing the tag. "Edsar!"

"No. Couldn't be," he replied.

It was. Edsar, the popular kung fu comedian from LAV school, was dead.

A lone rifle, bayonet fixed, was sunk blade-down into the sand. Atop the butt rested a helmet, a photo of Edsar in the elastic band around its brim. None of us held back our tears. We stood beside the rifle, bowed our heads, and listened to the words of the priest.

He spoke about honor, courage, and commitment . . . Edsar's Marine family . . . his wounded buddy, Frye . . . his family back home . . . and of everlasting peace. Shivers danced along my spine as the trumpet blew the first notes of "Taps."

That day I broke the vow I had made at my brother's funeral not to listen all the way through. It was painful, but I owed Edsar that much. As my body remained in the desert, my mind drifted back to the rainy April morning in 1985, to the memorial garden where I had sat crying before my brother's casket.

But Edsar had been my brother too. Somehow, I thought, Lenny would understand.

PART IV

VETERAN

TEN

SITTING ON THE BLEACHERS of the sandy theater, I indulged like a glutton, shoveling cheeseburgers in and pouring Coke down, my eyes watering from the unfamiliar sting. After eleven weeks in the field, Tent City was a vacation. Especially postwar Tent City, where the mission had switched from ramping up to winding down.

Finally, we were preparing for home. Our training schedule included leisure, recreation, sports, and any other opportunity to be social . . . and human. Parties. Music. Movies. Food. Drink. It felt good to be a spoiled American again.

"So what's playing?" I asked the Marine next to me.

"*Rocky* . . . after the lecture."

"What lecture?"

"You just rotated in, huh?"

"Yeah. . . . What lecture?"

"Battalion sends officers to talk about the move back to the world," he said. "You know . . . counseling shit."

The officer, a salty Vietnam veteran and reservist, soon stood before us, talking about the difficult transition from combat to home.

"You boys are going home to the biggest fucking party you ever saw," he told us. "And you're the guest of honor. The whole god-damned country's wrapped in yellow ribbons."

None of us had realized the magnitude of America's embrace of us as national heroes. Life in the field had insulated us from the news. Homecoming sounded great—the red carpet at the airport . . . welcome home parties . . . parades!

"Enjoy the attention! You deserve it," he continued. "But take your loved ones along for the ride. When the fanfare fades, they'll be all you have left. Don't fuck them over!"

His message was crude, but effective. It was time to begin thinking about Gina and Mom.

"Some strange shit will be going on inside you, Marines. But it won't be so bad if you know it's coming, and you deal with it. . . ."

Strange shit—that was Marine for *feelings*.

"When the homecoming honeymoon is over, you'll probably be mad as hell. . . ."

He talked a lot about the grieving process. Grief wasn't something I had ever done particularly well.

"Don't expect things to be the same when you get back. Then you won't be disappointed. The old lady fucked up the checkbook. . . . The kids'll listen to Mom more than you. . . . Your girlfriend's fucking your best friend. . . . That dick at work got your promotion. . . . And those antiwar professors dropped you from their classes."

He understood Marines, particularly Marine reservists. We weren't just going home for leave. We were going home for good. Back to our wives and children, family and friends, work and school . . . back to our lives. It would be absolute culture shock. The journey back into civilian mode would be just as difficult as the warrior transformation.

The cycle was reversing. The gears were downshifting. The warrior ego was letting go.

20 APRIL 1991

Our stay at Lejeune was much briefer on the back end of the war. With only four days to process off active duty there was barely enough time to get shitfaced and tattooed. By the time the buses rolled in at 0600, though, our seabags were stacked by the roadside, ready to load. Homecoming at Camp Upshur was only hours away. The morning formation was filled with nervous energy as Marines prepared for the long-awaited reunions with their friends and families. On the way to breakfast I had an unexpected reunion of my own.

Mobbing our way toward the chow hall along the corridor of barracks, I noticed groups of active-duty Marines clustered here and there, smoking and joking. There was no longer a noticeable difference between them and us. Our cammys were just as salty, mouths just as filthy, and stories just as grungy. But they knew who we were, and they stared. This was their intersection. Their barracks. Their territory. They were Morrison's rednecks.

Slowing, I wondered what would happen. Would it be an insult? Would they come to finish the fight they'd started five months before?

"Squad! Ahhh . . . tennn . . . huhhh!"

The small group locked their bodies as Morrison about-faced. What were they up to? Continuing on, watching and waiting, we passed with eyes right. Once we were close enough, his right sleeve snapped and his hand popped to his cover, fingers aligned with the brim. A hand salute! They remained locked in their salute as we passed, dead serious in their expression. We kept walking, cautiously waiting for the jeer that never came, the fight that never started. I regretted not stopping, or acknowledging his gesture with anything more than a sideward glance. Morrison would stay in my thoughts through breakfast that day, and during the journey home. Although I hadn't spoken a word to him since boot camp, what he did that day had communicated volumes to me, and made me think about my journey from spare part, beyond, and back again.

24 APRIL 1991

A standing ovation awaited as our buses thumped across the wooden bridge leading into Camp Upshur, more alive than I had ever seen it. There were yellow ribbons. White tents. A band. And the crowd! Windows dropped and heads poked through as Gunny Brandt called for us to keep our military bearing. He was no more successful than Capt. Cruz, who was trying in vain to assemble a formation. As we fell in, the crowd fell out, breaking off into waves, rushing, disbanding us.

The air was full of the smell of women's perfume. Gina's perfume. Then I caught a glimpse of her teary face, her outstretched arms, and felt hair mashing my face. Looking on I saw Mom, wiping her eyes, waiting patiently. I could hug them, but I couldn't speak. The words were lodged, stuck, trapped in my throat. Then the bullhorn sounded.

"Delta Company! Fall in! The sooner we form, the sooner we dismiss!"

Standing in formation, I wondered how I looked. Not like the last time they saw me, for sure. Better? Worse? Heroic and handsome? Or worn and haggard? I aimed for the middle, alive and well.

My face felt like leather—I had crows feet around my eyes, a scar on my eyebrow, and five o'clock shadow plus. I could taste the blood from my chapped lips, and smell the desert lingering in my cammys. It felt odd not having my knife strapped to my leg, my rifle across my back, or my gas mask on my side. As amputees still sense their ghost limbs, I still felt their presence. On my left bootlace my ID tag shone. I considered taking it out, but thought they wouldn't notice—and if they did they wouldn't get it. Inside my sleeve my shoulder burned from the new ink etched into my skin, a Ka-Bar knife with the inscription: SWA DESERT STORM USMC. My tattoo would remain covered, like so many other things, buried until later when, or if, I was ready to share.

25 APRIL 1991

I lay in my bed for the first time since returning home, a total stranger to everything around me, looking up and around, tossing and turning, thinking way too much before sleep. There were trophies on the dresser from my school days, but I couldn't recall when I had earned them, or even the sport. Scattered cassettes lay on the nightstand—music from a lifetime ago. My diploma hung crooked above me on the wall, a reminder of high school and who I had been before the Corps and the war. Those days now played in my head like old black-and-white movies on a television late at night, the fuzzy reception making them barely recognizable.

Flopping onto my side, I saw the picture of Gina on the shelf, giving me hope for better days ahead. But the poster of the Marine, the one with war paint on his face and rifle ready, was the last thing I saw before my eyes closed for the night. . . .

In my dream sandy trenches stretched forward, line after line, as far as I could see. I scrubbed the bolt of my rifle with a small green toothbrush, keeping it lubed, sand free, and ready for the enemy looming on the horizon. In the distance I could see glimpses of them, shadowy silhouettes crawling stealthily toward me, trench by trench. The Marines in the trench with me were strangers, and weren't concerned at all about the advancing enemy. Instead of preparing their weapons and gear they ate, drank, smoked, and even laughed. Growing ever more anxious, I dropped my bolt into the sand, rendering my rifle useless. Still the silhouettes kept coming, closing in on me.

My comrades laughed at my sandy bolt, and my futile attempt to scrub it clean. One stopped laughing long enough to take aim and fire, killing the enemy soldier climbing into our trench. Then he resumed laughing with his buddies. I stood and peeked over the trench. There were silhouettes everywhere. They were coming faster now, and I thought I was ready. My bolt was clean and back inside the receiver.

But my rifle still wouldn't fire. This time the problem was an empty magazine. The magazines in my pockets were all empty, too, though I hadn't fired yet. I asked the Marine next to me for some rounds. He laughed at me. I asked another and another. No one would share their rounds. Running hunched over along the trench, I finally found Dougherty, who gave me one of his magazines.

The enemy was closing in. Waves of them were rushing us, like an incoming tide, swelling from rain, intensifying by the minute. The Marines around me were now standing, locking bodies in their sights, firing and killing and cheering as the bodies dropped into the trenches to our front. Rounds were zipping overhead. Shouts from *us* mixed with cries from *them*.

Taking a knee, I attempted to insert the magazine that Dougherty gave me. After several tries my trembling hands dropped it into the sand, fouling it with earthy grit. That didn't stop the enemy troops from advancing. Realizing that there were too many to kill with rifles, the platoon sergeant began calling for machine guns and grenades. But I hadn't fired a single round . . . killed a single enemy . . . helped in any way at all. So in desperation I jammed the sandy magazine into the rifle, pulled the charging handle, and flipped the selector from "safe" to "burst."

A silhouette popped up only three trenches away, but managed to drop down before I could shoot. The next time he popped up I was ready, but when I squeezed the trigger, nothing happened—a jam. Knowing that this would be my last chance, I removed the magazine, cleared the jammed round, and slammed the magazine back in. When he popped up in my trench that final time, his rifle was pointed at me, and mine at him. The last thing I saw was his finger pulling back and a bright muzzle flash.

I awakened facedown on my floor, half under my bed and soaked in sweat, embarrassed, angry, and afraid. Embarrassed someone might find out . . . angry I couldn't control it . . . afraid it would happen again. Naively, I pulled the poster off the wall, as if it mattered. I had learned not to guess, or predict, or even to try to understand, my dreams.

At night the trenches came whenever the hell they wanted. And I couldn't do a thing about it.

JUNE 1991

Stepping onto the dry rotted door that still lay in the grass outside Second Platoon's barracks took me back in time to my first drill weekend. Twenty-one months had passed since I first smelled the dank air of the Upshur Quonset huts, heard the old wooden bridge rumble, and saw the parking lot fill with cars and laughter and cursing. It was our first drill weekend after returning from the war, and it seemed a lot like that first drill. It shouldn't have, though. After the war I had expected to join the other veterans, and storm around base like seniors on campus. I had expected drill would be a time of nostalgic reflection, and new kids, right out of boot camp and MOS school, would gather reverently to hear our stories. I had expected a welcome, a celebration, and a reunion of the band of brothers.

The barracks was eerily vacant. Sgt. Moss's wall locker door was wide open, a spiderweb inside where surplus gear once bulged its sides. I had hoped he would return, but deep down knew he wouldn't. He never saw himself vindicated through combat the way I did. He had focused instead on his shortcomings, and had opted out when his contract expired. Cpl. Shane had transferred to a grunt unit in Michigan. Bennett and Haley, along with the other Fox scouts, had returned to their unit in New York. Dougherty's locker was open and empty too. He had earned a slot in Officer Candidates School, leaving me as the only returning member of Red Two. My band of brothers was gone.

Nagel earned a medical discharge. Draper transferred to a different unit. Poole simply stopped coming to drill. Even Capt. Bounds moved on, along with Capt. Cruz and Gunny Brandt. Within a few months a quarter of our company disappeared. Some left legitimately, by end of contract or transfer. But many, like Poole, simply quit, abandoning their contracts, and accepting discharge under other than honorable conditions. The only Marine I recognized in First Platoon was Sgt. Krause.

"Normal attrition" was the official spin from our administration. Attrition my ass. Those who left were making personal statements: *I've served my time. One war is enough. I don't care . . . I'm fucking done.* It was a mass exodus.

AUGUST 1991

"Lance Cpl. Williams! Take charge of the platoon and carry out the orders of the day!"

Sgt. Krause headed toward the air conditioned headquarters building where he would spend the remainder of the drill, hobnobbing with the brass, pushing papers, and kissing ass. Not that I wanted him on the Ramp anyway. I preferred to be in charge of the platoon. The orders of the day, as they had been for the last two drills, involved meticulous washing, inventory, and maintenance on the three LAVs assigned to our platoon. But by the time his orders were translated through me to the crewmen, they were quite different.

We went through the motions of hosing the LAVs, a waste of time and water because they hadn't been driven since the last time we washed them. We then buzzed through the preventive maintenance checks and services. While I considered maintenance important, the complete checklist could be completed in a few hours. By lunchtime Saturday all three LAVs were scrubbed and serviced. Sgt. Krause would have stretched the work over two days. As a new crewman, before the war, I tolerated such redundancy. Many days I had sat and rubbed a rag over the same piece of gear for hours until the clock determined we were finished. Those days were over for me, and for the crewmen under me.

During midday Sgt. Krause visited the Ramp to check on our progress, angry to find crewmen running gun drills in the turret.

"Williams! Why aren't the LAVs on the wash ramp? Why isn't the gear laid out for inspection? Where's the discrepancy list? Where are the crewmen?"

"The LAVs are clean. The gear's accounted for. The discrepancy list was turned in to maintenance. The crewmen are in the turrets."

My quick-fire responses sent him over the edge. Sgt. Krause then made it his mission to find a flake of dirt on the undercarriage, or a piece of gear stored in the wrong place, or an omission from the parts order. This to justify making us wash, count, check, service, and list again. Once out of sight, however, we returned to our turrets. During this period of endless Ramp maintenance I made a discovery that changed my time in the reserves—collaboration with the Inspector and Instructor staff.

The I & I staff were the active-duty Marines who ran the base year-round in support of reserve drill weekends. In the reservists' world the I & I staff were all-powerful. On the Ramp the maintenance chief, Sgt. Jackson, reigned supreme. He could fail a vehicle for cleanliness, sending it back to the wash ramp over and over. He could deny us using time-saving tools, like ratchets, in place of the wrenches in the vehicle inventory. He could shut down the solvent tank that cleaned our weapons in seconds, instead issuing brushes and requiring hours of scrubbing.

After cleaning and maintenance I would send groups of Marines to work with the I & I staff. The goodwill paid off in big dividends, especially with Sgt. Jackson. The quicker we passed our inspections, the quicker he could get groups of Marines to work for him. Our inspections never went smoother. The concept spread to other platoons as well. Sgt. Jackson was the first I & I Marine to cross over, leaving behind the us-versus-them mentality that had separated active-duty and reserve Marines at Camp Upshur.

The same collaborative practices that had built bridges between the crewmen and the I & I staff, however, drove a wedge between Sgt. Krause and me. My ideas for improving training were no longer falling on deaf ears. The I & I staff listened to my suggestions, and I developed alliances with the people in power—alliances that were transcending Sgt. Krause's rank and control.

My passion for improving training was too much for Sgt. Krause. No longer the lemming of drills past, I respectfully but assertively challenged his authority whenever it impeded my idea of meaningful training. Moreover, I understood how to gain support for my ideas and turn them into action. Unable to control my rebellion Sgt. Krause did the next best thing; he transferred me into Third Platoon, under Sgt. Fields, a new-join grunt from the fleet.

Fortunately for me Sgt. Fields appreciated my initiative and encouraged me to lead. Unfortunately for Krause, the switch was a catalyst for my promotion. The next time our paths crossed, things would be different.

SEPTEMBER 1991

My first drill with Third Platoon brought a welcome break from the monotony of the Ramp. The weekend was devoted exclusively to qualifying on the rifle range, a monumental event in the Marine world. Rifle scores are part of Marines' permanent records, factored into promotions, and even worn as badges on dress uniforms. While the same significance is placed on rifle qualification in the reserves as the fleet, there is great disparity in preparation. Reservists get one day to snap in and qualify. Fleet Marines get a week or more. And we carried our scores, for better or worse, until our next qualification a year or two later.

Third platoon was assigned duty in the butts to pull targets in the morning, firing in the afternoon. At 0600 the targets went up and the first rounds popped overhead. *Pop! Crack! Zing!* The privates and Pfc.'s next to me lowered the target, pasted the sticker over the bullet hole, flagged the score, and raised the target. They moved effortlessly the way I once had in boot camp, ignoring the rounds just a few feet overhead. I offered little help. They were too busy to notice how I cringed and flinched and ducked when the sounds above matched the nightmare that was playing out in my head.

After six hours of pulling targets it was our turn to shoot, and we climbed from the shadows of the butts to the brightness of the grass above. Active-duty shooting coaches fanned out across the firing lines, issuing rounds, helping us fit our slings and adjust our sights. The layout of the range was exactly the same as I remembered from boot camp. The targets. The distance markers. The rules. And the safety officer's commands.

"Ready on the right. Ready on the left. All ready on the firing line. Shooters commence firing when your dog targets appear."

The torso-shaped silhouette rose above the grassy berm and the rounds from my rifle drilled into the black—all kills. We moved back a hundred yards and fired again. Another volley of rounds in the black. My good fortune carried me through to the last distance marker at five hundred yards. Walking back to the firing line, I realized my shots already qualified me as marksman, but I wanted to rate expert. Making all ten would give me a chance at high shooter. Waiting for the safety officer's commands, I lay on my belly, sighting in on the target.

Suddenly my nightmare resurfaced. I cannot explain why. . . . The wait . . . the pressure . . . the silhouettes . . .

My shooting coach handed me ten rounds to load into my magazine, and I froze, struggling to ignore my nightmare and concentrate. A minute later the loudspeaker jarred me alert, the rounds still in my hand.

"Ready on the right. . . ."

Far from ready, my fingers trembled as I pushed the rounds into the slot in the magazine.

"Ready on the left. . . ."

The rounds were hanging up on the lip, going in crooked, sloppy, and misaligned.

"All ready on the firing line."

I wasn't ready. I was panicked.

"Shooters, you may commence firing when your dog targets appear."

The Marine on my right fired first, and his silhouette dropped. Another popped up and he shot that one down as well. The Marine on my left fired too. The sound of rifle fire altered my perception, like the snap of a hypnotist's fingers, trapping me between the real world and the nightmare world.

No longer in reality, I imagined that my silhouette was closer than the others were. It seemed as if it were closing in—as it did in my nightmare. Thinking rationally now, I beat the magazine against my thigh to align the rounds. But my last slap was too hard, my fingers too shaky, and my magazine dropped to the grass.

Dropping it sent me back into the nightmare. I thought the Marine on my right was looking at me, laughing. As my mind's tricks continued, the silhouette looked closer still. Squinting hard to get a grip on reality, I jammed the magazine back in, pulled the charging handle, and released. It didn't sound right or feel right. It was supposed to clank, not clunk, slam home, not ease in.

The sane half of me keyed in to the safety tower, the call to cease fire drawing near. The other half imagined the silhouettes were closer than ever. So I flipped the safety off and pulled the trigger. Nothing happened.

Leaving reality, yet again, my silhouette was up now, and close. Marines around me were shooting theirs down, keeping theirs away, and laughing at my jammed rifle and me. Frustrated, I pounded my fist into the grass. The jolt shocked me back into reality, and I raised my hand to signal my jam to the shooting coaches. I looked right, but saw no shooting coach. I looked left. None were there either. The sweat rolled through my eyes and my heart pulsed in my trigger finger. I looked right again. Left again. No one was coming to help. Desperate, I left reality altogether.

The silhouette was before me, and this time I was determined to get it before it got me. Now I was not just imagining the nightmare, I was living it. My adrenaline surged, and I decided not to wait any longer. After ejecting the lodged round with my finger I slammed the magazine back in. This time the charging handle sounded right and felt right. I was aware enough to recognize that the others' rifles were quiet, their rounds expended, and their targets down. But I was not aware enough to know that time had expired, so my rifle came alive. One round traveled downrange. Yes! Then the second. I fired again and again and again, until the trigger clicked quietly, and the silhouette finally disappeared.

"Cease fire! Cease fire! All clear on the firing line!"

The range safety NCO ripped my rifle out of my hand while I was still dazed. Several Marines hovered over me.

"What the fuck's your problem, Crazy?"

Still confused, I stayed quiet.

"You can't raise your hand and then continue firing. That's a safety violation."

That shook me. Range safety violators are considered criminal almost.

Escorted from the range in disgrace, I waited for the CO.

"What happened, Lance Corporal?"

The truth was not an option. If he knew what was going on in my head he would have ordered me to get a psychiatric evaluation.

"I didn't know I couldn't change my mind," I said, hoping he'd buy into my excuse. "At first I thought I needed help, but then decided I could clear my own jam."

"Well, that was a costly mistake," he said, shaking his head to show his disappointment. "You'll go unqualified this cycle."

"Unqualified?" I challenged. "But I was qualified going into the last relay."

"Safety violators receive zero scores," he said flatly. "Rules are rules. . . ."

He could tell I was holding back steam and about to blow.

"Go ahead, Marine, let it out. I know it hurts."

He had no idea.

"I'm being punished for clearing my own jam."

He interrupted, "The rules are . . ."

I tuned out, holding my tongue. The CO's presence pissed me off more by the second.

"Just give me my zero and leave me alone . . . sir."

He gave me a patronizing pat on the shoulder, and then debriefed the instructor assigned to my relay.

"These reservists are fucking clueless."

SEPTEMBER 1991

Returning to campus at Towson State University let me know just how different I had become. The conversations of the students seemed much more juvenile and petty than I had remembered. Somehow the unfairness of pop quizzes, the latest fashions, and dating drama no longer seemed significant to me.

Ms. Morse, the physical-education office secretary, was the first to greet me. She walked around her desk and held out her arms for a hug.

"Buuuzzz!" She exclaimed, dragging out my name the way she always had. "Welcome home. How are you?"

"Well," I said, wondering how to answer that, "no one's shooting at me."

Ms. Morse looked shocked, not having expected that response. That "shocked" reaction was what I wanted from people when they asked the cursory *"How are you?"* question. It was important that they hear something from me other than the standard responses, "OK," "Good," or "Fine." People ignored those answers, and since I was still struggling to reintegrate into civilian life after the war, and felt neither OK, good, nor fine, I didn't want to be ignored. That response would become a trademark answer of mine for years to come.

My second encounter on campus happened in Professor Hayes's office, where she pulled my file and reminded me what assignments had been left incomplete when I withdrew the previous fall. Those assignments were barely recognizable to me. Conducting a biomechanical analysis of the placekick was the last thing I wanted to do. Then there was the observation journal, equipment modification, and final exam. Having to make up that work pissed me off. Was she serious? I barely remembered the name of the course, let alone all the textbook mumbo jumbo needed to complete it.

Dr. Hayes understood.

As I was preparing to leave, she gave me a hug and some off-the-record words of encouragement.

"Just focus on the analysis and the journal," she said, waiving the final exam. "I'm sure whatever you turn in will be A work."

Some of the other professors weren't as understanding as Dr. Hayes. The more liberal ones made their antiwar statements by holding me strictly accountable to make up everything I had missed, including exams. The worst was Dr. Leigh, a left-wing professor, with whom I had clashed ever since our first meeting a year before. Her first words to me during class the previous year had been "I don't like soldiers."

To that I had replied, "We should get along just fine, then. I'm a Marine."

She hushed everyone's laughter with a wave of her hand and a sharp retort. "I especially don't like smart-aleck Marines with dumb nicknames."

Since that first class Dr. Leigh had always seemed to find creative ways to denigrate the president, his policies, or the military in my presence. The fact that I had just returned from combat hadn't changed that.

"Withdrawing to play soldier is no different than withdrawing for medical reasons," Dr. Leigh said condescendingly. "Don't expect special treatment from me."

After muddling through my makeup work from the semester I had missed, I was able to begin student teaching. During my assignment at Oliver Beach Elementary School, Mr. DiPasquale, the fifth-grade social studies teacher, asked me if I would be interested in visiting his class to talk about my experiences in the Middle East. Together, we sorted through my artifacts, outlined my experiences, and put together a one-hour presentation titled "Middle East Culture and Customs."

Talking about the war to anyone but children was difficult for me. In front of the students I was perfectly at ease, and never offended by their questions. Their curiosity was innocent and refreshing, and because I was not embarrassed to talk with them, it was liberating. Although we always started the presentation talking about things like Arab dress, religion, and the desert climate, we usually finished with their questions about the realities of war.

"Did you kill anybody?"

"Did you get shot?"

"Did any of your friends die?"

"Was it scary?"

I developed creative answers that skirted the questions about killing and death, like "I didn't ever shoot anyone with a gun," and "No one in my platoon was killed." It was easier to be direct about my personal experience, which provided a much-needed outlet for me to express my feelings. That was something I could only do in front of a classroom.

"It was very scary."

"Being away from home made me sad."

"Sometimes I have bad dreams."

Over the next three years I would travel to dozens of schools across Maryland, Virginia, and Pennsylvania to share my "Middle East Culture and Customs" lesson. Sometimes I was in a classroom with thirty students, and sometimes I was in an auditorium with hundreds of students, parents, and teachers. There was even an occasional speech at a parade or high school graduation. My motivation then wasn't totally selfless. Public speaking, especially to children, became therapeutic for me.

After three years, however, interest in the Gulf War had waned. Students began confusing my war with wars past, and I soon found myself teaching history instead of discussing a relevant current event. In my mind the war was still relevant, and still current.

Each drill weekend I was still trapped inside my wall locker and footlocker, hours before formation, organizing, counting, and arranging my gear. While my compulsions were embarrassing, I couldn't stop myself. Nor could I stop my recurring trench nightmare from resurfacing. The dreams were most common as the drill weekend approached, as my mind was gearing up to enter Marine mode. During one of my worst nightmares I actually attacked Gina while she slept, punching her hard in her back. She played it off, making a joke out of it. It would be two more years until I faced the reality that my postwar anxiety was no joke.

MAY 1992

One of the prerequisites for earning a teaching certificate in Maryland is the completion of a course in special education: As part of the course requirement I was assigned to the Kennedy Krieger Middle School, a private school serving students with learning disabilities, autism, brain injuries, and behavioral disorders. Because they hadn't ever had a trained physical education teacher, I was welcomed enthusiastically by the students and faculty. That summer I was offered a job as the director of physical education for their new campus in East Baltimore. I accepted without realizing that one course in special education had hardly prepared me for the job—especially for teaching the students with behavioral disorders.

Off the record I referred to them as the fuck-you kids because that was their standard response whenever a teacher, or any authority figure, gave them a direction that they didn't like. At the time I hadn't a clue how to teach them. In the months that followed, I made it my business to talk with their social workers, crisis counselors, and teachers, to learn as much as I could about them. What I learned was not in any textbook I had studied while preparing to be a teacher.

Saying "Fuck you," I would learn, was one of the best ways for them to get what they wanted—to get out of work, to get back at a peer, to get some teachers to give them attention, and to send others away. Cursing and threatening, for many of our students, were their only coping strategies for life. In school they lashed out at their peers and teachers. At home they fought with their siblings and parents. On the corners they battled gang bangers, thieves, and junkies. And they wrestled with themselves, too, swimming upstream against the currents of temptation—easy drug money, dreamy highs, and the adrenaline rush of chasing, or being chased.

One of my favorite consultants back then was Dr. Sellers, our staff psychologist. We shared an interest in working with the fuck-you kids, although he used the more professional label "adolescents with conduct disorders."

"Being caring and compassionate is a good start," he said. "But to really break through with them, you've gotta have a hook."

APRIL 1993

Staff Sgt. Jackson parked the LAV right in front of our school, where it would rest as the featured attraction of our school's Spring

Fling Fair. He was happy to get off the base for a day and even happier to meet the pretty, young, single teachers. By noon students were swarming the vehicle, climbing through the hull, sitting in the driver's seat, and even traversing the turret. At one point Tavon, egged on by his buddies, traversed the barrel of the main gun so it followed our principal as he walked. Several teachers called for him to stop, but he didn't. Instead he gave his usual reply, "Fuck you!" as he kept the principal in his sights.

Tavon stopped laughing, though, when he saw Staff Sgt. Jackson sprinting toward him across campus.

"Get down here, son!" barked the staff sergeant, standing like a drill instructor, hands on his hips.

Tavon stopped moving the barrel, but waited for the staff sergeant's next move.

"Boy," he said, looking up to the turret like an angry father, "you've got five seconds to get down here or I'm coming up to drag you out."

To my surprise Tavon yelled out for everyone to hear, "Yes, sir!"

Then he climbed down and spent the remainder of the afternoon clinging to the staff sergeant's side. From time to time I heard him respond, "Sir," and he behaved like a model student until the end of the fair.

In the hallway walking back to class, though, Tavon was back to cursing at teachers, including me when I intervened.

"Why were you so respectful around the staff sergeant?" I asked.

His response would alter the course of my teaching career, and show me the hook I had been looking for.

"Because he's a Marine," he said, as if I didn't know. "That's what you're supposed to say to Marines."

Until then I had never considered mixing the Marine part of me with the teacher part of me. Most people in the school didn't even know I was a Marine. That is, not until I showed up for work the next morning wearing my dress blue uniform.

As I entered Tavon's classroom all eyes were on me.

Tavon decided to test me. "Look at Mr. Buzz, trying to look hard, yo."

Ignoring his comments, I launched into a brief speech about how physical education class was going to be conducted for the remainder of the year.

"Physical education as you know it is over," I commanded, using my most serious voice. "Starting today, you will have a choice of which type of class to attend."

Our students liked choices, and I had their attention. On the floor before them I laid a camouflage uniform, complete with cover, belt, and boots.

"Each of you will have the chance to earn this uniform," I continued, "if you choose to attend my boot camp."

Tavon spoke up again. "And what if we don't?"

"The other choice is ditto work in your classroom," I explained. "Ms. Veselich has been kind enough to give up her planning period for you."

As I turned to walk away, Tavon realized I was for real. "You givin' out uniforms, though, right?"

"I'm not giving away anything, Tavon," I said, fighting back the urge to smile. "If you want the uniform, then you'll have to earn it."

Tavon's sidekick, Rodell, looked at him curiously. "You goin'?"

"When you come to boot camp, Tavon," I said, not waiting for his response, "have the others stand on the yellow footprints in the hall outside the gym doors."

For the remainder of the school year every student in Tavon's class, the most challenging students in the school, chose to attend my boot camp. For ten weeks they marched, exercised, and memorized basic Marine Corps facts and the rank structure. They spent a lot of time digging on my quarterdeck, and with the brim of my cover against their noses, and they loved every minute of it. No one quit, was referred out of class, or was even close to a discipline problem (at least in my class). The program took the school by storm, and soon the gym was flooded with teachers, social workers, and psychologists—all trying to figure out why boot camp was working.

The teachers talked about the developmental progression of learning. The social workers attributed the success to the group process, and bonding. The psychologists saw it as a behavioral model based on a unique marriage of positive reinforcement and punishment.

One thing everyone agreed about, though, was that *it* worked—and that the school needed more of it, whatever *it* was. It would take me years to figure that out.

APRIL 1993

The word was the postwar budget was tight, which is why it took us ten drills to get our LAVs onto the firing range. It was about time. Our ATD was scheduled for July, and we had little time with the LAVs to prepare. As the only LAV veteran in the platoon I was appointed Sgt. Fields's gunner and would be tasked with platoon gunnery training. Teaching others was exactly what I wanted to do, so the drill promised to be one of the best since our return from the Gulf.

Things didn't turn out quite like I planned.

Friday night we prepped the vehicles and mounted up for the hour-long trip to the range. Once off road, Capt. Downes, our new company commander, ordered all vehicle lights off. Driving under blackout conditions, with night sights, was important for drivers. Knowing it was necessary didn't make it any easier for me to cope. It was the first time I had been in a LAV, at night, without being the driver . . . without being in control. Standing on the gunner's seat, exposed from the waist up, I strained my eyes forward. The dirt road was a patchwork of craters and mounds, pitching the LAV from side to side. Each tilt sent me down inside the turret, holding on for life, sure that we were rolling over.

"What're you doing, Williams?"

Sgt. Fields didn't know and I wasn't telling. There were a thousand excuses. My comm was down . . . my sights needed adjustment . . . my foot slipped . . . everything but the truth. Inside the turret my legs were locked under my seat, hands gripping anything solid to keep me in place. Scared out of my mind, and embarrassed, I wanted more than anything to tell the driver to turn on the headlights. Another pitch to the side. Another drop inside . . . legs locked . . . death grip. Finally, we arrived. The darkness hid my ashen face, trembling hands, and sweat-soaked uniform. Boots on dirt never felt better.

The early morning light showed all nine LAVs on the firing line atop the ridge, barrels extending over the canyon below; thousands of meters of open space littered with an assortment of trucks, armored vehicles, and tanks. Behind the LAVs was a mountain of ammunition boxes. The ammunition should have been expended before lunch on Saturday under normal firing conditions.

But our day on the range was anything but normal. Few of the guns were operational, none of the crews were proficient, and worst of all there was no firing plan. The only central authority on the range was the safety officer, tasked with ensuring rules were followed. The rules on the LAV range were as asinine as those at the rifle range. Once a LAV gun jammed, it remained on the firing line. Firing continued if the crew cleared the jam. Most of the time the crews required veteran gunners to come aboard and fix their malfunctions. Range rules required a cease-fire for Marines to enter and exit vehicles on the firing line. No sooner than one jam was cleared, another weapon would lock, and firing would cease again.

By lunch there was barely a dent in the mountain of ammunition, and the officers were anxious. We were only authorized to use the range until 2100 hours. Furthermore, the rounds had to be expended before the range closed because ordnance policy required all issued rounds be fired, not returned. Given our current rate of fire that was improbable.

As the clock ticked, the range safety officer relaxed the policy of shutting down the firing line every time a gun jammed. Instead, a brief cease-fire was called until the "down vehicle" moved to the end of the firing line, where Marines could enter and exit safely. By sunset all but one LAV was down. With more than a thousand rounds left the CO decided to use the lone LAV to simply blow rounds downrange. Sgt. Krause and Cpl. Ryder sat in the turret. I remained in the back of the hull, linking rounds and feeding them forward into the ready box. The main gun was able to fire two hundred rounds per minute when operated by a well-trained crew.

Dozens of Marines lay in the shadows along the wood line, eating and drinking, smoking and joking, watching and waiting . . .
some even sleeping. I didn't blame them. Some of them were officers, but not LAV officers. Few, if any, knew how to start the engine,
let alone operate the main gun. There were sergeants and staff sergeants among them too. But even the well intentioned offered little
help with the complexities of LAV gunnery. The majority lying in
the shadows were new-joins, sucked into the Corps by the glory of
Desert Storm hype. At twenty-five years old I already felt like an old
man compared to those starry-eyed kids. For them this was just
drill . . . reserve training at its best.

Sitting, exhausted and angry, amid the pile of empty ammo
boxes, I sorted through my thoughts and feelings. I was again growing to hate being a reservist. Most of my time now was spent on the
Ramp, washing hulls already cleaned, checking fluids already filled,
and counting the same parts over and over again. The few times we
had left the Ramp were disasters for me. Hallucinations on the rifle
range . . . panic attacks in the vehicle . . . and now even gunnery
was a joke.

What we needed were Marines like Capt. Ricks at Lejeune or
Staff Sgt. Rodriguez in Saudi. We needed Marines who had complete mastery of their field; leaders to mold the new kids; instructors
to teach them what they need to know when they're called to war.

I was reaching another crossroads. I couldn't imagine another
deployment with reserve-business-as-usual. More than half the veterans from the Gulf had already bailed for that reason. The alternative was to find the leaders and teachers we needed. My search
started as soon as we returned to Upshur that Sunday morning.

Capt. Downes understood our needs. He had served with us as
the TOW Platoon commander during the Gulf War, and replaced
Capt. Cruz when his tour ended. Capt. Downes deserved the promotion. He understood reservists and, more importantly LAVs.
Like Capt. Cruz he believed in realistic training in the field. The
problem was there weren't enough skilled Marines in the line platoons. Capt. Downes agreed with my concerns about training–
particularly gunnery training. He explained his vision for future

training, which involved a reserve master gunner that paralleled the
I & I master gunner. I didn't even know there was an I & I master
gunner.

I made it my business to meet him.

Later that day I stood outside Staff Sgt. Nicholson's door. It was
my first time in the training office, usually off limits to reservists. I &
I Marines didn't mix with reservists, a tribal dynamic I never fully
understood. My education began with the knock.

"What."

I stepped through the hatch and faced his desk, "Good morning,
Staff Sergeant."

Looking up from a pile of papers, he called, "What!"

"I'm Lance Corporal Williams. I want to be considered for the
reserve master gunner position."

"The reserve what? Master gunner?"

"The CO told me we were starting a new position called reserve
master gunner . . . someone to learn under you . . . and teach the reservists gunnery."

He hadn't heard about it. "Who told you this?"

"Capt. Downes."

He leaned back in his chair, hands behind his head, feet on the
desk. "Oh. That explains it. He's your CO, not mine. Until my CO
tells me otherwise, there ain't no such beast as a reserve master
gunner."

Appalled by his arrogance, I stepped up to his desk. "If you're responsible for our gunnery, then you should know about the cluster-
fuck on the range yesterday."

Now I had his attention.

"Most of the *gunners* don't know how to assemble the main gun,
time it, or install the chutes." I continued, "Few know which end of
the ammo belt to feed into the chutes, how to crank the rounds into
the receiver, or how to cycle the ghost round. And after they make
their best guesses the gun probably won't fire . . . and if it does it'll
jam . . . and only a couple of us know how to unfuck it once it does."

Staff Sgt. Nicholson was unimpressed. "I'm busy now, Williams.
Come back tomorrow and we can talk." Then came the conde-

scending sarcasm I had come to expect from I & I Marines. "Oh . . .
I forgot. You'll be off until next month. Too bad . . . I have the whole
day open."

His laugh was the last thing I heard on my way out.

My knock was the first thing he heard when he arrived for work
Monday morning. The three-hour drive was worth the look on his
face when I walked into his office.

"Still have the whole day open, Staff Sergeant?"

He laughed and shook his head in disbelief. "What the fuck are
you doing here?"

"I have an appointment with you to talk about the reserve master
gunner billet, remember?"

Staff Sgt. Nicholson, like Sgt. Jackson in maintenance, was more
bark than bite. He kept his word and spent the whole morning with
me, showing me his job as company master gunner. He knew gunnery, bragging he was the best gunner in the Corps. Serving with
2nd LAI, his was the active-duty company that deployed from
Lejeune just before we had arrived before the war. We spent hours
swapping stories. In between I learned about the gunnery curriculum, competency tests, qualification standards, and training aids.
Everything we needed. I also got an inside look at the mountain of
paperwork that kept Staff Sgt. Nicholson behind his desk, instead of
in the field where we needed him.

Staff Sgt. Nicholson introduced me to his CO and we talked
about the reserve master gunner idea. A reserve Marine was to be
trained as master gunner at Twentynine Palms during the July
ATD. It came as no surprise to me that Sgt. Krause had arranged for
his gunner, Cpl. Ryder, to get the job. Cpl. Ryder was a shit-hot gunner, and a veteran, but he was planning on getting out after ATD.
The news wasn't hard to spin in my favor.

"Train me and Cpl. Ryder during ATD . . . I'm his replacement."

Staff Sgt. Nicholson laughed, "Says who?"

"Says me. I'm the second-best gunner in the Corps."

Staff Sgt. Nicholson had clout. During Friday formation next
drill, Sgt. Fields congratulated me on my promotion to master gunner, along with Cpl. Ryder, and transferred me into Headquarters

Platoon. The surprised look on Sgt. Krause's face that day was priceless.

JULY 1993

The days leading up to the July ATD were particularly stressful. Gina and I were married 20 June, which gave us only a few days to honeymoon before my departure for two weeks of active duty in Twentynine Palms, California. Although Gina was understanding about my Marine obligation, as she had been since we met, I was becoming increasingly annoyed by it. Not even my wedding or my honeymoon could take my mind completely away from the anxiety I felt about going back into the desert, which in my mind would be reliving my combat experience. That was the kind of interference with my life that kept me on the verge of joining the exodus.

On the verge, that is, until I started working with Staff Sgt. Nicholson.

Staff Sgt. Nicholson was the reason I didn't quit the reserves. He was the real deal in gunnery—hard core. Finally, I had found a mentor who was willing and able to help me realize my potential as a Marine. Under his supervision I would become the Marine I had always wanted to be—a trusted and respected leader, capable of making a difference in the company's combat readiness.

Once in the desert of Twentynine Palms, Cpl. Ryder and I stayed glued to Staff Sgt. Nicholson's side. We were segregated from the line platoons, and worked as a three-man team immersed in the world of gunnery. Without the constraints of safety rules and bureaucratic regulations, the staff sergeant was able to teach us the way he had learned in the fleet—rugged . . . raw . . . and rogue.

Cpl. Ryder and I waited impatiently for our first day of firing with the staff sergeant. He opened the rear hatches of the LAV, the hull filled with ammo boxes, and smiled.

"Go for it, boys, let's see what you can do!"

Cpl. Ryder and I looked at each other stupidly, then back at the staff sergeant.

"Go ahead. We got the range all day."

Not since the Gulf had we been presented with boxes of ammo and the order to make our guns ready. Back then we winged it, never really knowing if what we were doing was correct, praying the gun would fire every time we pulled the trigger.

Staff Sgt. Nicholson stayed silent while we opened the ammo boxes and fed the belts into the ready box. He stayed silent while we failed to boresight the barrel, forgot to calibrate the sights, misconnected the links, neglected to check for grease, and skipped timing the receiver.

Nothing escaped him, though. He had a plan.

Cpl. Ryder took the driver's position and fired the engines while I powered up the turret and cycled the ghost round.

Staff Sgt. Nicholson dropped into the VC seat and called over the intercom. "You good to go?"

"Check!"

"Identify targets on your own and fire at will."

"Aye-Aye . . . On the way!"

The only thing on the way, however, was the misfire from hell. *Fucking great! A jam.*

"Piece of shit gun!" I said.

Staff Sgt. Nicholson called for Cpl. Ryder to shut off the engines and motioned me to the back of the LAV. Then he welcomed me to fleet-style training, slapping my helmet from my head.

"Don't you ever talk shit about that weapon system!"

Shocked and embarrassed, I looked to Cpl. Ryder for support, his eyes as big as mine. The staff sergeant continued.

"The only thing wrong with that weapon is you! That's how you prep for fire? And you two shit birds are the best in the company. No fucking wonder we can't get rounds downrange!"

Too late to maintain composure, I acquiesced. "I'm not sure what you want me to do."

"Climb up there and unfuck that gun!"

Cpl. Ryder joined me in the turret. Within minutes our uniforms were sweat soaked, and knuckles bloody. We tried every trick we knew to disassemble the gun, but nothing worked. After a half hour the staff sergeant took pity on us.

Looking down into the turret from above he called in, "There wasn't any grease on the bolt track. I dried it early this morning."

Like an engine operated without oil the gun's components were locked up.

Embarrassed again, I looked up through the hatch and confessed. "I don't know what to do."

The remedy was not pretty. It was downright dangerous. But I went along with it, rationalizing it as deserved punishment. Cpl. Ryder and I lifted the entire weapon out of the vehicle, without taking it apart, and laid it on the tarp to protect it from the sand. Who knew it could even be done? Then I inserted the long steel rod backward into the barrel until it stopped. Staff Sgt. Nicholson made the diagnosis by the length of rod left over.

"You got a round stuck in the barrel. Otherwise the rod would slide in up to this point."

Then came the crazy part.

"Use the sledgehammer to drive the rod down the barrel," he said. "It'll push the round backward until the receiver can grab it."

I was skeptical. "How do we know we're not driving the round back into the firing pin?"

"We don't. You should have thought about that before you fired my weapon dry."

He wasn't bullshitting, and took cover behind the vehicle while I pounded the high explosive round backward. With every strike I ducked, expecting the rod to blast outward. After several blows the round was back in the receiver and I hand-cranked it out. It was character-building experience, and a lesson I'd never forget.

"How'd you learn that, Staff Sergeant?"

He pulled my cover over my eyes in a fatherly manner, "Same way you did. . . . Nicely done."

That's the way Staff Sgt. Nicholson taught us everything about the gun. With each passing day our repertoire grew, along with our confidence. We became ammunition specialists, prepping and aligning rounds as they moved from crate to ready box. We learned to use prefire checklists, the way pilots did, to make the weapon ready. In addition to gun-specific training we became turret mechanics, optics techs, communications specialists, machinists, and electricians. We learned how to override sensors and jury-rig switches. We cleared jams by daylight and flashlight, at rest and on the move, from the gunner's seat and VC's seat. For the first time we understood how to align the sights with the main gun barrel and the machine-gun barrel. All this before firing a single round.

Once the firing started, we learned a whole new set of skills. No longer was success measured by simply getting rounds downrange; we had to hit targets . . . all sorts of targets. Armored vehicles with AP rounds. Trucks with HE rounds. Troops with the machine gun. We fired while stationary, moving forward and backward, accelerating and decelerating, at slow speeds and high. We fired under the cover of tank ditches and berms and through the concealment of smoke. And we destroyed everything in our sights. Cpl. Ryder and I became born-again gunners.

There were many more mistakes, slaps to the helmet, kicks in the ass, and hard lessons learned in the desert that summer. The hard work paid off at the end of ATD, back at Upshur, during the final formation. Capt. Downes promoted me to corporal and Staff Sgt. Nicholson presented me with a certificate of commendation for duty as the company master gunner. After the ceremony Staff Sgt. McGraw, the new Headquarters platoon sergeant, introduced me to Major Celeste, soon to be our new CO. It was my first salute and handshake with a major.

"Good afternoon, sir."

"Congratulations, Cpl. Williams . . . Master Gunner."

"Thank you, sir. If you ever want an orientation to the LAV, I'm your man."

Staff Sgt. Nicholson smiled at my confidence. "You know, sir, in the fleet the master gunner is always the CO's gunner."

Major Celeste concurred. "That sounds like a good policy to me. How about you, Williams?"

"A damned good policy, sir."

AUGUST 1993

The platoon sergeants and commanders looked at me strangely when I entered the boardroom for my first predrill meeting. It had taken me three years, but I had finally made it to the central command where decisions are made that trickle down into the barracks, Ramp, classrooms, and ranges. At last I would see behind the curtain and get the unfiltered scoop.

Major Celeste stood when I entered, greeting me with a handshake and personal escort to my seat.

"Everyone, please welcome Cpl. Williams, our new master gunner."

Sgt. Krause looked at me particularly hard, and I smiled back, placing my notes in front. Staff Sgt. McGraw, our new company gunny, walked over and shook my hand. Although in the fleet for eight years he looked no older than I, and showed me respect I had never experienced from a staff NCO.

"I'll expect a personal gunnery lesson, Cpl. Williams," he said, "when you have time."

Major Celeste gave each Marine the chance to react to the training schedule for the drill—rotate platoons through admin for record book checks . . . supply for new issue . . . medical for weigh-ins . . . the big classroom for MCI classes . . . everything but crewmen training . . . nothing about gunnery.

My reaction turned heads.

"Well, sir. This is a great training schedule for a headquarters company . . . but we're a light armored infantry company."

All eyes and ears were on me.

"Vehicle maintenance is listed as the default activity in between all our admin responsibilities . . . and gunnery training isn't listed at all."

The room hummed from sidebar whispers.

"Honestly, sir, I feel our priorities are ass-backward. . . ."

Sgt. Krause pushed himself away from the table, offended.

"Sir, we all agreed to the training schedule last month," he said. "It's fine the way it is."

Major Celeste looked Krause in the eye. "I believe the master gunner has the floor, Sgt. Krause."

Taking full advantage, I stood up and addressed the group.

"I need each platoon sergeant to identify their best gunners, and free them to work with me . . . they'll be our platoon-level master gunners."

Again Krause resisted, talking around me to the major. "Sir, we have a maintenance stand-down this drill. . . . We need every body on the Ramp."

"Not true, sir," Staff Sgt. Jackson clarified. "Williams and I worked out a system. All we need is three Marines per vehicle for four hours."

Again Sgt. Krause protested. "I don't have three crewmen per vehicle—"

"Sir, the plan requires three Marines, not three crewmen," I said, interrupting Krause. "Sgt. Krause separates scouts and crewmen for training."

"Sir, I won't have a corporal telling me how to run my platoon!"

Major Celeste looked to Staff Sgt. Nicholson. "How do you weigh in here, Staff Sergeant?"

"Master Gunner is a company-level billet, sir. . . . If it involves gunnery training, it's his job to tell the platoon sergeants how to run the platoon."

"Seems to me if platoon sergeants were running their platoons right, Sgt. Krause, we wouldn't need Williams," Major Celeste concluded.

That silenced Krause for the remainder of the meeting.

That meeting was the beginning of the end for Sgt. Krause. When his contract ended he declined reenlistment, no doubt partly because of me. Although I seldom agreed with Sgt. Krause, part of me missed him after he left. He was the last remnant of the original tribe—of the veterans. His departure marked the end of an era.

During the next two years Major Celeste and Staff Sgt. McGraw empowered me more and more as company master gunner. Working closely with the I & I staff, I made dramatic revisions to the policies regarding vehicle maintenance and gunnery. On the wash ramp, fire hoses replaced garden hoses. In the maintenance bay, crewmen and scouts worked side by side with the I & I mechanics to check and service the vehicles. Platoon master gunners received the same intensive training from me that I had received from Staff Sgt. Nicholson. They in turn trained the gunners under their charge.

At any given time, whether on the Ramp or in the field, gun crews trained, drilled, and tested to increase proficiency. Major Celeste spread our allotment of rounds for the year over several drills, allowing us more time on the ranges, focusing more on quality of skill demonstrated than quantity of rounds expended. Seldom did our guns go down for malfunctions, but when they did I had my head in the turret, identifying the deficiency and correcting it with training. When all the gunners and vehicle commanders were qualified, we trained drivers . . . then scouts . . . then mechanics, corpsmen, and even admin pogues. Sometimes I patted backs and sometimes I slapped helmets off heads, but everyone in the company knew what I was about and they respected me for it. All I ever wanted to do was to improve training, improve instruction, and hopefully improve the next generation's chances of victory and survival in the next war.

Things were never better for me as a man or Marine than during my last year with the unit. The awards, plaques, and commendations came monthly. I was happily married to Gina, up for promotion to sergeant, and at the top of my game as master gunner. No one was more surprised than Major Celeste, a lifer in the Corps, to learn I wasn't reenlisting.

We had shared many days and nights in the turret as VC and gunner, talking about God, Country, and Corps. Two years' worth. By my last drill, June of 1995, I was as close to Major Celeste as I had been to Sgt. Moss or Dougherty way back when. Our last conversation was memorable. A handshake. A hug. A salute. One last chance to reconsider. And the litany of reasons why I couldn't—to start a family with Gina . . . begin graduate school . . . add an extra weekend each month to my life. They were easy and light and true, although very much incomplete.

There were others—difficult and heavy . . . and unfortunately true. They were buried in a place, deep within, where I seldom went. Ashamed and embarrassed, I omitted any talk of compulsive rituals, flashbacks, and nightmares. He never saw me labor over my footlocker, cringe on the rifle range, fight my demons in the trenches, or lock my legs under the seat. Occasionally, though, he would catch me, unresponsive and staring, lost in that other world of sand and sweat, smoke and fire, fear and death. Those things, I thought, at least for the time, were better left unsaid.

EPILOGUE

It had been five years since my last nightmare, and even longer since I last looked at my Gulf War photo album, or rummaged through my seabags in the basement. After all that time I had finally managed to put my combat demons to rest. Until the around-the-clock media coverage during the buildup to Operation Iraqi Freedom woke them again, and my nightmares returned with a vengeance. Sometimes they were about the trench, while others were mixtures of my personal combat experiences and the battlefield coverage I was viewing on television.

Choosing not to watch, listen, or read the news was not an option for me. Breaking bulletins interrupted, preempted, or crawled across prime-time television shows. The radio, which once had helped me unwind during my hour-long commute, was now saturated with war hype and wound me tighter than ever. At work armchair generals would visit me in the office waving the daily newspaper, pointing, and asking things like:

"Did you see the latest?"

"Can you believe it?"

"What do you think about this?"

My reputation as a proud Marine kept me from answering honestly:

"No, I don't want to see the latest."

"No, I don't want to believe it."

"I try *not* to think about *that.*"

In January 2003 my war-related anxiety was building momentum. There were periods in which I would stay awake for days. When I did sleep, it would only be for three or four hours at a time, leaving me tired and depressed. I arrived at work late, left early, and in between spent little time thinking about anything but war—not the best circumstances for the principal of a high school.

My first bout with posttraumatic stress had lasted from 1991 through 1998, complicated and slowed by my ignorance, embarrassment, and denial. Back then I didn't understand my experiences in the Marines and the Gulf War, or their effect on me—at least not the way I did now. Now, I didn't know what to expect.

Following the Gulf War I had resisted reintegrating back into civilian mode after my drill weekends. During the twenty-eight days of the month when I wasn't drilling, I remained locked in the Marine mindset. While many reservists allowed their hair to grow as long as possible during the month between drills, I maintained my regulation buzz cut, abiding by the rigid standards of grooming and dress that the Marine Corps requires.

I was proud to be a Marine. Most everything I owned had the Marine logo ironed, embroidered, stuck, taped, or tattooed onto it. While running I listened to audiocassettes of drill instructors singing cadence. My alarm clock was programmed to wake me with the sound of a bugle blasting reveille. Dinnertime was called "chow time," going to bed was "hitting the rack," and *ooh rah* was a part of my everyday vocabulary.

Gina was often amused by uncanny ability to identify strangers as present or former Marines. I'd approach them at the mall, movie theater, or supermarket, and strike up a conversation about Parris Island, Lejeune, their war, or mine. Our talk would usually last longer than Gina could tolerate, and she'd politely pry us apart by saying something like "OK, boys, wrap it up. . . . We have to be going now." She thought it odd how complete strangers could have anything to talk about. But there are no strangers among former

Marines. Those chance meetings, for me, were like reunions with long lost brothers.

Publicly, it is easy to filter out the best parts of being a Marine and show them to the world—the sense of honor, pride, and camaraderie. But there is another side of being a Marine—the side that knows the ugliness of war—and with it comes fear, rage, agony, and sorrow. I once believed it possible to ignore these feelings, which left them just beneath the surface of my consciousness, a loaded gun ready to fire flashbacks and nightmares without warning. Many triggers had awaited me in the days, weeks, months, and years that followed my return from Kuwait.

The first month I was back, I found myself standing on Gina's front porch in Baltimore, with a front-row seat to the Fourth of July fireworks downtown as family and friends cheered the flashes and booms. I silently cursed those fireworks, because the rockets' red glare looked like those I had seen in my sights just weeks before, and the bombs bursting in air made me want to take cover. The Fourth of July has since become one of my least favorite holidays— now I go to bed after tucking in the kids, and hope to fall asleep before the sun sets and the first fuse is lit.

After that Fourth of July our annual family vacation in Ocean City, Maryland, became the next trigger. My first step onto the beach—with sand shifting beneath my shoes, a blinding reflection from the sun, and the heat radiating upward—took my mind back into the desert. I recall Gina's cousins, who were only children at the time, innocently asking me to dig holes in the sand so they could play soldier. Instead I chose to focus on reading a book, which would become my strategy for coping with the beach for several years to come.

My visits to the world of combat are never more real than when I watch war movies. Gina has seen how deeply those movies affect me, and she asks why I put myself through it. What I tell her is that I want to see if Hollywood got the details right, or that I am interested in the historical significance, or some other half-truth. The reality is that there is a part of me that needs to get back in touch with the raw emotion that those movies bring out. It's as if my anxiety about the war builds inside over time, like a volcano filling with pressure. I have spent many nights alone in my family room, after Gina and the kids are in bed, watching war movies and crying openly as the volcano within me erupts.

My choice to leave the Marine Corps Reserves had not been an easy decision. The pressure to reenlist is anything but subtle. Senior Marines put guilt trips on me, saying that I was fucking the company over, letting them down, and setting a bad example for the younger Marines. Then there was the formal "counseling" from the career planners, who first tried the retirement angle, and then the promotion angle, and when neither worked, they, too, resorted to browbeating me like the other jarhead lifers.

While emptying my wall locker and footlocker for the last time, I had felt the emotions welling up inside me, which I had held back only because other Marines were in the squad bay. Before leaving I walked the camp nostalgically, making one last visit to the big classroom, the headquarters boardroom, and the Ramp. The LAVs rested quietly there, beneath their thick green canvas tarps, like sleeping beasts, waiting to be awakened next drill. Driving across the Upshur bridge for the last time, my mind weighed heavily with relief and regret.

I hadn't been sure then that leaving the Marines was the right decision. It was a relief to live without the burden of monthly drills. But I regretted leaving the Corps before putting the war behind me. I had thought that each drill that passed helped redefine me as a Marine. I had counted on my promotions in rank and responsibility to distance me from the war and ease my anxiety problems. It had never dawned on me that drilling each month *was* my problem. That realization, like many others, would only come in time.

At school the lines between my identity as a teacher and Marine were blurred. After two years of running the boot camp program as an alternative physical education class for the students with conduct disorders (the fuck-you kids), it had evolved into a Young Marines program—the official youth program of the United States Marine Corps.

By 1995 my civilian role as commanding officer of the Young Marines program had surpassed that of physical education teacher, giving me reason to wear my Marine uniform to school more often than my gym shorts. I supervised daily routines, like raising and lowering the flag, taught military science classes, ran social-skills counseling groups, coordinated weekly community service field trips, and led outdoor adventure trips in which we climbed rocks and rappelled down cliffs. Young Marines was the most popular extracurricular activity in the school—and the most effective means of touching those students who were hard to reach.

In September of 1995 I enrolled in the master's program in school counseling at Johns Hopkins University. The counselors at Kennedy Krieger, who'd gone through the program, told me a few things to get me started: which professors to take and which to avoid, the major counseling theories, and the pioneers in the field. But they forgot to mention an important requirement for becoming a therapist.

Dr. Miller was the first to break the news to me, as we were all sitting in a circle facing each other on the first day of class. "The first thing to know about group therapy is what it feels like to be *in* group therapy," he told us.

The group therapy class opened my eyes to many parts of myself that I hadn't understood in the past, especially the recurring trench nightmare. Dr. Miller encouraged me to talk about feeling unprepared, incompetent, and powerless during the war—the themes he believed were fueling my nightmares. These feelings were difficult to admit, even to myself, but by the end of the semester my conscience was purged. Dr. Miller's theory was that such intense feelings needed to come out one way or another—consciously through talking about them or unconsciously by dreaming about them. Dr. Miller was right. After the course my nightmares slowed, and eventually stopped.

The diagnosis course was another eye-opening experience for

me. This semester was the first time I had heard the acronym OCD (Obsessive Compulsive Disorder). Obsessions, I would learn, are repeated *thoughts*—and include the irrational need to have things in order. Compulsions are repeated *behaviors*, and also include the act of repeatedly organizing and ordering objects. Reading about OCD behavior was like reading about myself, and it made me want to learn more about the condition. After class I talked with Dr. Miller about my bizarre behavior in the Corps—the mortar rounds that had to be stacked, the endless Scud drills in Tent City, and even my predrill rituals with my wall locker and footlocker.

Dr. Miller called my behaviors "OCD tendencies," which by my time in graduate school did not interfere with my life enough to warrant a full OCD diagnosis. In my case the symptoms increase with stress, which explained why they peaked during boot camp, LAV school, the war, and then monthly just before drill. He guessed that OCD had been a part of my personality since childhood, and probably always would be, ebbing and flowing in response to the stress in my life.

At age thirty-five I'm still managing my OCD tendencies. The strategy that works best for me is called "replacement," and involves trading more time-consuming and cumbersome rituals with quicker, simpler ones. So instead of organizing and inventorying everything in my house, my focus narrows to just keeping the desktop clear in my study. And instead of poring over every detail of my dress and grooming, as I had for years (courtesy of Drill Instructor Sgt. Talley), my focus becomes the Marine Corps eagle-globe-anchor tie clasp I wear each day at work. Wearing it makes up for anything about my appearance that is unsatisfactory by Marine standards.

By the time I earned my counseling degree in May of 1998, I was finished with nightmares and flashbacks, and had my OCD behaviors under control. The counseling program, with all of the coping strategies and self-awareness that it provided, was partly responsible. Another factor was time. By then seven years had passed since

the war, and three years since my last drill. The event most responsible for helping me move past the war, though, was the birth of my
son, Tyler. Becoming a father would eclipse the war in significance,
giving me a new sense of purpose, and a better reason to wake up in
the middle of the night.

During the summer of 1998 I was offered a position as a coun-
selor in a public school. What I learned, though, was that leaving
Kennedy Krieger was not so easy. It would mean, among other
things, leaving my lifeline to the Marine Corps—which was how Dr.
Miller described my affiliation with the Young Marines program. He
helped me realize how being commanding officer of a Young
Marines unit satisfied my need to stay connected to the Marine
Corps, as well as to fill the role of the "big brother" I had lost. I declined the public school offer and remained with Kennedy Krieger.

My work with the Young Marine students at Kennedy Krieger
School earned me recognition as a National Teacher of the Year, as
well as a promotion to assistant principal of Kennedy Krieger's new
high school. My new role didn't allow enough time to run the
Young Marines program alone, so I began searching for a full-time
Young Marines coordinator. In September of 2000 I found her—
First Sergeant Vivian Price-Butler. The first sergeant had more than
twenty years' experience in the Marine reserves and, like me, had
been activated for the Gulf War in 1990. Under her leadership the
Young Marines program would expand its scope to include students from first grade through twelfth, and become one of the foun-
dations in our school system for maintaining order and discipline.
By her third year First Sgt. Price-Butler had become an institution
at Kennedy Krieger, and a favorite among students, faculty, and
parents.

But in the winter of 2003 the first sergeant's reserve unit was
gearing up, organizing MORDT stations, and spending their drills
in the classroom getting war briefs. No one at school knew that, and
she didn't talk about it. Nevertheless, as I watched the news, and listened to President Bush's press conferences, I recognized the pattern.
Thoughts of the Gulf War began creeping into my head. Then the
day came that I had known was coming—the day the first sergeant

handed me her orders to report for active duty in the Persian Gulf, and hugged me good-bye.

To our students the first sergeant's activation meant an interruption in their schedules. To our staff it meant the need to find substitutes to assume her teaching responsibilities. For me it meant a return to the trenches.

During January 2003 the President was on television every evening, via sound bite or satellite, warning Saddam, warning the world, and instilling fear in us all. His voice sounded eerily like his father's had thirteen years before, during my war—that *other* Gulf War. It was never my intention to watch the coming war unfold on television, because I knew it would uncover thoughts and feelings that had taken me years to forget. But occasionally, an image or a headline would seduce me into staying tuned. I would tell myself that watching for a minute or two couldn't do any harm. Little did I know that the minutes would become hours, and the hours would become days, and that the harm would be a painful return in mind and soul to my war gone by.

Staring at the television like a zombie, I wouldn't hear my five-year-old son, Tyler, asking me to play with him. Nor would I hear my toddler, Sophia, crying for a bottle, or a diaper change, or a hug after a fall. And I wouldn't hear Gina asking for help with the kids or the house or the yard. Watching the war unfold on television was like taking a virtual trip back in time, back into the Marines, back into combat. And with that trip came all of the emotions that had taken me so long to forget.

One news clip showed a Marine hugging his wife good-bye at Camp Lejeune, which reminded me of the sadness I had felt saying farewell to Gina. Another showed troops with starched cammies and fresh faces filing onto planes that would take them to war. Then a day later, the news would show those same troops arriving in a tent city halfway around the world, with wrinkled cammies and anxious faces. I knew that anxiety well, and was now experiencing it again.

In the days that followed, the news stories became progressively more intense and combat oriented. Although all news about the military buildup was interesting to me, I focused on stories covering grunts and armor. They weren't hard to find. On television during any given night that winter there were troops training in the desert—humping, digging, and shooting, on foot and aboard vehicles, in the daytime and at night. I watched enthusiastically, hoping to hear the roar of the LAV's diesel engine, the whine of the turret traversing, or the *thump, thump, thump,* of its main gun firing. But I wasn't prepared for the variety of emotions I would experience when I finally did.

In the beginning of the ground war I was jealous that those troops were getting the glory and respect that I had once enjoyed. Then, when I saw the improvements in their weapons, gear, and vehicles, I grew resentful—especially the thermal night sights that were far superior to the passive night vision sights that we had used. I should have felt happy to be watching the action from the safety of my home, and grateful that others would be fighting while I remained with my family. But I felt neither happy, nor grateful. Mostly I felt angry.

I was angry that our troops had to go back to the desert to take care of business left unfinished by the war I had fought. Angry that Delta Company was deploying without me and my expertise as master gunner. Angry that a new generation of warriors might get slaughtered for a questionable cause, but at the same time angry that they might upstage our performance, liberating Baghdad in less time and with fewer casualties than we had while freeing Kuwait. Realizing how irrational those emotions were made me angrier still.

I stopped watching the television coverage before the ground war even began, but by that time my emotions had already been stirred from hibernation. Dr. Miller once told me that posttraumatic stress could be covered, but never erased. By mid-January the blanket had been stripped away, leaving me to deal once again with bothersome compulsions, sleepless nights, and a flood of memories that filled my head day and night.

Unlike the past, when I simply wished those feelings and memories would go away, this time I embraced them and channeled my energy into something productive. That's when I decided to finish writing a passage about boot camp that I had begun shortly after returning home in 1989. Back then I'd had no purpose for writing it, other than to document my first training day on the Island. That passage would become Chapter One of this book, and the section I wrote that first day at my computer in January of 2003 would become Chapter Two.

Writing those chapters, however, only occupied me for a weekend, and the seemingly inevitable war that was coming would keep me on edge for months. As February approached, I could only sleep a few hours at a time, my head filled with thoughts about the Marine Corps, the reserves, and the war. Wide awake, in the middle of the night, I would find myself in my study, sitting at my computer, and scanning the shelves. The flag from Lenny's funeral was there, and a picture of me with Sgt. Moss in front of our LAV. Behind the glass doors of the display case was my Gulf War memorabilia, a minimuseum in which I could lose myself for hours at a time. Then the memories poured out of my head, and my heart, and my fingers, and spilled onto the keyboard.

Although writing this book had consumed my life for many months, it was well worth the sacrifice. Aside from its therapeutic value it gave me a chance to reconnect with some of the Marines with whom I had served during the war. The book gave me a reason to call Doug Moss, whose number I received from a mutual friend. I hadn't spoken with Doug in twelve years, but once we got over the shock of hearing each other's voices, we talked for hours. Since our reunion I have had the privilege of serving as the best man at his wedding, and continue to communicate with him weekly by phone and e-mail. Doug now works in the computer industry and lives in northern Virginia with his wife and son.

The second Marine I contacted was Jim Bounds, my platoon

commander during the Gulf War. Thinking that he might have forgotten me, I introduced myself as Lance Cpl. Williams . . . from First Platoon . . . during the Gulf War. He remembered me, and welcomed the opportunity to review the manuscript. Over the next few days I received a series of e-mail messages, each with his commentary on the book. Interestingly, it was the first time I had ever communicated with him directly about the events that occurred leading up to and including the war. He qualified a lot of my experiences with background information that only officers would have known about at the time. While investigating the shooting at the police station in Kuwait, for instance, he witnessed a brutal interrogation of Palestinian prisoners. Today, Jim is an attorney and lives in northern Virginia with his wife and children.

I also contacted Ray Celeste, the company commander during my last year as a reservist. Although I hadn't spoken with him since we ran together in the Marine Corps Marathon in 1997, I figured he was still on active duty—he was a career Marine. After searching a military database I found his number, and learned that he was now Lt. Colonel Celeste, working in the Marine Corps's office of legislative affairs in Washington, D.C. Since our days at Camp Upshur I have admired him as a Marine and a scholar, which made his acknowledgment of this book's merit one of the best compliments I have received.

Lt. Colonel Celeste gave me the e-mail address of Eric Downes, who had served as commander of the TOW Platoon during the Gulf War, and our company commander afterward. While Lt. Colonel Downes was complimentary of my writing, he explained how different his perspective of the war was from mine. He also told me that he had shared my story with a captain who was formerly an enlisted Marine during the Gulf War, and had served as gunner on a LAV. The captain, he said, described experiences similar to mine. When I asked for the captain's e-mail address I realized who he was talking about—Lance Cpl. Dougherty.

My conversation with Mike Dougherty was the most awkward among the Marines I would contact. His voice sounded different

than I remembered, more "officerlike" in tone and cadence. Moreover, his attitude was one of indifference about our experiences as
reservists, and the Gulf War in general. I understood how that could
happen. Since the war had ended, he had become an officer, served
as an infantry platoon commander, and was now working at Quantico, Virginia, in intelligence. While being a reservist and fighting in
the Gulf War had defined me as a man and Marine, that time was
merely a fraction of his time in the Corps. He indulged me in a few
laughs and shared a few stories, but I sensed it was a stretch for him
to recall his lance corporal days.

After calling every "John Shane" in Michigan, I finally found the
right one. John was as dry and reserved on the phone as I remembered him to be in person. Unlike Mike Dougherty, John and I re-
connected on a personal level, the way that Doug and I had. We
have talked several times on the phone since then, and plan to stay
in touch. John works in the appliance industry and lives in Michigan
with his wife.

Writing the book also gave me a chance to reflect on the different
perspective that I have now, thirteen years later, about being a reservist during the Gulf War.

Ours wasn't the most polished performance, especially in the
early days of Operation Desert Storm. At times we were downright
pathetic. Even at our best we were barely worthy of mention in the
annals of modern warfare. But we didn't make excuses. We learned
from our mistakes and forged ahead, making up lost ground on the
job, in the field, and under fire. Of Marines it is said they are the few
and proud. Among them I think we were the fewer and prouder.
There was nothing *spare* about our role in the War. Our transformation from civilians into warriors did not happen in the rear area behind the active-duty Marines. We were right there beside them,
sometimes in front, watching and waiting ... cursing and sweating ... fighting and killing ... bleeding and dying.

So, too, have thousands of reservists in the war in Iraq. Considering the offensive and defensive engagements during the combat phase of the war, as well as the guerrilla warfare that followed, it was amazing that my former company suffered no casualties. I think their fate lay partly in the hands of God, and partly in the peacetime training that built their confidence and skill as warriors. Concerning the latter I'd like to think that my contributions during the last decade played a small part in making that so.

I have also spent considerable time reflecting on what being a Marine has meant to me. The Marine Corps has been, is now, and will likely always be the most influential institution in my life. As a child it gave me a way to connect with my brother and the hero I looked up to. As a wayward adolescent it gave me much-needed direction and a reason to stay on course. As a young adult it gave me a blueprint for being a respectful boyfriend, disciplined student, and productive employee. I still rely every day on the values I learned in the Marine Corps—as a faithful husband, responsible father, and positive role model for high school students.

In August of 2003 I resigned from Kennedy Krieger and accepted a position as an assistant principal with Harford County Public Schools in Maryland. Thus far, being away from the Young Marines program has done little to separate me from the Marine Corps. On the first day at my new school I met Ms. Tackett, a teacher whose husband was serving in Iraq as a LAV gunner with Bravo Company. During our first parent night I found myself bonding with a group of fathers who were former Marines. Shortly after, I met Sgt. Duplessis, the Marine recruiter who sets up shop in our school's lobby each month.

At home, too, the spirit of the Marine Corps is alive and well. Tyler digs through my seabags, dresses like a Marine, and marches around the house barking out orders to imaginary troops. Sometimes we visit my Marine display case in the study, because he thinks the uniforms and gear and photos are cool. He asks a thousand questions about war, and I try to explain it in terms that a five-year-old can understand. When Gina isn't around I let him push the button on my drill-instructor action figure, which curses and screams like drill instructors do, and we laugh together.

Sophia, too, is undeniably the daughter of a Marine. "Ooh rah" was the third intelligible thing I ever heard her say after "Momma" and "Dadda." While Gina loves the Marine Corps (as much as any Marine's wife can), she hugs Tyler and Sophia and tells them that her babies are not going into the Marines. For me it's not important whether they join the Marines—or any other branch of the armed services, for that matter. I will love them no matter what.

But now this book will be ready for them to read, and to help them answer knowledgably, should the yellow footprints call.

AUTHOR'S NOTE AND ACKNOWLEDGMENTS

THIS BOOK DESCRIBES my development as a Marine reservist, and my personal journey before, during, and after combat. The events depicted are true, though constrained by my memory and perspective. The characters are real, although I have changed some names and biographical details.

This book would not have been completed had it not been for the time and space given to me by my wife, Gina, who has demonstrated she can raise the kids and run the house without me; by my son, Tyler, who has sacrificed more than his share of daddy time; and by my daughter, Sophia, who is old enough to recognize when I'm not there, but too young yet to understand why.

I am grateful for the guidance and support of my agent, Joe Veltre, who was the first publishing professional to believe in my story; also at Carlisle and Company—Michelle Tessler, Michael Carlisle, and Pilar Queen.

I am indebted to my editor, Brendan Cahill, who worked with me line by line to make my writing the best it could be—a master teacher in his own right; Ray Lundgren, for creating the perfect cover; Craig Schneider for his copy edit expertise; and the talented team of professionals at Gotham Books including Patrick Mulligan, Joseph Mills, and my publisher, Bill Shinker.

Sincerest thanks to those readers who provided valuable feedback as the chapters developed—Patty Laibstain, Lisa Muccino, Barb Veselich, Mary Ramos, Linda and John Brandenburg, Sarah Heneghan, Ben Rodriguez, Debbie Chain, Melinda and John Knopp, Denise and Dick Meyers, Angela Meyers, Dick and Clara Howlett, Laura and Donnie Falcone, Julia Falcone, Robin and Randy Weagley, Carl and Clara Del Gallo, Giulio and Arlene Del Gallo, Carl and Dawn Del Gallo, Jane and John Peplinski, Ken and Kelly Brandt, and Jim and Joanne Phillips.

Special thanks to the board of directors and staff members of Baltimore Medical Systems Incorporated (BMSI) for their support of my work; the administration of Kennedy Krieger High School: Robin Church, Gabrielle Miller, Andy Hubner, Aaron Parsons, Renard Adams, Rick Abbott, and Scott Steppa—for their patience and understanding; Vivian Price-Butler for inspiration; and Ed Bigley for sage advice and moral support.

I wish to express my gratitude to the following Marines for providing checks and balances to my perspective: first and foremost my friend, Doug Moss; Ray Celeste, Jim Bounds, Eric Downes, John Shane, and Mike Dougherty.

DATELINE

WARRIOR

SEPTEMBER 1990:	Check-in at Camp Upshur for first drill weekend after LAV school
18 NOVEMBER 1990:	Phone call from Sgt. Moss–official activation for war
22 NOVEMBER 1990:	Withdraw from classes at Towson University–last day on campus
23 NOVEMBER 1990:	Check-in at Camp Upshur for mobilization to active duty
26 NOVEMBER 1990:	Road-march convoy from Camp Upshur to Camp Lejeune
27 NOVEMBER 1990:	Weapons Company merges with Fox Company to become Delta Company
29 NOVEMBER 1990:	First day of our twenty-eight-day training period at Lejeune
26 DECEMBER 1990:	Last training day at Lejeune–board TWA flight to Saudi Arabia
27 DECEMBER 1990:	Arrive in Saudi Arabia–Tent City at Jubail
31 DECEMBER 1990:	First combat experience–Scud alarms
2 JANUARY 1991:	Leave Tent City for field positions and training
6 JANUARY 1991:	Grunt training and trench clearing
11 JANUARY 1991:	Return to Tent City in Jubail
17 JANUARY 1991:	Desert Storm begins–the LAVs arrive
29 JANUARY 1991:	Hunter is wounded by friendly fire
8 FEBRUARY 1991:	Surrendering Iraqis pass through our command center–Sgt. Moss is demoted
22 FEBRUARY 1991:	Vehicle rollover
24 FEBRUARY 1991:	Ground war begins
25 FEBRUARY 1991:	Blue One kills Iraqis in the mail truck
28 FEBRUARY 1991:	Palestinian children attacked for seeking food

4 MARCH 1991:	Red Two takes fire in Kuwait
5 MARCH 1991:	Cpl. Shane and I explore the Kuwaiti house
12 MARCH 1991:	Combat funeral for Lance Cpl. Edsar

VETERAN

1 APRIL 1991:	Return to Tent City in Jubail
20 APRIL 1991:	Return to Camp Lejeune
24 APRIL 1991:	Return to Camp Upshur
JUNE 1991:	First postwar drill weekend
AUGUST 1991:	My transfer to Third Platoon
SEPTEMBER 1991:	I go unqualified on the rifle range
APRIL 1993:	LAV live-fire
JULY 1993:	ATD in Twenty-Nine Palms, California
AUGUST 1993:	First drill as company master gunner
SEPTEMBER 1993:	I create the boot camp program for at-risk adolescents
JUNE 1995:	Last drill weekend
SEPTEMBER 1995:	I become CO of Young Marines Central Maryland
SEPTEMBER 1995:	I enroll in master's program in school counseling at Johns Hopkins
JULY 1998:	I become assistant principal of Kennedy Krieger High School
SEPTEMBER 2000:	First Sgt. Price-Butler becomes CO of Young Marines
JANUARY 2003:	First Sgt. Price-Butler prepares for activation
JANUARY 2003:	I begin writing *Spare Parts*

With Lenny after his graduation from Parris Island,
September 1975

On the yellow footprints after graduation from Parris Island,
August 1989

Training as a mortarman during the winter of 1989 before reassignment to an LAV platoon

With Gina, taken on the way to report for active duty at Camp Upshur

First day at Tent City in Jubail, Saudi Arabia,
27 December 1990

Company area within Tent City

The "shitter" and "pisser" within Tent City

One of the last days in the Kuwaiti Desert just before returning to
Tent City, March 1991

New Year's Eve 1990—when I stayed awake practicing the masking procedure
(and the night I proposed to Gina)

NBC gear: gas mask with hood, Cipro pills, NAP pills, and Atropine injectors

In the driver's compartment of the LAV with Sgt. Moss in the vehicle commander position

Atop the troop compartment of the LAV

With Sgt. Moss and the LAV in Kuwait following the ground war

The crew of Red 2 the morning after the rollover—Dougherty far left, Cpl. Shane far right

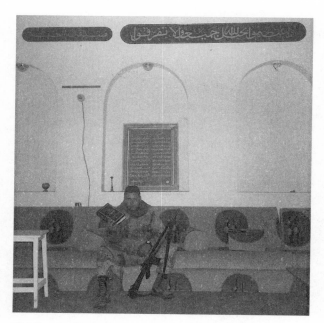

Holding the Koran in the living room of the Kuwaiti house

Evidence of torture in the bathroom of the Kuwaiti house

Boarding the plane for the flight home, 19 April 1991

Arrival home, 24 April 1991